P9-CMY-022

RUSSIAN
ALTERNATIVES
TO MARXISM

THE UNIVERSITY OF TENNESSEE PRESS : KNOXVILLE

RUSSIAN *ALTERNATIVES* TO MARXISM

CHRISTIAN SOCIALISM
AND IDEALISTIC LIBERALISM
IN TWENTIETH-CENTURY RUSSIA

By George F. Putnam

Library of Congress Cataloging in Publication Data

Putnam, George F   1923–
  Russian alternatives to Marxism.

  Bibliography: p.
  Includes index.
  1. Socialism in Russia—History. I. Title.
HX724.P87   335'.00947   76–49606
ISBN 0–87049–206–3

FOR LOUISE

PREFACE

AT THE BASE OF THIS BOOK lies my desire to understand late-nineteenth-century and early-twentieth-century Russian culture. As anthropologists use it the term *culture* embraces the entire creative activity of human groups as they seek ordered, satisfying lives in particular environments. Of course, to speak of understanding *the* culture of late Czarist Russia in these terms would be absurd. I employ the word in the more limited traditional sense of efforts by creative individuals to express in philosophy, religion, literature, and the arts the central beliefs and attitudes, values, hopes, and institutional predilections of their societies. This work deals with a specific, though central aspect of that activity—non-Marxist religious, philosophical, and social thought.

I have listened attentively and critically to the dialogues of that time involving spokesmen for various components of Russian culture. The many-sided discussions involved Russian Orthodox officials, monks, parish priests, and theologians, urban "rationalized" professors and liberal politicians, poets, novelists, and literary critics, and the Russian radical intelligentsia, Marxist or otherwise. From their juxtaposition of basic elements of Russia's thousand-year cultural heritage, we can gain something more than a one-sided, ideological insight into those things which were possible for Russia and those which were not, as the fateful year of 1917 approached. In addition, we can acquire a real understanding of what was lost or repressed in Russian culture, what needs or desires may lie unfulfilled, because of the particular ideas and attitudes of those who emerged as Russian rulers after 1917.

The thinkers studied here sought to point out a new path for early-twentieth-century Russia. Some did so from a rigid attachment to one "basic" side of Russian culture and others from a perspective which sought to harmonize several, and they all, including the Marxists, failed, but did not think and write in vain. For in their efforts, they cast light on the various needs, hopes, and accomplishments for which a lasting productive Russian culture would have to provide some outlet. While Russian culture is my subject and I would not like to claim an excessively wide application for its articulation, the issues being considered were both universal and central to the survival of civilized man as he has been for some thousands of years.

Fears of the disappearance of the "person," the impossibility of "community," and the triumph of "scientism" inspired the Russian discussion. These lie at the heart of the malaise of the most "developed" late-twentieth-century societies. Christianity may have lost its power to bind. Liberal politics seems unable to deal with the inexorably widening range of human wants. Marxism has become almost unrecognizable in the hands of twentieth-century romanticists. Yet, in discussing their interrelations, early-twentieth-century Russians raised issues and perspectives central to the modern search for a new path. A new myth, if there is to be one, in terms of which a recognizably human world might be preserved must be a modified expression of past successful modes by which men have managed to live with the world, themselves, and other men. Some of the most civilized of these found expression in the intellectual exchanges which this work considers.

The prospective reader should know that this is an essay on past thought about Russian culture. I do not make a *systematic* effort to relate the ideas discussed to class backgrounds or interests. This does not mean that I believe that ideas, much less the Idea, determines human history or that most men, most of the time, can think solely within the "laws of thought." In principle, socioeconomic information can add to understanding, but the level of data usually included in works in intellectual history and that which would be possible here explains little. It may be better to describe and analyze as well as one can the ideas under examination. To explain how they are related to

viii

social-economic forces and interests is a task which no one yet knows how to do.

I have used the Library of Congress transliteration system for footnoting and bibliography. In the text itself, I have used Anglicized forms of Russian names, i.e., Merezhkovsky, not Merezhkovskii.

Needed and much appreciated financial support came from the American Philosophical Association, the American Council of Learned Societies, the Inter-University Travel Committee, and the Fulbright Committee. The last two made possible a productive stay in the USSR. I am grateful to those scholars who supported my applications for these grants. I also wish to thank Dean Robert Bader and the History Department of the University of Missouri at St. Louis for their contribution toward the publication of this book. Mainly, I wish to acknowledge my debt to my wife, Louise, who worked tirelessly to prepare this work for publication. More important, without her presence in my life, the book would not have been written.

GEORGE F. PUTNAM

St. Louis, Missouri
January, 1976

CONTENTS

Preface   *page* vii

I   Philosophy, Religious Thought, and Social Life   3
       Alternatives to Marxism   7
       Idealism, Religious Thought and Ideology   16

II   Problems of Idealists: Novgorodtsev and Bulgakov Before
       1904   25
       Russian Idealism and Its Critique of Positivism   28
       Paul Novgorodtsev: Kantian and Christian   34
       Serge Bulgakov and Vladimir Soloviev   44

III The St. Petersburg and Moscow Religious-Philosophical
       Meetings and Societies (1901–1914)   56
       The St. Petersburg Religious-Philosophical Meetings
         of 1901–1903   61
       The Moscow Religious-Philosophical Society
         (1905–1908)   69
       The St. Petersburg Religious-Philosophical Society
         (1907–1908)   78
       Russia, Its Church and Its People   85

IV   Serge Bulgakov's Christian Socialism   93
       The St. Petersburg Religious-Philosophical Society
         (1908–1910)   96
       Bulgakov and Russian Liberalism   99
       Christian Socialism and Social Democracy   106

V   Novgorodtsev's Idealistic Liberalism   122
       Novgorodtsev As a Russian Liberal   124

xi

	The Lost Illusion of Social Harmony	128
	The State and the Citizen	134
	The Individual and the Society	137
	Culture, Personality, and the Social Ideal	143
VI	The Priest and the Professor	152
	Modernization and the Free Person	155
	The Church and the Academy	159
	The State and the People	164
	The Revolution of Sensibility and the Gnosis of Modernity	172
	Notes	177
	Bibliography	199
	Index	225

RUSSIAN
ALTERNATIVES
TO MARXISM

Chapter I

PHILOSOPHY, RELIGIOUS THOUGHT, AND SOCIAL LIFE

As in all Europe, an exhilarating but disquieting feeling of impending change dominated Russian life in the last two decades before 1914. Despite czarist insistence that bureaucratic government would continue essentially unchanged, it appeared plainly incompatible with the more pluralistic society emerging in tune with rapid industrial expansion. In the midst of continuing peasant revolts, and accelerating worker demonstrations and uprisings, particularly after 1901, revived revolutionary political thought and action became dominant among opponents of the regime. More secondary and technical schools and more diversified opportunities for productive work greatly increased the number of persons who challenged the bureaucracy in that manner. At the same time, the innovative spirit manifested itself in a bewildering variety of literary, artistic, and philosophical conceptions, most of which were far from realistic in any direct sense. Perhaps more than was customary in modern culture, artistic creativity and philosophical speculation interacted with socially oriented thought.

Creative individuals and a small minority of the educated turned to new directions in art, music, literature, and philosophy, particularly in St. Petersburg and Moscow. To name but a few, the painters Leon S. Bakst and Mikhail L. Larionov, the composers Igor F. Stravinsky and Alexander N. Scriabin, the poets Alexander A. Blok and Andrei Belyi, and the philosophers Vladimir S. Soloviev and Leon I. Shestov produced highly original work between 1890 and 1914. Painters and composers, in particular, benefited from the largess of wealthy, aes-

3

thetically astute patrons, some of whom also subsidized journals of a mainly intellectual, even political, content. In drawing rooms and salons philosophers, poets, political thinkers, and others carried on wide-ranging, serious discussions of all sides of Russian and Western European culture. Members of those St. Petersburg and Moscow circles fostered and reacted to an intoxicated anticipation of a great transformation in European culture and the part that Russian creativity would play in it.

Romantic perspectives featured much that was new as creative artists and philosophers vigorously attacked naturalism and positivism. They claimed for themselves the ability to penetrate the banality and ugliness of everyday life on all social levels, to present to those capable of seeing it—the aesthetic elite and the unspoiled masses— the reality behind reality. Viacheslav I. Ivanov, Dmitry S. Merezhkovsky, Vasily V. Rozanov, Zinaida Hippius, Larionov, Scriabin, and Soloviev all sought to express the inexpressible. They joined a mainstream of Western European thought in the last third of the nineteenth century and struck at the dominance of positivist and naturalist attitudes among Russian intellectuals and artists of the same period.

Like their Western counterparts the Russian Neoromanticists influenced the outlook of educated society less than the brilliance of their perspectives and their own excitement might suggest. In particular, positivist, utilitarian, and Marxist points of view continued to dominate liberal and revolutionary social thought. But among realistic politicians and social thinkers there did arise idealistic and religious critiques of positivism not entirely independent from the less mundane forms of cultural expression. Thinkers like Paul I. Novgorodtsev, Serge N. Bulgakov, Peter B. Struve, Nicholas A. Berdiaev, Serge N. and Eugene N. Trubetskoi, Simon L. Frank, and Vladimir F. Ern attacked positivism in general and Marxism in particular. They pointed out the inherent weaknesses of Marxism, both as philosophy and as a world view compatible with the struggle for freedom and justice in Russia, and offered alternatives. Idealistic liberalism and Christian socialism were the two most important nonpositivistic options which arose from the tangled cultural and political life of *fin de siècle* Russia.

When discussing Marxism, the idealistic liberal Paul Novgorodtsev

4

and the Christian socialist Serge Bulgakov referred almost exclusively to the writings of Karl Marx. Bulgakov had studied Marx's writings during adolescence and polemicized as a Marxist between 1897 and 1900. As a legal philosopher and student of the history of social thought, Novgorodtsev devoted a large section of his book, *On the Social Ideal*, to the explanation and criticism of Marx's ideas. But both lived and thought in the midst of the controversies among proponents of the several varieties of Russian Marxism: orthodoxy, revisionism, economism, Bolshevism, Menshevism, and empiriomonism. In the period before 1904 they spoke out against the particularly deterministic Marxism which was directed during the 1890s at indigenous "populist" Russian revolutionary ideas and practices, and which received classic formulation in the writings of George V. Plekhanov.

In 1895, Plekhanov published his *In Defense of Materialism*. In this work, the most influential of all Russian Marxist (as distinguished from Leninist) writings, Plekhanov espoused a highly positivistic, deterministic doctrine.[1] Directing his fire at the romantic subjectivism of "populist" writers, the author offered to young revolutionaries an interpretation of history which could give them assurance that their cause had the sanction of science and would inevitably triumph. The prime mover of human development was changes in the means of material production. Possession or lack of these—slaves, land, industry—determined the economic relations between social classes and inspired class struggles. In any society the dominant class dictated the acceptable forms of political order, legality, philosophy, literature, art, and other aspects of culture. It employed that "superstructure" to safeguard and sanction its control of the material means of production. The scientific "laws" of history guaranteed that ultimately control of production would pass to society as a whole, and a socialist order would result.

In Plekhanov's theory, the individual played no independent role. No matter how enlightened, forceful, or self-sacrificing, the person could not alter the sequence of events in terms of his own aims and purposes, though he might positively or negatively affect the pace of development. *Epistemologically*, though Plekhanov tried to avoid the naïve "copy theory," he could not explain knowledge as other than the result of an unmediated contact between material man and the

5

material world. Consciously or unconsciously, an individual's thought reflected his class position and hence his material interests. This meant, further, that there could be no universal *Ethics*. Though Plekhanov struggled throughout his life with the philosophical difficulties inherent in these views, they represented the main elements of Marxist philosophy to most early Russian adepts. Plekhanov's was the Marxist "positivism" against which religious thinkers and idealistic philosophers polemicized in the late nineteenth century.

After 1905, Novgorodtsev and Bulgakov confronted developing Marxism-Leninism and the "Marxism" of the empiriomonists, particularly Alexander A. Bogdanov, Anatole V. Lunacharsky, and Vladimir A. Bazarov. Lenin's voluntaristic thought and activity particularly aroused them. They denounced the undemocratic organization and mode of operation he imposed on the Bolshevik faction of the Russian Social Democratic Workers' Party, and his determination to inspire and use peasant revolution, regardless of theoretical considerations or the fate of Russia. On the other hand, they denied that empiriomonism offered a useful corrective to Marxist materialism. It was true positivism in that it discarded all metaphysics, materialistic as well as idealistic. It absolutely rejected the reality of substance and denied to man knowledge of anything beyond his experiences. It even treated scientific theories as essentially heuristic devices and mathematical concepts as but "auxiliary concepts."[2] To Lenin the attempt to base Marxism on the ideas of Richard Avenarius and Ernst Mach was but another form of idealism.[3] To Bulgakov and Novgorodtsev it represented a flight from philosophy, which destroyed the only essence which made philosophy meaningful, the *substantial person*.

Early-twentieth-century Russian alternatives to Marxism extended from largely aesthetic approaches to ideas closely connected with practical politics and social theory. Three major forms of thought appeared: (1) "Godseeking," mystical literary speculation on religious and philosophical topics, seeking to delineate a *new religious consciousness*, upon which a new world of peace and freedom might be erected; (2) *Christian socialist thought*, seeking to bind together Orthodox Christian theology, modern idealist and Marxist philosophy, and social action; (3) *idealistic liberalism*, based on rigorous Kantian and Neo-Kantian epistemology and ethics, while seeking to reconcile both with modern demands for the fulfillment of the many-sided person and the well-being of the masses.

6

ALTERNATIVES TO MARXISM

Most important among the "Godseeking" writers were Merezh-kovsky, Hippius, and Rozanov, who, with church officials, created the St. Petersburg Religious-Philosophical Meetings of 1901–1903. Merezhkovsky and his wife, Hippius, helped inspire the early-twentieth-century symbolist movement in Russian literature. Hippius may be considered a symbolist poet, while Merezhkovsky, despite his limitations as poet and novelist, was an original and influential literary critic. He provided journals, themes, and slogans in terms of which major cultural activities developed. Rozanov, who cannot be identified with any school, was a determined irrationalist and lyrical stylist, whose sexually-saturated religious visions strongly impressed not only ordinary readers, but also philosophers, poets, and critics who rejected their message.

In 1901, Merezhkovsky, Hippius, and Rozanov joined representatives of the Orthodox Church in the St. Petersburg Religious-Philosophical Meetings. The ensuing discussions initiated a searching examination of the role of the church in twentieth-century Russia. Many of Russia's most perceptive intellectuals pursued that subject in books, articles, and the post-1905 Moscow and St. Petersburg religious-philosophical societies. In this study the largely aesthetic ideas and attitudes of the Merezhkovskys will not be fully examined but will be referred to in their organizational and catalytic function.

Writers on religious-philosophical topics presented three potentially fruitful assessments of Russia's needs in the early twentieth century. Merezhkovsky and his associates began and ended with "the new religious consciousness." They claimed that Christianity had not yet appeared in its final form, but would embody new revelations, which would bring it into fruitful connection with modern human demands for cultural autonomy, sexual liberation, and political-economic freedom. The Moscow philosopher Vladimir Ern best represented a group which agreed with Merezhkovsky that many contemporary practices of the Orthodox Church required change. But he maintained that the divine revelations on which Christianity was based were final and sufficient. Christians need but return to their early communal and expectant way of life to bring to fulfillment the ancient dream of a kingdom of God on earth.

Both idealistic liberalism and Christian socialism embodied the

7

ideas of men much involved in efforts to reform the Russian political and social order. Some of them had embraced Marxism, but by the mid-1890s were engaged in a sharp idealistic critique of Marxist determinism and relativistic ethics. In 1903 these "ex-Marxists," Struve, Frank, Berdiaev, and Bulgakov joined Novgorodtsev, Bogdan A. Kistiakovsky, Serge A. Kotliarevsky, and other liberals and moderate socialists in the Union of Liberation, which became a major intellectual and organizational vehicle for the spread of liberal ideas. In the same year under the editorship of Novgorodtsev, the group published *Problemy idealizma (Problems of Idealism)*, a collection of essays intended to show the superiority of idealism over Marxism and positivism in general as a philosophy of freedom.[4] However, in the collection it was obvious that there was a sharp distinction between proponents of secular idealism and those who believed that idealism could be valid only in a religious framework.

As exponents of anti-Marxist arguments, the most prominent from the religious side were Bulgakov and Berdiaev and from the secular idealist side, Novgorodtsev, Struve, and Frank. Of the two religious thinkers, Bulgakov presented the most important ideas for an understanding of Russian cultural and social life at the beginning of the twentieth century. Berdiaev's aristocratic individualism or mystical anarchism removed him and his thought too radically from this world to have much social impact. On the other hand, Bulgakov's Christian socialism, rooted both in Russian religious experience and modern thought, is the most conscious and complete expression of that point of view ever produced in Russia.

Among the idealistic liberals, Novgorodtsev was the most important philosopher. He pursued epistemology, ethics, and metaphysics throughout his career as a professor of jurisprudence at Moscow University and director of the Moscow Commercial Institute. Before 1903 his close associate, Peter Struve, was perhaps a more active epistemologist and metaphysician, but he was not a consistent philosophical idealist.[5] And, after 1903, Struve concentrated almost entirely on journal and newspaper polemics on the political and social questions of the day. Simon Frank, also a well-known liberal intellectual, was not a committed idealist; indeed, during the entire period to 1914 he consciously worked through philosophies of many different schools en route to this mature system of Christian real-idealism.

No other liberal with idealistic leanings came close to matching the

8

sustained philosophical attention and mature political thought which Novgorodtsev displayed in his major works. His works contained the most generally accepted principles of idealistic liberalism, but he went beyond general statements in an attempt to synthesize idealist thought from Immanuel Kant through Johann Fichte and George William Frederick Hegel to the Neo-Kantians. He tried to maintain what he believed to be the correct aspects of Kant's epistemology, ethics, and political theory, while adjusting his formalistic ethics and rationalistic view of man's nature and needs to conform to nineteenth-century experience and thought. Though seldom directly stated, Orthodox Christian belief set limits on the form that his synthesis could take. That he did not succeed in constructing a universal theory from such radically different ways of looking at the world does not detract from the value of his effort for the student of Russian culture.

With idealistic liberalism and Christian socialism, Novgorodtsev and Bulgakov sought to solve a dual problem. Politically, *idealistic liberalism* embodied the social, political, and economic doctrines associated with early-twentieth-century European liberalism, with differing emphases reflecting peculiar Russian conditions. As its philosophical base, idealist modes of thought replaced forms of utilitarian positivism. *Christian socialism* shared with secular socialism a marked distaste for liberal individualism, but held that the only secure basis for freedom under socialism was a Christian commitment resting on love. But, beyond the question of the fate of freedom in Russia, Novgorodtsev and Bulgakov confronted the broader crisis in philosophy, embodied in the late-nineteenth-century belief that all problems could be solved by correct application of the methods of natural science. They insisted that Christian thought and philosophical idealism provided men with autonomous approaches to knowledge. Science could take its place as one of man's greatest achievements, essential to his spiritual as well as material progress, but it was unable to answer ultimate epistemological, ethical, and ontological questions.

As defenders of the autonomy of the person, Novgorodtsev and Bulgakov joined major critics of late-nineteenth-century European culture. At least since John Stuart Mill, Western European liberal thinkers had sought to safeguard the complex thinking-feeling personality from an impersonal economic order and the "tyranny of the

9

majority'' by use of idealistic philosophy.[6] Christian socialist ideas had been expressed in France since the 1830s in the writings of Félicité Lamennais, Phillipe Buchez, and the Saint Simonians.[7] Christian socialism became an important movement in England in the 1850s under the leadership of Charles Kingsley and Frederick Denison Maurice; the latter originated the term ''Christian socialism.'' It played a major role in the very influential writings of John Ruskin and William Morris.

In Germany and Central Europe, Bishop Wilhelm von Ketteler organized a Christian socialist movement as part of a revival of German medieval Catholicism. Toward the end of the century, Christian socialism became a part of the popular Pastor Friedrich Naumann's attempt to establish a nationalist movement embracing Christian, socialist, and democratic principles.[8] Concurrently, churchmen like Herman Kutter, Leonhard Ragaz, and Emil Fuchs sought to commit their churches to social action.[9] Ragaz organized a broad-based movement, some of whose clerical members actually joined and worked with the Social Democratic party. In Western societies, at the end of the nineteenth century, idealistic liberalism and Christian socialism could attract a substantial following from intellectuals, the educated middle classes, and even working class populations. In Russia it was much more difficult to inspire such support.

An idealistic liberal or Christian socialist defense of the person could have an attractive progressive tone in Europe from England to Austria. In increasingly democratic England and France, idealistic liberalism could appear as the guardian of individual liberties and cultured creativity against pressures to conform to the ideas and behavior of the multitude. In Russia, where the basic human needs of the majority still remained unsatisfied, it might have seemed, at best, an untimely statement of noble principles and, at worst, an expression of the self-interest and uneasy conscience of the privileged. Christian socialist thought in the West expressed a call to deepen human experience and arouse communitarian feelings in a utilitarian, callously individualistic culture. But in Russia it would strike many as an assertion of the continued dominance of an intolerant church, the state to which it was subject, and the social order it sanctioned. Novgorodtsev and Bulgakov spoke for important elements in Russian culture, but did so in terms of a critique of late Western European liberal societies in a society and intellectual climate perhaps more attuned to a "scientific" critique of a decaying old regime.

Both idealistic liberalism and Christian socialism continued major traditions in Russian thought. Monks of the Russian Orthodox church continued until the late nineteenth century to repeat social attitudes expressed centuries before by Fathers of the Church, such as Saint Basil and Saint John Chrysostom. Both had sharply criticized as man-hating robbery the selfish pursuit of private property and exploitation of the poor.[10] In addition to this sense of moral outrage, Bulgakov shared the belief of nineteenth-century Slavophiles that Orthodox Christianity was the core of a Russian culture superior to legalistic, competitive, and individualistic Western Europe.[11] Like them, he believed that Orthodox Russia would make a unique contribution to the spiritual development of man. Archimandrite Alexander M. Bukharev, Fedor M. Dostoevsky, and Soloviev were his late-nineteenth-century mentors.

Dostoevsky remained a kind of "Christian Socialist," even after his imprisonment in Siberia and turn to conservatism. After 1861 he vigorously attacked any secular ideology which rested on the idea of the goodness and eventual perfection of man. In his polemical writings he ardently supported "Autocracy, Orthodoxy, and Nationality."[12] But he never discarded the faith in the ultimate brotherhood of man which had brought him to the Petrashevsky Circle.[13] And in his last writings, he still seemed to suggest that a golden age might emerge from a Christian transformation of man by childlike love. Particularly attractive to Bulgakov were Dostoevsky's ridicule of secular utopias, his psychological dissection of the motives of their proponents, and his demonstration of the superiority of faith and love to reason in understanding the world.

Vladimir Soloviev, who was very close to Dostoevsky, strongly impressed Bulgakov in two ways. He believed that Soloviev had shown that religious faith was compatible with modern philosophy and science. More than that, only by religious faith could science establish necessary connections between its "laws" and the world. Soloviev's work enabled "sophisticated men" to overcome the split consciousness which debilitated their energies and kept religion from playing the integrative role in their lives that it should.[14] Secondly, Bulgakov believed that Soloviev had shown how the struggles of

secular reformers and revolutionaries were necessary to the spiritualization of man. This made it possible for the religious man to accept
and support their work, even though its purveyors attacked Christianity and used violent means contrary to its spirit. But Bulgakov believed that moral denunciation was not enough and that Soloviev paid
too little attention to the concrete facts of the Russian economy and
politics.

Despite the overwhelming importance of Western thought and
politics to Novgorodtsev's idealistic liberalism, he was part of an
eighteenth- and nineteenth-century tradition in Russian thought.
From the time of Peter the Great (1689–1725), Russian thinkers had
employed two major bases of liberal thought, natural law and
utilitarianism, to defend the autonomy of a secular ethics and politics.
Originally employed to buttress Peter's claim to absolute authority,
as in the writings of Vasily N. Tatishchev and Theofan Prokopovich,
natural law and utilitarian arguments took on a more liberal cast
toward the end of the eighteenth century. The eighteenth-century
Enlightenment strongly affected the writers who began the modern
liberal movement in Russia, Nicholas I. Novikov and Alexander N.
Radishchev.

Radishchev accented rationalism and the principles of natural law
in his writings between 1773 and 1790 on government and society. He
urged Catherine II to substitute rational government for arbitrary
despotism resting on bureaucratic corruption, demoralizing class
privilege, and exploitation of the enslaved peasantry.[15] The employment of reason would lead to understanding of the natural laws which
gave to each control over his own person and the products of his
labor. They were eternal and unchanging. Radishchev used utilitarian
arguments to buttress his appeal to principle. If the peasants were
freed, agricultural production would rise greatly and peasant revolts
would cease to drain resources and weaken the government. If the
empress, her advisers, the administration, the courts, and the church
were "enlightened," the strength of the state could not but increase.
Novgorodtsev used similar arguments one century later, but unlike
Radishchev did so on the basis of an idealistic ontology and epistemology.

The liberal ideas of the Enlightenment continued to attract educated Russians throughout the nineteenth century. The most important liberal thinkers of the period, such as Timofei N. Granovsky,

Constantin D. Kavelin, and Alexander D. Gradovsky were professors and not philosophical idealists. Each of these, like Novgorodtsev, cherished the principle of individual freedom and denounced the use of abstractions to justify the imposition of limits on liberty. The same holds for the brilliant and very influential writer, Alexander I. Herzen, although he is considered not a liberal, but an originator of Russian socialism and populism.[16] The most prominent Russian idealistic liberal thinker before Novgorodtsev was unquestionably his older contemporary Boris N. Chicherin, a historian, political philosopher, and professor of legal history at the University of Moscow until 1868.[17]

Novgorodtsev saw in Chicherin one of the greatest spokesmen for the *personalism* which he considered the primary basis for a liberal philosophy and social order. That the individual person had absolute significance, that the personality was a unitary, metaphysical essence, was the firmest conviction of both. Despite his Hegelianism, Chicherin emphasized the Kantian position that man's freedom consisted in his ability to make moral choices and that this presupposed an infinite (noumenal) element in man beside the finite (phenomenal).

Chicherin also held positions which Novgorodtsev could not accept. He did not share Chicherin's attachment to Hegel's dialectical logic and the identification of thinking, material, and social processes associated with it. On the more concrete level, Chicherin was a more conservative liberal than Novgorodtsev. He assigned high progressive meaning to human inequalities, fearing greatly that interference in the economic and political struggles of individuals would weaken productivity and liberal order. In his twentieth-century welfare liberalism, Novgorodtsev polemicized directly against Chicherin's laissez faire attitudes. But beyond the specific philosophical and political similarities and differences of the two lay a fundamental existential fact. Both were strongly religious men who nonetheless believed it possible to express basic philosophical and political beliefs in purely secular terms. Yet at the same time religious commitment played a determining role in their approaches to politics. On that level, Novgorodtsev remained closer to Chicherin than to fellow liberal thinkers and politicians, such as Ivan I. Petrunkevich, Alexander A. Kizevetter, Paul N. Miliukov, and Struve.

Novgorodtsev and Bulgakov presented points of view that had been important in Russian cultural life for almost one century. Bulgakov's conviction that Russia could survive modernization only within the framework of the Orthodox Christian religion had existed continuously since the reign of Alexander I (1801–1825). Novgorodtsev's fundamental principle that the freedom and autonomy of the individual under law was the ultimate aim of good government had an equally long history. But both attitudes had existed almost entirely as ideas expressed with varying degrees of brilliance and depth in literature, lecture hall, or salon. No one who understood the nineteenth-century Russian state and Orthodox church could consider political liberalism or a Christian social movement possible.

By the early twentieth century, both a serious Christian and a liberal thinker could be more sanguine. It was unlikely, but possible, that by basing itself on a mass Christian resurgence, a *movement* which would socialize the means of production and introduce democratic reforms might be able to play a major role in an orderly modernization of Russia. Similarly, as economic development and social tensions speeded up, a liberal could well expect the creation of a constitutional government. A democratically elected representative assembly, civil liberties, and considerable social legislation would not seem an unreasonable hope. As more and more of Russia's millions received at least a secondary education, both could expect that modernization could go on in a relatively stable environment in which their forces could grow. The cumulative effect of post-1860 economic advances and political reforms seemed to have set the stage for progressive change. But progressive change had its traditional self-conscious definers and warriors, the radical intelligentsia. Novgorodtsev and Bulgakov challenged not only the unyielding bureaucratic government but also that group.

The term "radical intelligentsia" refers to that small number of Russians who considered the utter destruction of the nineteenth-century, political-social order the only means by which freedom and justice for all could be obtained. No single psychological portrait, body of ideas, or mode of action can accomodate all the intellectuals between Vissarion G. Belinsky and Lenin who could be considered "radical intelligents," but a sort of "ideal type" existed whom Russian writers in the late nineteenth and early twentieth centuries thought they could describe.

Though usually, if only partly, university-educated, the "intelligent's" knowledge of philosophy, history, economics, and natural sciences did not go very deep. He considered himself a materialist, worshiped science, and scorned all metaphysics and religion. He believed that he acted for the good of the "people," but on the basis of "rational egoism," not duty or altruism. Socialist institutions appeared to him to be the only acceptable way of ordering economic life, while he considered other institutions, such as property, marriage, and the family to be relics of a bygone era of patriarchal domination. Art, music, and literature earned his scorn if they did not present materials clearly useful in furthering the revolutionary struggle. To him "scientific" historical study showed that men acted in terms of universal laws which were leading them to a peak of eternal happiness. Martyrdom and the infliction of suffering and death on others were necessary if "progress" demanded them.

As far as the *radical intelligent* appeared concretely and not simply in the "ideal type" constructed from the psychology, ideas, and actions of Paul I. Pestel, Michael A. Bakunin, Belinsky, Nicholas G. Chernyshevsky, Dmitry J. Pisarev, Andrei I. Zheliabov, and others, he was likely to be found at the beginning of the twentieth century in the Social Democratic and Social Revolutionary parties or among anarchists. These were the implacable enemies of everything connected with the "system." They expressed contempt for those liberals or even moderate socialists who wished to reform Russia, sometimes greatly, but not by violence and protracted class war.

The radical intelligentsia, even in the heyday of the "nihilist," did not dominate Russian culture and thought. Men and women had maintained a rich humanistic culture throughout the nineteenth century, in the bureaucracy, the universities, the world of literature, the medical and legal professions, and the educated society of the capitals. But the radical intelligentsia had in familiar ways arrogated to itself the role of idealistic champion of the poor and oppressed. It could not make that claim without challenge in the increasingly complex society at the end of the nineteenth century.

Late-nineteenth-century modernization in Russia provided more varied career opportunities and widened intellectual horizons for the educated. The number of doctors, lawyers, professors, journalists, engineers, and other professionals grew, while the attraction of the way of life and modes of thought of the "radical intelligentsia" declined. As products of this development, Bulgakov, Novgorodtsev, and many others sharply opposed Russian Marxists, seen as the

15

twentieth-century descendants of the "radical intelligentsia." They denounced the "intelligenty" as conservatives whose perpetuation of old modes of thought and action actually hindered progressive development. At the same time, it seems almost certain that the degree to which they tried over and over again to refute the political and philosophical positions held by radicals betokened a deep fear that just these positions would most successfully mobilize and channel the deep hostilities of the Russian masses toward any kind of political-social order built around Western European culture. Idealistic liberal and Christian socialist alternatives to Marxism sought to safeguard freedom and culture by separating intellectuals and the educated from the radical intelligentsia.

Problems abound for the modern student of philosophically idealist and religious social thought. The radical secularism and positivism of the modern world refuse to include such thought among the multiple realities of everyday life. There is an almost universal consensus, imbibed in the very air men breathe, that idealism and religious thought are compensations for failures to find satisfaction in the "real" world. At least since the appearance of the French *idéologues* of the early nineteenth century, thinkers have sought a scientific method by which all thought, but particularly idealistic and religious ideas, can be derived from a given thinker's "real" social and economic position in the world. Accordingly, in an otherwise very good study of Russian thought of the late nineteenth century and early twentieth century, Soviet scholars label the idealistic and religious currents of the time "Noble landholder, liberal-bourgeois, and bourgeois-democratic currents in philosophy and sociology in Russia."[18] However, their volume does not show that the concrete, complex thought of Novgorodtsev and Bulgakov can be assigned to these categories. Such descriptions do not aid comprehension of ideas. They inhibit rather than encourage thought.

IDEALISM, RELIGIOUS THOUGHT, AND IDEOLOGY

The thought of Bulgakov and Novgorodtsev cannot be described simply as class ideology. They produced ideologies in an imprecise, general sense of that term—reasoned exhortatory explanations of the kind of social order each thought best for a free and just Russia. Like all such prescriptions, their writings were subject to the many determinations extant in the phenomenal world, including social class. But idealistic liberalism and Christian socialism were not ideologies in the more restricted sense that they were merely ideal expressions of conscious or unconscious Russian bourgeois or landowner class interest.

Bulgakov urged immediate state ownership of industry and transfer of all land to peasant proprietors and proposed eventual nationalization of the land. Novgorodtsev held views which were characteristic of influential middle class segments of Western societies of his time. But there was no large, independent, economically powerful class in late-nineteenth-century Russia which would feel that their interests were being supported by the kind of welfare-state liberalism Novgorodtsev proposed. Nor can it be shown that Russia was caught up in a mystical, world historical process in which non-Marxist thought played an essential role as a "false consciousness" leading its bearers to inevitable self-destruction.

Since the end of the nineteenth century, Marxists and others have tried to search out and specify the social-economic *bases* of thought. In the procedure known as the *sociology of knowledge*, some have tried to do so objectively. Although approaches of this kind can be traced back to the very beginning of modernity in Bacon's comments on the *Four Idols*, they derive mainly from Karl Marx's *substructure-superstructure* theory, to which Marx himself was not faithful and which few social thinkers or philosophers would accept today.[19] There is a long jump from the statement "social existence determines consciousness" to the proof or even demonstrated probability that all philosophical, religious, or artistic interpretations of human life are simply masked expressions of social-economic interests. A very large body of literature on this theory exists, but there is no successful application of it resting on a detailed empirical examination of just how the "substructure" and the "superstructure" are connected; indeed, the more literal and direct the approach, the more barren the results.[20]

Karl Mannheim's effort to construct a theory based on Marx's dictum failed. He was unaware of the degree to which such an effort must rest on the most basic psychological and linguistic research and could not handle the philosophical difficulties raised by his largely literary approach.[21] Moreover, the class categories he employed were defeated by the very nature of modern, particularly post-1848 thought. Workers and peasants did not produce systematic written thought, and, though "aristocratic" approaches to modern life can be found, these do not reflect noble class ideologies so much as individualistic reactions to industrialism and "leveling" in the garb of outraged aestheticism.[22] The truth is that in modern "bourgeois" intellection there is room for an enormous variety of thought between the poles of unrestrained subjectivity and laboratory science objectivity. From Bohemian to staunch defender of hearth and home, from anarchist to the most fervid defender of authority, from cosmopolitan to nationalist, from romanticist to the most unbending positivist—all can represent tendencies let loose by the collapse of the old order and the emergence of the middle class epoch.

To a large degree nineteenth- and twentieth-century thought expressed middle class civilization's search for a firm identity. In the "market place of ideas" all points of view, from the most subjectivist to the most rigorously objective, are commodities eagerly purchased by those who wish desperately to know what they are. What Mannheim took for a "free floating," non-class-determined intellectual stratum is really a most inescapable part of middle class culture.[23] Modern intellectuals and artists search for truth in a culture where all tables, be they Judeo-Christian, Enlightenment, or Marxist, have been shattered. To impute class interest to all who seek to reestablish or refurbish old tables is to use an ideological ploy rather than to engage in a difficult analysis. To deny the reality of the search is to place modern individualists on opposite sides of a barrier, across which communication is impossible and where mute stares of bitter hostility mask supplication for mutual understanding.

Despite the failure of Marxist "unmasking" and the rather small return from the substantial effort of sociologists of knowledge like Mannheim and Max Scheler, scholars continue to feel that there is a social dimension involved in the genesis and meaning of ideas. I would ask, "how could it be otherwise?" But to explain the connection is inordinately difficult, although one thing seems clear: students must get away from the simplicity and vagueness of Marx's time-bound categories and approach the problem more scientifically. It may be that at the conjunction of modern psychological, linguistic, and anthropological science there may lie a helpful explanation of the relation between an individual's social experience and his ideas. Work published in recent years by Jean Piaget, Basil Bernstein, Mary

Douglas, Madeleine Mathiot, Paul Friedrich, and Ernest Gellner suggests that this may be true.[24] However, not all of these seek and none would claim to have demonstrated in a reliably scientific manner the connections we need.

Of course, more basic than the efforts of Marxists and others to dismiss idealistic and religious thought as ideology is the modern tacit conviction that such thought must be treated in "compensatory" terms. Many intellectuals write about religious thought as either a naïve or self-interested rationalization of religion, which is seen as a group of dogmas, rituals, and institutions brought into existence mainly to recompense the majority of men for their alienation from economic, political, and personal self-determination.[25] Many go on to identify idealistic philosophy with religion and religious thought. Using the "compensation theory" in this way is simply to apply negative connotations to what the religious thinkers being criticized and many wise men view as a *fact*. Limited man finds it difficult to understand his place in an obdurate world in which events continually mock his sense of justice. He seeks not compensation in the negative sense, but fulfillment in what he is.

Other alleged paths to human fulfillment, such as "historical materialism" and "psychoanalysis" are not less "compensatory" and magical. To paraphrase what Alexander Herzen long ago asked, "Why is it superstitious ignorance to believe in God and enlightened wisdom to believe in History?"[26] Certainly those aspects of religion—a Father-God, Eucharist, Immortality—which are repugnant to "enlightened" moderns can be "bracketed" while a general theory of man and society connected with them can be confronted with experience and evaluated.[27] In any case, basic religious positions share with the basic assumptions of secular world hypotheses, such as positivism, materialism, and idealism, the quality of being neither provable nor refutable.

Many modern thinkers also treat philosophical idealism in largely compensatory terms. Writers from Heinrich Heine to Martin Malia have interpreted the great intellectual edifice of German idealism of the nineteenth century as largely a reaction to the feeling of impotence felt by German intellectuals of the French revolutionary period.[28] Unable, because of the lack of a revolutionary middle class and the presence of an inert peasantry, to gain the political freedoms attained through political struggle by the British and the French, the

German thinkers took refuge in philosophical theories in which Truth, Beauty, and Freedom could be acquired in nonpolitical ways.

One could adhere to the rigorous call of duty, treating all men as ends rather than means, advancing slowly toward a kingdom of ends where the higher values would reign. Or the individual could cultivate the *schöne Seele*, which regarded political despotism and social injustice as unimportant in relation to the cultivation of a *prekrasnaia dusha* through friendship, love, and art. Or the person could succumb to extreme subjective idealism, which denigrated experience in the phenomenal world to such a degree that he could think of the world in any way that seemed most desirable and comforting. Marxists extended this approach and made it "scientific" when they explained idealism as the compensatory philosophy of a weak or decaying bourgeois class, which could not bear to look at the real world, where its power was being eroded by economic weakness and concomitant revolutionary action.

This interpretation of German philosophical idealism has much validity, but probably at the same time manifests the modern intellectual's overly political-economic posture toward the world. Philosophical speculation can be and often is an autonomous activity, which has attracted some of the finest minds of the civilized world. If carried on far enough, it raises questions about man and the world, which are better explained by idealism than by either common sense or some form of mechanism.[29] The relevant question is not whether a philosophical position correlates with some class position or some concept of world political-economic development, but whether it helps us understand the time and place in which it was written, and seems to have offered the people of that time and place helpful perspectives on the problems that faced them, including that of finding a satisfying way of understanding their position in the world. As things now stand, subjectivity in judgments about the nature and functions of ideas cannot be avoided, but can be reduced to a minimum by honest effort and resolute care to avoid the politicization of thought.

Finally, students should be wary of too facile identification of philosophical idealism with religious thought and practice. In order to attain consistency and universality, both do require a transcendental realm, an area beyond direct human experience in the phenomenal world. However, there is a sense in which they are more inimical to one another than either is to the mechanistic theories which they both oppose. The more religious thought approaches acceptance of the world in its common sense guise, in which God is experienced as a Person and things and persons are experienced as real, though limited, the more it diverges from philosophical idealism. And conversely, the more idealism replaces the personal God with an abstract Idea or Mind and becomes involved in ever more sophisticated epistemological reasoning, the more it diverges from the common sense view of the world which the Christian doctrine tends to share with various forms of mechanism.[30] Expressed as the difference between "religion" and "religiosity" this incompatibility played a central role in separating the idealistic liberal from the Christian socialist in early-twentieth-century Russia. The religious thought and philosophical idealism espoused by modern Russian intellectuals should be viewed not as "compensations" but as two of many reactions to the onrush of modernity.

Modernity increasingly denigrates the subjective desires of individuals in favor of what appear to be the objective needs of the economic life and social organization of greatly increasing populations. The stronger the pressure, the more middle class persons desire that their inner thoughts and feelings should be attended to. They demand that organization, systematization, and measurement should not crowd out, render impotent, or explain away the human subjectivity of the person. Of course, they themselves pursue "rationalization" relentlessly in an effort to control nature and society. To an extent the good nineteenth-century bourgeois citizen tried to compartmentalize this fissure in the middle class spirit, dividing his life into two separate parts, the one of science or business, *occupational*, and the other of art, music, and the theater, *cultural*. Another indication of the polarity was the designation of the first as "man's world" and the second as "woman's world." Both the idealist liberal Novgorodtsev and the Christian socialist Bulgakov suffered from this ambivalence.

Intellectualized religion and philosophical idealism are the most respectable modes of defense of the person against the encroachment of rationalization. They are most respectable, because they themselves are systematic organizations of thought and feeling, which try to mobilize rationality in their service in order to demonstrate a kind of objectivity in which the "person" will still have an autonomous place. In the first case, the autonomy of the person rests on the objectivity of God and His order; in the second, on the objectivity of the idea and its logic. Both were able to picture Marxism as simultaneously deterministic and relativistic, destroying both the autonomy of the person in the name of efficient, social-economic organization and his link to humanity in the name of class epistemology and ethics. Defense of the person against "thinghood" drew Novgorodtsev and Bulgakov toward each other, while the respective natures of their conceptions of the "person" drove them apart. But their confrontation was not simply that of Athens and Jerusalem.

In idealistic liberal and Christian socialist thought the very core of European "bourgeois thought," *individualism*, made its last stand in Russia, where it had never been a dominant cultural fact. Concern for the "person" and individualism are different; indeed, in some interpretations, conflicting positions. But concrete manifestations of the first involve acceptance or rejection of various forms of the latter. The term "individualism," like most nominatives in the modern social-political vocabulary is debased coinage, meaning many things to many men. As far as the meanings which engaged the attention of the thinkers studied here are concerned, they largely rejected the *economic individualism* of early- and middle-nineteenth-century Europe. Nor would they accept *aesthetic individualism*, which celebrated the artist's search for truth as an ultimate value, requiring no justification other than the approval of the artist and his elite clientele. But their writings elaborated a variable mix of four interrelated forms of individualism: Kantian, Romantic, Nietzschean, and Christian.

Kantian individualism, fundamental, though not fully acceptable to Novgorodtsev and rejected by Bulgakov, required that each man seek to embody the good will, so that his moral judgments in particular situations might be taken as universally binding.

Within limits both accepted the claims of *romantic individualism*, which insisted on the individual's right to pursue the fulfillment of all sides of his personality and to reject any social, political, or economic force which would seem to thwart such development. Romanticism's late-nineteenth-century variant, *Nietzschean individualism*, placing the self-reliant Apollonia-Dionysian individual in sharp opposition to mass man, found some support from Novgorodtsev, Bulgakov, and others as a defense of high spiritual values. Finally, *Christian individualism*, in which each person's primary task is the salvation of his soul, but with that salvation requiring social concern and action, strongly moved Bulgakov and affected Novgorodtsev, whether in directly Christian formulations, Neoplatonism, or the German idealism of Fichte.

A complex interchange about the fate of Russia engaged Novgorodtsev, Bulgakov, and Russian Marxists between 1895 and 1914. None of the combatants doubted that Russia was undergoing great change and would continue to do so in the twentieth century. The fateful question was: under which auspices would institutional change take place and what would be the basic "world hypothesis" around which Russian culture in the broadest sense would be unified? The idealistic liberal and the Christian socialist polemicized together against Marxism and, at the same time, against one another. These clashes involved more than the intellectual quarrels of individuals. They entailed the claims of political parties, social forces, and major Russian institutions to define major aspects of the new Russia.

The church, the academy, and the Socialist parties contended for leadership in a modernizing Russia. Serge Bulgakov attempted to build a social movement around a reformed Russian Orthodox church. On pluralist principles, Novgorodtsev did not believe in the organization of political parties around specific institutions. But like most idealistic liberals, he was a man of the *academy* and he believed that the culture based on the principles of individualistic humanism, which the universities had to offer, was the correct basis for a modernized, progressive Russia. And, of course, the Social Democratic party had a world-cultural point of view and mission, which it sought to establish as the basis for a new Russia. The claims of the liberal and the Christian socialist are the subject of this book.

Although the time period under study is short (twenty years), important changes took place in the ideas of Novgorodtsev and Bulgakov. Decisive points were the apparent triumph over the bureaucratic government in 1904–1905; the sobering experience of the restricted authority of the first two Dumas, 1906–1907; and the deepening of the reaction after 1907 and especially after the death of Peter Stolypin in 1911. Chapter two presents the philosophical views of each in the period before 1904: Novgorodtsev's Neo-Kantianism and Bulgakov's understanding of Soloviev's thought. Chapter three offers an analysis of the major concerns of the St. Petersburg and Moscow religious-philosophical societies (1905–1914). These provided the personal and intellectual environment in which the ideas of

23

Bulgakov and Novgorodtsev developed after the shock of the Revolution of 1905. Chapter four discusses the development of Bulgakov's Christian socialism between the Revolution of 1905 and 1914. Chapter five does the same for Novgorodtsev's idealistic liberalism. In chapter six I seek to show the place and importance of idealistic and religious critiques of Marxism in early-twentieth-century Russia.

Chapter II

PROBLEMS OF IDEALISTS: NOVGORODTSEV AND BULGAKOV BEFORE 1904

BETWEEN 1900 AND 1904, Paul Novgorodtsev and Serge Bulgakov contributed decisively to the Russian critique of Marxist theory and practice. Novgorodtsev studied and taught the history and philosophy of law at Moscow University. Politically, with other professors he helped organize a liberal movement capable of bringing pressure to bear on the bureaucratic government. He also lectured in a liberal vein to Moscow workers and to audiences in provincial towns.

Bulgakov served as a professor of political economy at Kiev University and continued in books and articles the critical examination of Marxism which he had begun in the mid-1890s. Both spoke and worked for a new, modernized, and free Russia.

At the turn of the century the signs of the impending crisis of the old regime became increasingly noticeable. The progressive impoverishment of the Russian peasantry had reached the point where the continued productive existence of the class was threatened. In their everyday life they manifested drunkenness and brutal interpersonal relationships which suggested utter demoralization. The violent peasant uprisings, which had characterized rural life since 1861, rose in number and destructiveness in the early years of the new century. Although Russia's twentieth-century instability arose from several interrelated problems, that of the peasant was most important. At the end of the nineteenth century no social thinker could offer a philosophy or mode of action without taking into account the state and attitudes of the peasants. A fundamental difference between Nov-

25

gorodtsev's idealistic liberalism and Bulgakov's Christian socialism hinged on just that factor.

Depression between 1900 and 1904 sharpened the discontent of the industrial working class. The great industrial advances of the 1890s had sharply increased the size of the urban proletariat, which suffered from the low wages, bad working conditions, and abysmal housing characteristic of the early stages of the industrial revolution everywhere. Over two million workers suffered cruelly in St. Petersburg and Moscow. By official, probably low figures, the number of strikes increased from 19,000 in 1900 to 87,000 in 1903. Perhaps the most dangerous aspect of the situation was the government's stubborn refusal to carry out reforms. Trade unions remained illegal, while the existing laws regarding the pay and health of workers were not enforced. Government intransigence contributed substantially to the growth of organized revolutionary and radical liberal political movements.

Marxist, peasant revolutionary, and liberal parties rapidly became a permanent part of the political scene. The Russian Marxist Social Democratic Workers' party held its First Congress in Minsk in the first days of March, 1898.[1] Arrests soon followed, agitation and propaganda among workers made little headway, and instead splits over ideology and tactics quickly emerged. Nonetheless, the party remained in being with a potentially powerful appeal to workers. At its Second Congress in 1902 the party split into the Menshevik and Bolshevik factions, the latter led by the authoritarian Lenin and dedicated to violent revolution. In the same period other opponents of the regime formed the Social Revolutionary party. Stemming in the 1890s from the indigenous Russian revolutionary tradition, the party, formed in 1901, looked toward the peasants rather than the industrial workers as a base for a mass revolutionary uprising. Like the Social Democrats, the Social Revolutionaries demanded sweeping political, economic, and social reforms and aimed at the creation of a classless socialist society. The party included a terrorist wing, which carried out many assassinations, adding much to the general air of crisis in Russia between 1902 and 1911.

In the first years of the century, Bulgakov, who had been a Marxist, moved toward a radical liberal position which would associate him with the more moderately liberal Novgorodtsev. They worked together in the Liberation Movement which emerged between 1902 and

26

January 1904 under the leadership of Struve and Miliukov.[2] This political organization included nobles and others whose experience in the *zemstvos*—the local elective assemblies decreed in 1864—had led them to seek national liberal reform, including at least a consultative assembly. They were joined by intellectuals and many more professionals and white collar workers who hoped to establish a party for those who desired liberal political and major social reforms in Russia. By 1904, then, opponents of the regime had created both revolutionary and liberal organizations which might bring together worker and peasant discontent to press for major change.

In 1903, Bulgakov and Novgorodtsev shared a complex cluster of ideas and attitudes, the core of which was philosophical idealism. Yet, as evidenced in *Problems of Idealism*, the single most striking idealist manifesto of the period before 1905, and in their other important writings, differences of principle between their conceptions of idealism were likely to destroy any long-term cooperative effort in philosophy and politics.[3] As is often the case in human affairs, they came together in large degree as polemicists against a common enemy. Both feared that European positivism was spreading deterministic attitudes which would undermine the freedom and dignity of the human person. But they held opposed views on the degree to which an idealistic philosophy had to fashion its ontology, epistemology, ethics, and social thought on the mysteries of Christianity.

Before 1904, Bulgakov had become a self-consciously Christian philosopher, a disciple of Vladimir Soloviev, and Novgorodtsev had settled into an eclectic idealism, resting mainly on a Kantian base. The son of a priest, Bulgakov neared the age of forty with what was clearly a final return to the Christianity of his home and early education, which, like Soloviev and many others, he had deserted in adolescence for materialist conceptions. These had seemed a better basis for the struggle for freedom and justice in Russia. Although he no longer believed that to be so, up to 1904 he remained a socialist, though not yet a "Christian socialist." Novgorodtsev neared the same age with a fixed and learned commitment to Kantian philosophy, which remained the basis of his world view, even as he tried to "modernize" it with Hegelian, romantic, and Neo-Kantian perspectives. There is nothing in his writings to suggest that he had even been intellectually and emotionally attached to any body of ideas other than deeply rooted Platonism. At the very base of his personality lay

27

Christian beliefs and feelings, but he would not employ them in his writings as principles from which philosophical deductions could be made. Probably, he had also never wavered from his liberal political views.

RUSSIAN IDEALISM AND ITS CRITIQUE OF POSITIVISM

Novgorodtsev and Bulgakov often pictured themselves as members of an embattled minority defending their truth against dogmatic, entrenched positivism. In doing so, they accurately described the position of all idealist philosophers of their time. But their attitude stemmed directly from experience, real and vicarious, of the Russian intellectual atmosphere of the previous generation and the continuing presence in Russia of a vocal, often abusive, and intolerant positivist wing of the intelligentsia. The latter shared the general European conviction that in positivism they had grasped the key to universal truth. They were shocked and insulted by philosophers who cast doubt on their "scientific laws" of human development. Coming from an "idealist" perspective, such criticism was bound to arouse hostility and counterattacks. Thoroughly discredited by the inferior imitators of Hegel, "idealism" struck positivists as, at best, dreamy, well-intentioned literature posing as philosophy and, at worst, as the weapon of obscurantists trying to forestall the progress of knowledge and human well-being.

Novgorodtsev remarked that early-twentieth-century students might find it difficult to believe the monopoly which positivism had enjoyed among Russian intellectuals of the previous generation.[4] Moreover, the fierce dogmatism and abusiveness of the positivists, while no longer uncontestably dominant among Russian intellectuals, still characterized the reactions of many and hindered dispassionate study of philosophical questions. Idealists still encountered the same kind of virulence which an anonymous young "intelligent" had expressed toward the public lectures of the philosopher Pamfil D. Yurkevich in the 1860s. After accusing him of failing to see that a logical argument cannot refute a "fact," the writer went on, "I have the honor to warn you, dear sir, that, if in subsequent lectures you do not stop your cynicism, will not refer to materialism with respect, you will hear, not hissing, but whistling. But you will do even better if you become conscious of your impotence and cease to lecture, which would spare the public great errors and yourself vexing suspicion."[5] In fact, Yurkevich's "cynicism" lay in his critique of illogicalities in Chernyshevsky's *Anthropological Principle in Philosophy*. At least through the 1880s in the philological and juridical faculties of Moscow University, almost every professor referred contemptuously to metaphysics and considered Comte's law of human development from theological to metaphysical to scientific stages a fundamental truth.[6] A similar dominance of positivist views held at St. Petersburg University. Only scattered voices could be heard defending idealistic principles.

However, by the end of the century, the best philosophical minds in Russia had adopted various forms of idealism. From the 1870s V. Soloviev and Leo M. Lopatin at Moscow University and Michael I. Vladislavlev and, in the 1890s, Alexander I. Vvedensky at Petersburg attracted several students who became prominent idealist philosophers.[7] In the same period, Soloviev, Nicholas N. Strakhov, and Rozanov brilliantly defended idealistic points of view in salon society and in the press, while Chicherin published several important works of which idealism was the premise.[8] In 1884 professors at Moscow University formed the Moscow Psychological Society, providing a highly professional forum for the discussion of philosophical questions from all points of view.[9] Under the chairmanship of Nicholas Ia. Grot, from 1887 to 1899, the membership of the society expanded greatly, and it sponsored public lectures and books which popularized idealistic philosophy among educated Russians.

The society's greatest achievement and the greatest force for the spread of idealism in Russia was the publication from 1889 of the journal *Voprosy filosofii i pskikhologii (Questions of Philosophy and Psychology)*. Combining philosophical rigor and attention to agelong human problems, articles in the journal found a growing audience among educated Russians. Nonetheless, the attitude to idealism in the pages of most "thick" journals remained hostile and caused Novgorodtsev to say that "not much can be done immediately to overcome that tradition of Russian thought which links freedom with positivism and sees other forms of thought as reactionary."[10] That assumption made it difficult for idealists to gain a hearing for their philosophical critique of positivism and their presentation of an idealist alternative. They vigorously pursued that end in *Problems of*

29

Idealism, a work which illustrates both the sharp differences among the views of its authors and the grounds for considering them together as idealists.

Bulgakov and Novgorodtsev remained "idealists" in the technical sense that they believed that mind played a dominant role in the construction of reality as humans know it. They shared the basic idealistic premise that man's knowledge cannot be satisfactorily explained on either an empiricist or a materialist basis. Despite the degree to which psychological and social factors shaped individual attitudes toward everyday life, man's independent mental activity constructed that scientific understanding of the world which made human survival possible. In the same way both idealists believed that there existed objective ideals which men could pursue, despite the degree to which their thoughts and actions were determined. Both shared the view that these ideals were ultimately the good, the true, and the beautiful, and that human life was a drama revolving about the pursuit of these ideals in a recalcitrant world. In addition, they shared the conviction that repressive and outmoded social, political, and economic institutions not only destroyed heroic struggles for freedom but also distorted human nature. Made mutually hostile by material suffering and injustice, men could not advance to the kingdom of realized values. The Russian idealists sought to show that positivism was ontologically, epistemologically, and ethically false and, therefore, not able to provide a consistent basis for the struggle for freedom.

Most fundamentally, the idealists attacked the monism of Marxism and other positivist philosophies. They considered dualism the law of the world.[11] Rooted, ineradicable dualism, of theoretical and practical reason, of fact and value, of the *is* and the *ought* made rationalist epistemology necessary to counter subjective psychology, demanded the categorical imperative to combat man's asocial sociability, and required metaphysics to overcome the feeling of *Angst*, which arose from the disparity between man's impotence and the infinitude of his need to know his place in the world. Monistic philosophy failed on all three counts.

Positivist epistemology exposed clearly the dangers inherent in expanding the authority and use of natural science beyond its inherent limits. It held that all that could be known was the tangible, the measurable, the calculable. Some, dogmatic materialists, argued that there was nothing else *to be known*, while others, agnostic positivists, claimed to hold no opinion on this "metaphysical" point. To the idealists, both disregarded or denied some of man's most precious knowledge and most valuable experiences. And positivists compounded this stubborn ignorance, for that is what the idealists held it to be, by subscribing to the "copy" theory of knowledge, the notion that ideas in the mind embodied valid knowledge insofar as they exactly reflected objects in the external world.[12] It was as though Kant had never carried out his philosophical counterpart to the French Revolution.

The idealists also accused the positivists of a "vulgar materialistic" reduction of the psychic activity of the mind to that of the brain. According to the latter, all the contents of the mind came from the external world, entering through the action of external stimuli on the sense organs, becoming representations, and finally, by some unknown, but scientifically discoverable process of association, ideas. To the idealists, as to opponents of more refined behaviorism since, this reduction seemed pitifully inadequate to deal with the enormous complexity, subtlety, and mysterious beauty of the great creations of human mental activity on which the existence of civilization depended. This fear engendered by positivistic "metaphysics" and epistemology gained intensity when confronted by its utilitarian ethics, for that was both less theoretical and more directly involved with mankind's undoubtedly natural desires for happiness.

If positivists determined the truth of an idea by its faithfulness as a copy of its real counterpart in the outside world, they judged the *value* of an idea or action in terms of its usefulness. When talking about an individual, "useful" meant, in the ancient hedonistic or more recent Benthamite formula, that it produced more happiness or satisfaction for him than pain. When speaking of social groups or man as a whole, "useful" meant, in the modern utilitarian expression, "the greatest good of the greatest number," or in still more modern evolutionary language, "contributing to make the group more fit in the struggle for survival." In either sense, the idealists believed that the hedonistic-utilitarian ethics missed the very essence of morality, that "morality is an autonomous *quality* of the human soul. It is impossible to derive it from such non-ethical conceptions as satisfaction or happiness."[13] The *ought* and *is* were forever irreducible to each other.

31

The logical error of trying to derive the *ought* from the *is* vitiated utilitarianism, but other arguments could also be brought against it. Men do not seek happiness, but objects, and they derive happiness from the search perhaps more than the acquisition. In addition, much human experience suggests that to pursue happiness consciously is the surest way not to find it. And Jeremy Bentham's *Felicific Calculus* was doomed to fail because happiness, or pleasure, as J.S. Mill's effort to rescue it in *Utilitarianism* showed, is not unitary, but qualitatively different for different human activities. These arguments were directed against the highly individualistic form of utilitarianism, which became social only on the discredited principle of the additive nature of experiences of happiness. The idealists also rejected more altruistic forms, which saw the main standard of morality to be the degree to which one helped the downtrodden, thus increasing the amount of happiness in the world.

The idealists would admit to no real difference between Marxism and Spencerian evolutionism with regard to ethics. True, the latter employed biological metaphors like "quantity of life" as standards of progress and hence of the ethical, while the former spoke of "truly liberated social man." Spencer espoused individualistic competition as the road to satisfaction for all, while Marxists spoke of individual fulfillment in a classless society and excoriated competition. But both claimed to establish morality on a scientific basis by substituting for empirical utilitarian reasoning the deduction of moral rules from biological or sociological laws. From the point of view of the idealists, these substitutes represented no real improvement over customary hedonistic or utilitarian measures of value, for they perpetuated the root error, the derivation of morality from being, the denial of its autonomous character.

If anything, the Marxist or Spencerian evolutionist view erred more radically than narrow Benthamism, for it subjugated moral choice, as well as all life, to necessity in the form of a scientifically determined process of development. The evolution of the species became the ultimate criterion, a great plan which subsumed and gave meaning to all individual acts and choices. All idealists believed that monist ontology, reflexive epistemology, and utilitarian ethics led inexorably to the destruction of freedom inherent in the *one great plan*. When applied to men in their private striving for truth and in their relations with their fellows, they transformed science into "scientism," the opinion that the methods of laboratory science could be employed successfully to understand all aspects of human life.

Novgorodtsev and Bulgakov admired and practiced the science, that mixture of empiricism, rationalism, and "tacit knowing," by which men had conquered the natural world and had acquired the beginnings of knowledge of the social order. But they insisted that positivists, having succumbed to scientism, could not logically present their ideas as a defense of human freedom and altruistic action for others. In short, they contended that the kind of behavior considered a highest good by the Marxists was, whatever else it might be, not moral. Moreover, in ethics "scientism" was not scientific.

The idealists' critique of positivistic ontology and epistemology strikes the late-twentieth-century mind as basically sound. But, though logically valid in its own terms, their assault on utilitarian ethics does not convince. The suspicion lingers that a life of personal sacrifice for the well-being, including happiness, of others has some moral value. That it may be inspired by feeling, indeed, as Nietzsche said, feeling which deceives itself, that it may give the actor self-esteem and happiness, and hence may result from self-interest, need not deprive it of moral value. Self-overcoming may be the main thing demanded by morality, but not only self-overcoming attained by submission to the rational law of duty, but also the self-overcoming for the service of others taught by some utilitarians. No doubt this leads to subjectivity and can be claimed as a motive by the cruelest of murderers, but to deny morality to all acts in which self-interest of some kind can be unearthed leads to the kind of psychological analysis in which Nietzsche excelled and the consequent ethical relativism. This is a dilemma to which Novgorodtsev in particular was very much alert, and which neither he nor twentieth-century thought has been able to overcome.

Nineteenth-century thought complicated the European conception of man and set the stage for the tenuousness of ethical doctrines in the twentieth century. Since the seventeenth century most thought not committed to institutionalized authority had agreed that ethical prescriptions had to serve, or at least not hinder, the fulfillment of the individual personality. As long as the individual was seen largely in terms of the *cogito ergo sum*, it could be believed that rational ethical injunctions would be both universally valid and conducive to individual fulfillment. However, when the notion that men had a right to

33

demand satisfaction of their urgent affective needs gained credence, it became much more difficult to specify universally applicable norms.

By the 1870s the full relativistic consequences for ethics of the emergence of the more subjective romantic man became apparent and were articulated by Friedrich Nietzsche. The German philosopher challenged men to replace discredited tables by man-created moral codes, oriented to the satisfaction of human capacities for courage, sensitivity, and nobility. But the very nature of the romantic demand rendered this extremely difficult, if not impossible. The problem became not simply that men could no longer believe in the absolutes for which they seemed to yearn, but also that the kinds of self-fulfillment which they came to demand could not be generalized, even in relativistic terms.

The subjective needs of men are so varied that no ethical statement can possibly encompass them. Under such conditions, perhaps, socially-dedicated action acquires as much right to the label of "highest good" as does the "examined life." Novgorodtsev's eclecticism tried unsuccessfully to embrace both perspectives, while Bulgakov tried to recapture the whole man in an updated Christian framework. Their efforts should not be described as "bourgeois thought," but rather, insofar as they relate to something other than an individual search for a consistent and operative truth, as voices of the claims for social leadership by two institutions, the academy and the church, in a society which was far from bourgeois.

PAUL NOVGORODTSEV: KANTIAN AND CHRISTIAN

A professor of jurisprudence and a philosopher, Novgorodtsev was born in 1866 in the town of Bakhmut, a provincial center of approximately 8,000 people in the Ekaterinoslav government. He early showed signs of scholarly interests and aptitudes in his performance at the Ekaterinoslav gymnasium.[14] In 1884 he entered the juridical faculty of Moscow University, from which he graduated in 1888 as a candidate for a professorial post in the history and philosophy of law. Between 1888 and 1896 he traveled and studied abroad in France and Germany, working mainly in Freiburg, where he came strongly under the influence of the Neo-Kantians. On his return to Russia, he began to lecture in Moscow University. In 1897 he received the degree of master of state law for his dissertation, "The Historical School of

Jurists.'' After having defended and published in 1901 his ''Kant and Hegel and Their Teachings on Law and the State,'' he received the doctor's degree from St. Petersburg University. In 1903 he was designated professor extraordinary at Moscow University and in 1904 received the appointment as *professor ordinarius.*

One former student reports that he was a very popular professor, combining encyclopedic knowledge with a striking professorial appearance, an excellent lecturing style, and exceptional polemical ability.[15] Another points to his particular successes in the higher women's courses of Vladimir I. Gere. ''Who among them was not 'in love' with the 'raven head' with the Assyrian beard and the deep-seated eyes, when, with a small brief case in his hands he appeared at the lectern and, having trimmed neatly the pages of his manuscript, began his lecture in a velvety baritone?''[16] According to this former student, Novgorodtsev was the major exception to the generally low level of the Moscow Juridical Faculty in the mid-1890s. During that period he also administered a lecture bureau which provided scholarly speakers for lectures in provincial towns.[17] Socially, he participated in the high-level intellectual life characteristic of friendly gatherings in the apartments of such scholars as Vladimir I. Vernadsky, Alexander A. Kornilov, and Vasily O. Kliuchevsky. During the entire period of his academic activity, Novgorodtsev remained, also, closely connected with the liberal wing of political thought and action in Russia.

In 1901–1902, Novgorodtsev, as a ''liberal intellectual,'' helped found the Liberation Movement. In 1904 he was an important figure in the Union of Professors, which became part of the liberal pressure groups of the Union of Unions. In the same year he played an active role in an activist Moscow University faculty-student organization and was its chairman when Serge Trubetskoi went abroad. As a member of a brain trust he helped plan political programs and campaigns for liberal politicians.[18] However, no memoir or historical account of the political activities of the years up to and including 1904 reports political leadership on his part. One writer suggests that his wife, Lydia Antonovna, (Budilovich), a close, active supporter of Miliukov, strongly influenced his decision to enter politics.[19] A measure of Novgorodtsev's basic disinterest in active political life is his writings, three large volumes and numerous articles on questions of political theory and philosophy in which, in the midst of a Russia torn by political party strife, terrorism, and government reprisals, he makes only theoretical reference to competing doctrines.

Novgorodtsev was an outstanding professor and impressive administrator, but a deeply private man. There is nothing in his writings or those of the few who wrote briefly about him that would suggest that he was married with four children, nor that he was a regular participant in Moscow social life. In his small apartment on Troitsky Street he lived under exceedingly modest, almost ascetic, isolated conditions, in an atmosphere of great intellectual rigor. In his public life at the university and in politics, he never placed his inner feelings and deepest beliefs before other men. He lectured brilliantly, and gave much of his time to careful grading of papers and personal meetings with students, whom he met in his apartment each Sunday between eleven and two.[20] But one student remembered in those meetings a mixed ambience, on the one hand, softly-tender, while, on the other, restrained and chilly.

Similarly, in his seminars, attended by Marxists, *narodniks*, and idealists, Novgorodtsev maintained outward restraint and a refined, even-tempered, rigorously demanding approach to the subjects (those treated in this book). Yet he aroused in his students a feeling that internally, burning convictions were at work. All of his associates remembered him mainly as a strong, disciplined character with hidden depths of understanding and spiritual experience. As a teacher, lecturing or tutoring, as an intellectual disputant, as a political and educational administrator, and as a writer, Novgorodtsev remained an essentially private man who elicited warm friendship from some men, but whose deeper personality remained exceptionally guarded from public view.

Before 1900, Novgorodtsev had developed his mature philosophy, a modified, but still dominant, Kantianism. He tried to construct a logically satisfying philosophy in which religion and idealism would have a place, but which would remain true to the hard empirical and causal view of the world which science seemed to demand of the educated man. He suspected that this philosophy might not be compatible with political influence in Russia. In Western Europe, as Polanyi points out, men pledged fealty to a scientific outlook, but conducted their lives on the basis of deeply implanted ethical convictions, ultimately based on religion, and fortified by centuries of philosophical expressions of religious norms.[21] Though he fought for popular sovereignty, Novgorodtsev feared that the great mass of the Russian population did not possess such inner controls. He felt that the spread of scientism, a positivistic-deterministic approach to the world, might have free reign in Russia, for it would not find barring its hegemony the *inner man*, where the basic idea of human dignity continued to reign. But because of his strong Orthodox Christian commitment, Novgorodtsev feared this less than other idealistic liberals. He could believe that not only Western secular culture, but also Russian religion respected, above all, the *person*.

Novgorodtsev was a devout member of the Russian Orthodox church and a Kantian philosopher. To a large degree he avoided expression of his private and deeply personal Christian belief in his philosophical works. To him religion, and particularly Russian Orthodoxy, brought men together in ritual and prayer so that they could feel and to a degree manifest Christ's love. That experience provided the ultimate base on which social life rested, but in historical time on this earth it could not eradicate the social instability and conflicts arising from man's dual nature. Novgorodtsev believed that neither religious practice nor its relation to social life could be explained in analytic discourse by secular individuals. He shared a characteristic Russian Orthodox attitude that manly seriousness and modesty demanded that belief should not be trivialized by disputations in social gatherings and the secular press. So Novgorodtsev's social theorizing remained philosophical, especially Kantian, and provided only the smallest glimpse of his Christian commitment.

Nonetheless, Novgorodtsev's Russian Orthodox convictions contributed to the tension which threatened to tear apart his Kantian-based idealistic liberalism. In his attempt to provide a liberal philosophy for twentieth-century Russia, Christian personalism clashed with Kantian individualism. Kantian rationalistic epistemology conflicted with the more personal, integral ways of knowing associated with Christianity and its secular derivatives like German romanticism and Ivan V. Kireevsky's Slavophilism. So also, a Christian ethic based on love could not exist without contradiction with a Kantian reverence for the rational law of duty, although the two could partially coincide. As Novgorodtsev altered his Kantianism in terms of nineteenth-century romanticism and historicism, he at the same time manifested a basic struggle between rationalistic and Orthodox Christian attitudes toward the world.

The notion of the "person" central to European culture derives from Christianity. The Christian person is "a rational, indivisible, individual substance," created in the image of God.[22] A human becomes a person to the degree that he purifies himself of those aspects of his being which link him with the common nature of man.[23] The latter forms the basis of *individualism*, in which each man is a willful egoist seeking with clouded understanding to assert himself against nature and other men. The person strives for harmony, though not that of the anthill. Christian personhood manifests itself in a universal harmony in which each man is uniquely himself. As more and more of the variety of the world is brought into it, the more complete the harmony becomes. Unattainable in historical time, the goal of harmony is what the person seeks and approaches through religious faith and grace. Novgorodtsev understood the person in this way, as "the end and criterion of progress."[24] To be a person was to have "the highest, deepest, most inclusive experience of the real." These are not Kantian statements, nor would Kant say that "the principle of personality is the single moral norm." Epistemology, ethics, and a concept of the person are intertwined components of any world view, and a rooted Christian commitment can coexist but awkwardly with "Religion within the limits of Reason alone."[25]

Nonetheless, Novgorodtsev held that his social philosophy rested firmly on Kant's notion of the person as noumenon. Kant's concept of that aspect of man, in which he is free from the determinism holding in the phenomenal world, is closely related to Christian conceptions of free will. But for Kant, man was most free, most a "person" when he acted rationally in respect for the law of duty. Kant distrusted, restricted, and distorted man's affective approach to the world. Novgorodtsev understood him to mean that a man was most a person when he was most like other men, when he engaged in the logical, rational operations common to all normal men. He argued that such an accent on cognition as man's most distinctive trait undercut each man's uniqueness, that which most clearly represented his personhood. Kant's man as *noumenon* remained for Novgorodtsev the guarantor of human freedom, particularly in confrontation with all positivist philosophies. But he himself criticized it very severely in the liberal philosophy he tried to develop.

Similar conflicts to those revolving about the idea of the *person* could arise between Novgorodtsev's oft-repeated Kantian epistemology and his Christian belief. Novgorodtsev said that in relation to Christian mysteries he accepted Saint Anselm's dictum, *credo ut intelligam*: to believe so that he could understand.[26] He also praised integral knowing, a simultaneous act of the reason, will, and emotion, as a major characteristic impressed upon persons formed in the Russian Orthodox church. Yet many times he thoroughly endorsed Kant's epistemology and accented its superiority to positivist theories which, in one way or another, relied upon the "copy theory" of knowledge. He did not doubt that knowledge of the natural world, including man as physical and psychological being, resulted from the impression of the forms and categories of the mind—causality, time, space, and others—on the chaos of sensible experience.[27] That man as *noumenon* could *know* the good and the right by use of his practical reason and that this could guarantee the objectivity of norms also seemed proven by Kant.

Christian knowing and Kantian epistemology are not necessarily contradictory. Participation in Christian rituals and prayer may prepare the soul and even bring about a direct experience of truth. Kantian criticism, then, could be a way for a man filled with the light to cognize and express knowledge of himself, others, and the world around him. But the kind of immediate knowing which mystics have sought for centuries is of a different order from that attainable by Kantian rationalism. When Novgorodtsev described Kant's Reason as the "light . . . which exposes at one glance," he used a metaphor more applicable to Christian than to Kantian knowing. To many religious men much less mystical than Dionysius the Aeropagite, Kantian rationalism might appear restricting and distorting. Indeed, modern scientific minds hold that to make sense of myriads of "facts" by deduction or induction requires emotional, aesthetic, and intuitive reactions and "tacit knowing."[28] Novgorodtsev intended to satisfy the claims of both modes of knowing and to show the lineaments of a social order in which both would be productive. As such, idealistic liberalism would suffer from the intellectual lack of focus characteristic of eclecticism and a concomitant weakness in seeking the support of real political forces.

In ethics, Novgorodtsev also based his thought on Kantian principles to which he could not remain faithful. Like Bulgakov and other Russian Orthodox intellectuals, Novgorodtsev placed great emphasis on the fact that religion involved much more than teaching ethical

39

principles. He believed that the essential quality which Russian Orthodoxy aroused in practicing believers was love.[29] Under the impact of Orthodox ritual and prayer, a feeling of love enveloped the whole man, making it possible for him to live peacefully and productively with others, despite inevitable inner struggles and conflicts of interests. The predominance in a person of this feeling toward others would lead to an altruistic ethics substantially different from that embodied in Kant's ethical teachings.

Kant believed that rather than basing his social acts on the untrustworthy feeling of love, social man should cultivate the good will, reverence for law. He should accept the duty to act always so that he could will that his action could be subsumed under a law binding on all men. That decision was to be made on purely rational, formal grounds.[30] Utilitarian considerations, feelings, and motives were to be especially avoided, for, at best, they had nothing to do with the morality of an act. Novgorodtsev often praised the wisdom of this basic Kantian attitude, but he held that it required modification if it were to encompass the complexities of man's ethical life in a liberal, free society. Moreover, in trying to apply the standard in concrete cases, men would fall into utter subjectivism. Because of his exaggerated formalism, Kant had shown no way to avoid such inconsistency.

Kantian ethics had been criticized by his contemporaries, Johann W. Goethe, Friedrich Schiller, Friedrich D. Schleiermacher, and Hegel, for its formalism and excessive rigor. From his Orthodox Russian point of view, Novgorodtsev applauded their criticisms and sought to reconcile his basic Kantianism with them.[31] Goethe, Schiller, and Schleiermacher had tried to show that benevolence, sympathy, love, and noble purpose could be the basis of ethics, that Kant's attitude made a mockery of much of the good done by man in history. But most of man's history disgusted Kant, who believed that dedication to the ethics of duty would make progress at least possible. Novgorodtsev would follow Goethe and Hegel in saluting Iphigenia for confronting harsh *Moralität* with *Humanität*.

Hegel sought to overcome Kant's formalism by showing how rules of ethical behavior differed in terms of the time, place, conditions, nations, and social classes in which they developed. For an individual they represented the impact of the many forces which had formed him. They could not be subsumed completely under the rational law of duty. Hegel showed that Kant's formulation of the latter placed an

40

impossible task before men, for "it is inherently self-contradictory to seek any moral legislation, which would have to have content, from this practical reason, since its essence consists in not having any content."[32] Before 1905, Novgorodtsev placed this statement at the very center of his effort to make Kant's ethics active in the political world. But, he cautioned that, although Hegel's attack on Kant's formalism was valid, he had placed man so much under determination by social and national forces that his freedom had been destroyed.[33] In an effort to reconcile his basic Kantianism with Hegel's objective idealism, Novgorodtsev turned to the Neo-Kantians, particularly to their development of Kant's natural-law doctrine.

Novgorodtsev considered his restatement of the principle of natural law to be his outstanding contribution to political philosophy. As a natural-law theorist he contributed to a mainstream in twentieth-century legal thinking. As a Russian idealistic liberal he tried to employ the doctrine to reconcile Kantian formalistic rigor with the emphasis on the concrete of nineteenth-century romanticism and historicism. To do this, he argued that Kant had strongly implied what the Neo-Kantian Stammler made explicit, "natural law with a changing content."[34] The latter became an instrument for bringing phenomenal content into Kant's ethical principles without endorsing Hegelian determinism and utopianism. Similarly, it made it possible for Novgorodtsev to accept the historical-judicial school's emphasis on historical experiences, while avoiding its positivism. For a Russian Orthodox thinker drawn to Kantian sobriety, the notion of natural law with a changing content made possible a liberal progress theory. It pointed toward a *summum bonum* in a world where good and evil commingled in all human actions and would do so until the end of time.

The concept of natural law has appeared in theories of law, society, and government at least since the Stoics. Although many different ways of using the notion can be distinguished, a normative characteristic has dominated.[35] Thinkers offered "natural law" as a standard by which existing behavior and institutions could be evaluated. But what was the standard, the "natural"? For many it was a universal unchanging "human nature." Unfortunately, neither history nor science has been able to produce any acceptable criteria by which one description of "human nature" can be shown to be universally true.

Most important in the seventeenth and eighteenth centuries in the

West was the idea that humanity's most uniquely determining attribute was *reason*. Enlightened philosophers claimed that most institutions and beliefs of the people of the time were irrational, "unnatural," and that, properly educated, Europeans would cast them off in favor of rationalistic, "natural" arrangements. Novgorodtsev called this a "naïve faith."[36] For a corrective he turned to Kant and the Neo-Kantians.

Kant wrote little about natural law, but Novgorodtsev considered his contribution decisive. In his philosophy of Right, Kant stipulated that a natural law relating human affairs rested on a priori principles, those which applied to man "as long as he possessed freedom and a moral consciousness."[37] Recognition of natural laws arose from rational consideration of the grounds of human moral action. More precisely, natural laws were those which were universally and rationally necessary for a legal order in which men could exercise their moral freedom. They were criteria for evaluation of political law.

From Novgorodtsev's point of view, it was part of Kant's genius that he did not offer a genetic description of how natural laws arose and manifested themselves in human institutions. But he believed that Kant's natural law, like his categorical imperative, was unduly formalistic. No way was shown to relate the formal principle to the concrete political experiences and purposes of men. Kant's approach denied the right of culture-bound humans to turn their values into eternal contents of natural laws, but was so abstract that in practice it encouraged subjectivity.

The Neo-Kantians, Paul Natorp, Rudolph Stammler, and Wilhelm Windelband were showing how to bring natural law into connection with the customs, habits, and living needs of people.[38] Natural law posited a highest good for mankind, in Stammler's term, a *social ideal*, a "community of freely willing men," similar to Kant's "kingdom of ends." However, unlike Kant, they believed that certain concrete institutional and legal principles embodied "natural law" for their place and time. They represented a temporary "highest end" toward which men strove until greater perspective enabled them to see a higher end. The higher end could be glimpsed by the application of the critical method to the conflicts and mutual relations in a specific society. And so empirical advances could be made toward a "highest end" which could be unattainable on this earth.

Eager to unite philosophy and politics in Russia, Novgorodtsev did not see in the 1890s that "natural law with a changing content" would be either too empirical or too formalistic. It could lead to a claim of universality for the values of a class (Marxism), a nation, or a culture (Windelband). Or if restricted too much from concrete embodiment, it would easily become what it had been for Kant—a group of highly abstract principles. It could lead to the relativism of the historical school of jurists, or back to Plato, with his eternal forms, never fully embodied on this earth. There could be little doubt about the direction Novgorodtsev's thought would take when choice became imperative. When the optimism surrounding the Revolution of 1905 ebbed, he would fall back on a Kantian statement which he repeated more than once, "The moral state of man in which he must always reside is *virtue*, that is, the moral determination to *struggle*, and not *holiness*, in the form of apparent possession of a complete purity of the will."[39] Both his religious and his idealistic convictions would push him toward "manliness," full recognition of the tragic sense of life.

Conceptions of human nature and related epistemological convictions bear heavily on social theory. They limit the goals attributable to a society and help define what means should be safeguarded, encouraged, or employed to attain them. Novgorodtsev's Orthodox Christianity and his Kantianism, while compatible in important ways, brought unresolvable tension into his idealistic liberalism. Christian knowing transforms the soul, whereas that of Kant does not. All rational men may know the law of duty, but not all rational men can know the will of God. A Kantian society would seek cohesion from the commitments of rational individuals and leadership from experts, the most successful products of rationalistic education. Rationalism would be its cultural keynote and all customs and traditions the targets of institutional "rationalization."[40] An Orthodox Christian society would seek to unite men in prayer, participation in the sacraments, and spiritualized good works. It would distrust "experts," would place ritual at the center of education, and would safeguard old usages from the all-out onslaught of rational systematization. And the form of knowing implicit in the Christian view of the person espoused by Novgorodtsev leads to perspectives on the future of man which, as a Kantian, he would not accept, for which in fact, as a Kantian, he castigated others, Comtian and Marxian.[41] Seeking to satisfy the needs of both Kantian individualism and Christian personalism, he produced an eclectic liberalism in some tension with the social and

43

political facts of early-twentieth-century Russia. Indeed, knowing by believing and believing by acting are Christian conceptions in some ways more compatible with Marxist thought than with rationalistic individualism. Perhaps this is one of the reasons why Bulgakov initially found Marxism so attractive and why, having found it unsatisfactory, he rapidly moved past philosophical idealism in his search for an intellectual basis for the freedom struggle in Russia.

SERGE BULGAKOV AND VLADIMIR SOLOVIEV

In the period before 1904, Bulgakov moved from Marxism to idealism. However, his idealism sharply diverged from that of Novgorodtsev. He employed Kantian epistemology and ethics to criticize and eventually reject Marxist philosophy, but once having abandoned Marxist metaphysics, he rather rapidly moved toward another.[42] Kantianism was too narrow in its conception of man, too technical and abstract in its epistemology, too rationalistic in its ethics, and too tentative in its approach to ultimate salvation to satisfy him. Novgorodtsev experienced the same feelings, but much less sharply. With the liberal's perhaps essential attitude that tolerant study and expression of different opinions and ideas can always lead to acceptable compromises, he sought to reconstruct liberal theory on a Kantian base. Bulgakov became a disciple of Soloviev, an idealistic philosopher with mystical visions of the gradual advance of humanity toward *Godmanhood*. Though the end for man was to be religious transfiguration, Soloviev argued that secular reform and revolutionary movements played an indispensable role in the process. This fit well with what Bulgakov sought at the end of the nineteenth century—a philosophy which would discard the materialistic determinism of Russian Marxism, while attributing an important role in human development to the progressive activities of political men.

Bulgakov was born in 1871, into the family of a priest in the city of Livna in Orel. His life as a child was saturated with religion, his father being a provincial priest and both parents "being penetrated by church faith in a simple and naïve entirety, which permitted no questions and at the same time no freedom and weakening."[43] The religious atmosphere deeply impressed him, and he later found in it "my own deep nature, my calling, my element." He lived in the

44

modest circumstances of a town priest, in a wooden, simply furnished, five-room house with no pretensions to affluence, but in immeasurably better circumstances than the majority of the townspeople among whom he lived. Resentment of the well-to-do landowners of the district and their cultural heritage of literature, art, and music dominated his social attitude, as it did those of common people. At one and the same time he felt union with the poor through a shared Christian culture and ''shame and social repentance'' because of his superior circumstances.

At the age of thirteen, Bulgakov entered the Orel Theological Seminary, intending to follow in his father's footsteps. However, like so many educated young people in Russia, he rebelled against a state resting on the misery of the masses and a church which blindly served that state and appeared indifferent to the cruelty and injustice of the social-political order. Bulgakov turned to materialism and Marxism, which he accepted as both a scientific theory of the development of freedom in history and a morally elevated guide to practice. In 1888 he transferred to a gymnasium at Elets and then in 1890 on to Moscow University, from which he graduated with distinction in law in 1894. After work on his master's degree, he went to Germany in 1897. Upon his return to Russia in 1901 he was appointed to the Chair of Political Economy at the Kiev Polytechnic Institute, where he remained until 1905. By education and profession Bulgakov was well prepared to undertake serious social theory.

During the 1890s, Bulgakov participated in the theoretical debates revolving about Marxism, both as applied to Russia and in the wider area of European social thought. With regard to the first he published numerous articles and in 1900 a scholarly two-volume study, *Kapitalizm i Zemledelie (Capitalism and Agriculture)*, criticizing on the basis of empirical study both Marxian ideas on the necessary direction of agricultural development and Herzen's idealization of the Russian commune.[44] A major conclusion of that work was that in the first stage of a revolution in Russia, peasant ownership of small farms should be encouraged. Only in that way would the peasant gain self-respect and the chance to become part of a stable, productive society.

Bulgakov participated in the polemics of the 1890s among European Marxists concerning the nature and continuing validity of Marxism. Could ideals be derived from scientific Marxist historical materialism? Was Marxist determinism consistent with individual freedom? If not, could it be combined with Kantian or Neo-Kantian critical philosophy, so that a thinker could at one and the same time offer a scientific analysis of the development of social forces and a reasoned demonstration of the freedom of the moral will? Bulgakov began as a firm exponent of determinism, but gradually changed into an idealistic and religious opponent of Marxism.[45] Marxism remained for him a scientific doctrine explaining the dynamics of social life, but he denied to it any capacity to explain man's values, ideals, and ultimate fate. Eventually he was to label it an evil force standing in the way of man's spiritual progress.

In July 1903, Bulgakov joined Struve, Frank, Berdiaev, Novgorodtsev, and others in the Liberation Movement. At that time, he was considered one of the "socialistic intellectuals" joining this attempt to unite various types of moderate socialist and liberal opponents of the bureaucratic regime. He helped define the group's effort to establish an antigovernment movement which would force the government to introduce much-needed reforms, but which would avoid violent revolution.

Bulgakov identified two purposes of the "Russian idealism" which he largely espoused before 1904. First, it rejected the aridity of Neo-Kantian epistemology in favor of "transcendental realism in epistemology and ontology, spiritualism in metaphysics, and a more or less closeness to Christian theism understood as the religion of God-manhood."[46] Secondly, it tried to shake the faith of Russian intellectuals that only a positivist philosophy could serve the cause of political, social, and economic freedom in Russia. The first aim had been partly accomplished by *Questions of Philosophy and Psychology*, while the second had been begun in *Problems of Idealism*. But the great majority of Russian intellectuals remained philosophically positivist and politically suspicious of idealism.

Positivistic opponents ranging from liberals to mechanistic and contextualistic Marxists denounced idealists as quietistic, anti-egalitarian opponents of democracy.[47] One Marxist opined that they were "lackeys of the bourgeois" and "weaknerved faddish decadents," whose God was "'a priori' against direct, universal suffrage."[48] Idealistic arguments that man should seek progress through personally accepting the universal moral law or that the person's primary duty was to seek the salvation of his soul were interpreted as

46

"in reality" a surrender to maintenance of the bourgeois order resulting from fear of democratic politics.[49] The best which avowed
positivists would say of the idealists was that their turning away from
the world to indulge in philosophical-religious searching might un-
earth insights which would help future man. But this possibility could
not override the criminality of preaching soul-searching and Kantian
moral rectitude to millions who lacked food, shelter, and clothing, the
essential bases of a human life.

Bulgakov believed that *Problems of Idealism* could not shake these
mistaken convictions, because it lacked a unified overall view and
most of its contributors stopped at abstract philosophical idealism.
He asserted that the latter was no more able than the positivism of
Comte and Spencer to answer the ageless human problems which it
was philosophy's duty to confront. If it was to express the truth and
be a real force in life, idealism had to move on to religion. "To me
personally the meaning of the idealistic movement at the present time
is decided by its religious value and is defined in dependence on the
degree to which it can serve the interests of a religious renaissance."[50] So the emerging religious philosopher directly denied to
Problems of Idealism the calling which its editor, Novgorodtsev,
attributed to it: that of presenting a secular idealistic philosophy
which, without specific religious affiliation, could provide a valid
understanding of the world and basis for the freedom movement in
Russia.

To seek an understanding of the world from Soloviev rather than
Marx entailed a major shift in perspective and language. But, for
Bulgakov, the change was easier than one from Marx's social theory
to that of Novgorodtsev. He had become a Marxist for two basic
reasons: As a "social science," it appeared to lay bare the dynamics
of the economic relations on which capitalist society rested. In the
process, it indicted the perpetrators of enormous suffering in Russia
and described concrete institutional changes to overcome it. By 1903,
and to some degree, throughout his life, Bulgakov believed that Marx
offered a valid, although limited, analysis of social-economic phenomena.

Marx also offered an all-encompassing explanation of man's pris-
tine innocence, his fall, his purification and return to a world of
harmony and freedom. Bulgakov had begun to deny this aspect of
Marx's teachings as early as 1896, and by 1903 had found in Solo-

viev's thought a convincing alternative to it. Like many others, he had exulted in a "scientific" theory which, at the same time, unraveled the mystery of man's fall and redemption. But, to a thinker deeply concerned with the latter, dissatisfaction with Marxism soon sets in. There is no empirical or logical reason to think that Marx's five stages of historical development—primitive communism, slave society, feudalism, capitalism, and socialism—inevitably lead to a transfigured man.

The path from necessity to freedom, from history to nonhistory, cannot be determined solely by human ends, means, and struggles. If a thinker demands a philosophy embodying a link between the profane and the sacred, the metaphysics of Soloviev is preferable to that of Plekhanov. But it is also preferable to that of Novgorodtsev, who shared Bulgakov's scorn for utopian thought, but insisted on radical separation of the profane and the sacred. Before 1905, the liberal idealist said little about the doctrine of human progress to perfection on this earth. Perhaps this idea was so intrinsic to late-nineteenth-century liberalism that he did not wish to alienate associates and give aid and comfort to enemies. But, Bulgakov found the essential error of Marxism in its historical theory. Neatly reversing Feuerbach, he asserted that it rested on blind faith, an outgrowth of the misery and hopelessness of men in their own time and place.

Bulgakov directed his sharpest barbs at the modern delusion that progress was inevitable and linear. He first denied to positivist progress theorists like Auguste Comte, Herbert Spencer, and Marx their identification with the most powerful symbol of the day, *science.* Belief in progress to a perfect consummation was not scientific, but a religious faith, the "Religion of Humanity."[51] In order to maintain the will to live, men needed to believe that their ideals would one day be embodied in human life but, despite its enormous contributions to human well-being, science could not provide the ground for such belief. Saint Augustine was right and the modern *raisonneurs* wrong; faith came first, then conviction, and eventually knowledge. But humanity could be no God, for from the secular point of view, it was a reification, no more than the collectivity of individual men, displaying their weaknesses and limitations.[52] Men could act progressively in the world only in terms of a higher ideal outside humanity. To try to build an ersatz religion around humanity was to fall into the toils of bad infinity.

Pavel A. Florensky, in an argument which Bulgakov fully accepted, applied Georg Cantor's discoveries regarding infinity to the problem of human progress. In his great work, Cantor distinguished between *potential* and *actual* infinity.[53] The first defined infinity as the embodiment of continual, unending, limitless change, "a variable finite magnitude increasing beyond all finite limits." Its most basic manifestation was eternally flowing *time,* in which each moment devoured the last, forever. Florensky sought for striking metaphors for this and found them in the torment of Tantalus (itself accepted as a positive symbol of man's eternal striving by Camus), the vessel of the Danaïdes, and, most vividly, in the essence of the devil as seen by Buddhists. The devil was "an eternally hungry monster, with a fat head, a savage visage and enormous stomach, which is never filled. It had dry, skeleton-like members and was naked, covered with hair, with . . . a narrow mouth. Eternally hungry and thirsty, once a millenium it heard the word, 'water.' But, when it appeared before the monster, the water turned foul."[54] So it was that natural, sinful man's ideals and hopes, when apparently realized on this earth, inevitably turned into evil torments, leaving men ever hungry for true salvation. Positivism committed its proponents, both scientists and social thinkers, to the idea of *potential* infinity. In that guise infinity eternally mocked the idea of human perfection on this earth.

To Florensky, Cantor's conception of *actual* infinity seemed to make human striving meaningful while maintaining mathematical rigor. *Actual* infinity postulated a fixed construct, greater than any finite constant, no matter how large it might become. Actual infinity designates a fixed number while potential infinity denotes an endless process. A circle defines an actual infinity, for an infinite number of points may be inscribed within it, each of which, however, is fully defined. Most important from the standpoint of discourse about man's condition and fate, *actual* infinity provided a logical meaning for the *concept*. As Friedrich Schelling showed in *Bruno*, "the concept sums up a multitude of representations, which do not appear to be finite. But, since the concept, by its essence, is fully defined and given it can be nothing other than a case of *actual* infinity."[55] Rational and irrational numbers, a line, a circle, a concept—all of these can be viewed either from the standpoint of potential or of actual infinity. But only the existence of actual infinity would enable men to attribute progressive meaning to the infinity of human states manifested in the historical process.[56] Therein lay the tragic flaw of all positivistic progress theories—they could not specify mankind's actually infinite limits, God, Platonic ideas, the moral law.

Religion and idealism provided the only valid basis for the idea of progress—universals, the reality of actual infinity. Positivism, though it did so (the perfect man) had no right to postulate universals. Since no perfect man existed in the external world (the example of Jesus Christ, of course, was neither available nor acceptable to positivists) the concept of a perfect man could never arise except as a vague subjective notion (again unacceptable to the positivists). Enlightenment, Marxist, and Spencerian theories of evolutionary progress to a perfectly harmonized human order could not be sustained. Either the myth of Tantalus described the fate of mankind or human fulfillment demanded and reality included essential nonpositivistic elements.

Bulgakov offered other arguments against the positivists' secular idea of progress, all revolving about their assumption that the ultimate goal of progress was complete happiness.[57] The nature of future man's happiness could not be known. Even if glimpsed, it could not be logically pursued, because of the prevalence of unintended consequences in history. If acquired as viewed by hedonistic philosophies, it was self-contradictory. The means, heroism, sacrifice, and struggle, were directed toward an end of satiety, a life of pleasure, without struggle, without care, the "ant hill" of Dostoevsky, a state which made meaningless the values to which the best representatives of hundreds of generations of humanity had subscribed. Could the aim of progress be the mindless herd of which Nietzsche spoke, wandering about with neither cares nor memory?[58] Or, if it were conscious men, what would be their moral stature if they accepted "happiness" in full cognizance of the enormous suffering with which it has been purchased? Would this be the "perfect" mankind toward which progress was allegedly directed?[59] Most fundamentally, even assuming that there could emerge a "perfect" humanity, on which logical grounds could it be demanded of the individual that he sacrifice himself for it?

Perhaps Bulgakov and other antipositivists followed Hermann Lotze's argument on this point. That philosopher believed that to demand that an individual strive for a goal of mankind was logical nonsense "unless it could be shown in what manner the individual could avail himself of this goal for himself."[60] He went on to argue that there was but one way that men could be sure that every individual would participate in the future happiness or perfection of mankind. This was to assume personal immortality. "Just as every individual has a perfect right to renounce his own claim, so every individual has a right to expect and demand a fair share in the future happiness or perfection of mankind."[61] And, if no guarantee could be given that that expectation and demand would be met in some way or other, the individual had a perfect right to turn his back on the very concept of history and its goal and to assert its complete irrelevance. For his part, Bulgakov would recognize but one absolute duty of the individual to mankind: to respect the freedom and spiritual self-development of the *person*. He believed that the philosophy of Soloviev showed how this goal implied social struggle and progress, but not the attainment of a secular utopia.

Bulgakov held that Soloviev had successfully connected the truths of philosophy and religion and integrated both with the truths of practical life. As such, he was exactly the philosopher Russia and the world needed in the beginning of the twentieth century.[62] Soloviev had been able to present religious truth in a way acceptable to the modern scientific and rational mind and to show the degree to which only Christian belief and practice could make possible the solution of the social, political, and economic problems on which so much modern energy was expended.[63] He embodied the essence of the Russian approach to life's problems and the solution of the problems which had tormented all people in all ages. That his mysticism repelled many clearly indicated the poverty of the age.

In his doctrine of *total unity*, Soloviev epistemologically reconciled empirical, rational, and metaphysical approaches to the world. Not scientifically demonstrable itself, it had to be taken on faith, for without it the world and man himself disintegrated into a chaos of unconnected parts. Total unity was *real*, in the sense that it existed prior to any nominalistic accumulation of cases. Yet it was immanent to all cases. Faith in unity made the philosophical and scientific enterprise possible, for without that faith men would be unable to make the hypotheses and design the experiments which led to knowledge. Man as a knower apprehended the world through an integrated act of thinking, willing, and feeling and, in so doing, gradually uncovered the unity which made its own discovery possible.

The absolute all-unity of being confronted men in three ideas: good—satisfying to the nature of the will, truth—to that of the reason, and beauty—to that of the emotions. That is, one divine principle manifested itself in three different ways, although man, internally fragmented in his fallen state, experienced them as three conflicting elements of his personality. Man's actual discovery of the unity of his being was gradual, taking place as he developed toward Godmanhood, the emergence of which would signal God's and man's triumph over human egoism and willfulness. With it would come triumph over evil and man's return to unity, with himself, the world, and God.

Soloviev's refusal to explain away evil greatly impressed Bulgakov. Evil was neither a mere goad inducing the individual to live by the formal law of reason, nor a motive force in a world-historical process over which man had no control. Soloviev accented both its inescapable "realness" and its utter irrationality. Evil was neither the "absence of good," nor a temporary phenomenon to be eliminated by material progress or evolution. There was in it something which could never be explained or justified in rational terms within the time span of the world.

Soloviev saw that the solution to the problem of evil had to be eschatological. Given the presence of the irrational component of evil in all human actions, all efforts directed toward its destruction were themselves built on willful egoism, force, and violence. Only the termination of the world and the appearance of a new kingdom in which men were radically transformed could bring about the final triumph of good over evil. Fallen, sinful man could conceive of this blessed state and hence of the reality of evil because in him there existed *Sophia*, or Wisdom.

In Soloviev's anthropology, Sophia linked God with mankind and acted to bring man to the Divine. By pitting himself against God, nature, and other men, egotistic man had fallen away from his ideal self, from the world soul of which he was a part. In both body and soul, he was foreign to Sophia, but she increasingly drew him back to the world soul, ideal humanity. The aim and meaning of the historical process became, then, to regain unity, to escape the chaos of separated elements which resulted from the fall from divine unity. The historical process became "the spiritualization of man through his internal assimilation of divine principles." That is, man, the passive principle, reacted with the Divine, the active principle, to introduce active unity into the world.

But man's role in the return to unity extended beyond passivity. His active egoism held it back, while his God-given love, assured of fertility in life by Christ's Atonement, urged him to bring together again in total unity that which he, in his fallen state, had dispersed. Soloviev believed that the secular struggles in the world for political, social, and economic justice played a major role in this process. From this point of view, Bulgakov found the secular idealism of Novgorodtsev too abstract and his liberalism too pedestrian to bring about the qualitative change in man which Christianity showed to be certain. Not only was Bulgakov encouraged in this direction by Soloviev's mystical philosophy but also by the perspectives developed by the St. Petersburg Religious-Philosophical Meetings of 1901–1903 and the new journal *Novyi Put'* (*New Path*), with which he became associated in 1904.

Beginning in 1903, Bulgakov's intellectual activities became inseparable from the religious-philosophical societies. He viewed with approval the discussion between intellectuals and churchmen at the St. Petersburg Religious-Philosophical Meetings; but he criticized them, as well as Soloviev, for "lack of interest in and contact with concrete historical, social, and political problems."[64] At the Kiev Polytechnic Institute he organized meetings, at which a few scholars discussed the interrelations of religious, philosophical, and political questions. Toward the end of 1902, these were transferred to the institute's large auditorium, where they attracted a variegated group of students and even a few workers.

As Bulgakov propounded his theory that a socialist progress theory without a religious basis would be futile—indeed, highly destructive—he debated with the empiriomonist Marxists Nicholas V. Valentinov (Vol'sky) and Lunacharsky.[65] This began a period in Bulgakov's life in which he dedicated substantial effort to the organization of religious-philosophical societies in Kiev, Moscow, and St. Petersburg. The political events surrounding the 1905 Revolution provided the hopes, tensions, and eventually disillusionment which sparked much of the discussion at the societies. But Bulgakov and others involved in those exchanges passed beyond the transient cir-

cumstances of the day to confront questions of religion and philosophy of more fundamental relation to the nature and survival of
Russian culture.

By 1904, Bulgakov and Novgorodtsev had presented the philosophical bases of their alternatives to Marxism. Novgorodtsev had
shown that, whatever modification he might introduce, he would not
stray too far from Kant's rationalistic individualism. The conflict
between Christian personalism and Kantianism was fundamental but
was muted by his refusal to employ Orthodox Christian feelings and
beliefs in his argumentation. Not only nineteenth-century intellectual
and political developments but also inner Christian conviction im-
pelled Novgorodtsev to accept alterations of Kantianism that accented the moral goodness of sympathy and benevolence and the
impact of social realities on the person's developing ethical consciousness. The same combination of religious belief and historical
awareness supported one of his most basic positions, that the pursuit
of utopian final solutions to the problems raised by man's "asocial
sociability" were futile and dangerous.

In the year of *Problems of Idealism*, Bulgakov firmly asserted the
principle that any valid idealism had to be religious idealism. Moreover, religion had to be *real* religion, in which humans sought true
membership in a church, through prayer to and sacramental contact
with the living God.[66] In that church men would seek salvation and
not the mere bolstering and refinement of their ethical sensibilities.
Bulgakov believed that only religious idealism could save philosophy
from the sterile juggling of concepts characteristic of the imitators of
Hegel and the epistemologists. He continued to feel that Marxism
offered the most accurate analysis of the social-economic dynamics
of the modern world, and that liberal demands for representative
government and civil rights required immediate satisfaction. But
neither Marxism nor liberalism could provide the unifying philosophy
so desperately needed by twentieth-century man.

Concomitantly with the development of forms of antipositivist
idealism, another group of antipositivists claimed the attention of
educated Russians. Dmitry Merezhkovsky, Zinaida Hippius, and
Vasily Rozanov led a group of writers who, in association with
Orthodox church officials, organized the St. Petersburg Religious-
Philosophical Meetings of 1901–1903.[67] They raised in striking fash-

ion the basic questions of the place which Orthodox Christianity might have in a modernizing Russia. The meetings also provided a model of the way educated Russians of many backgrounds might exchange views on that topic. They set the stage for the Moscow Religious-Philosophical Society (1905–1914) and the St. Petersburg Religious-Philosophical Society (1907–1914). Though the latter societies emerged in a different political environment and pursued partially different aims, they continued to investigate, before a wider public, the place of Orthodoxy in Russian culture.

The ideas of Novgorodtsev and Bulgakov developed in conjunction with the exchanges originating in the religious-philosophical societies. In October 1904, Bulgakov became associated with the Merezhkovsky group as political editor of its journal *New Path*; and in January 1905, editor of its successor, *Voprosy Zhizni (Questions of Life)*. In 1905 he played a leading role in the formation of the Moscow Religious-Philosophical Society and in 1907 he helped found the St. Petersburg Religious-Philosophical Society.[68] There is no doubt that his direct involvement with the Merezhkovsky group in 1904 set in motion his rapid transformation from a socialist thinker with religious sensibility (like Lunacharsky, for example) to an Orthodox Christian thinker deeply concerned about social justice.

As far as can be discovered, Novgorodtsev neither delivered a paper nor participated in any religious-philosophical society. Yet his writings, in which he very seldom mentioned the societies, show awareness of their themes and discussions. Moreover, his late major work, *On the Social Ideal*, embodied a criticism of doctrines offering ways to reach a ''paradise on earth'' just as applicable to the eschatological prophecies of Merezhkovsky, Ern, and Belyi as to the secular utopianism of Marx or Spencer. Analysis of Novgorodtsev's idealistic liberalism and Bulgakov's Christian socialism requires familiarity with the activities of the religious-philosophical societies.

Chapter III

THE ST. PETERSBURG AND MOSCOW RELIGIOUS–PHILOSOPHICAL MEETINGS AND SOCIETIES (1901–1914)

IN THE RELIGIOUS-PHILOSOPHICAL MEETINGS (1901–1903) and societies (1905–1914), Russian intellectuals sought to delineate the place of Orthodox Christianity in a modernizing Russia. Discussions and many associated books and articles treated several related topics, such as the nature and mission of the Russian church, the religious beliefs and attitudes of Russian peasants, the degree of mutual influence between the culture of the educated and that of the people, and the relation of religious challenges to authority to revolutionary ideas and action. These were all questions which no social theorists in early-twentieth-century Russia could ignore.

The speculations at the religious-philosophical societies particularly interacted with the thought of Novgorodtsev and Bulgakov. In his idealistic liberalism, Novgorodtsev presented an alternative to Marxism which rested on Western European history and thought to such a degree that it demanded confrontation with the questions raised at the religious-philosophical societies. The gap between the apocalypticism so prominent there and his own basic Orthodox Christian commitment also played a major role in his thinking. As for Bulgakov, direct involvement in the religious-philosophical societies hastened his return to the church. As an organizer and major participant between 1904 and 1914, he developed the view of the true nature of the church and the basic truths of Marxism that defined his Christian socialism. Of course, neither the societies nor Novgorodtsev and Bulgakov could escape the impact of the Revolution of 1905. Of particular importance to Novgorodtsev and Bulgakov was the fate of liberalism, its victory and defeat in the period 1905–1907.

In the St. Petersburg Religious-Philosophical Meetings of 1901–1903, Merezhkovsky, Hippius, and Rozanov asserted that Orthodox Christianity embodied man's best hope of combining modernization with freedom. However, they claimed that the Russian Orthodox church had become a soulless, bureaucratic institution that denied to man the fulfillment of legitimate aesthetic, intellectual, social, and sexual needs. The church embodied the attitudes and usages of a passing phase of human cultural and religious development, while the writers had glimpsed new revelations that would usher in a new higher stage of the path to the divinization of man. Only if it could listen to, understand, and embrace the message of the new voices could the Russian Orthodox church play a positive role in the fast-approaching transfiguration.

Representatives of the church scorned the idea that they stood for an outmoded phase of the Christian drama of human salvation. Nonetheless, at the meetings and in clerical journals most churchmen discussed seriously and some approved of specific points of the intellectuals' critique. Yet even where pursued, mutual understanding foundered on the almost exclusively aesthetic approach of the writers. Like Thomas Carlyle, Nietzsche, and Charles Baudelaire, they felt repelled by the ugliness of modern cities, industries, and working class lives and the triviality of an "elite" culture based on the cash register and "healthy thought." And like Sören Kierkegaard, they asserted that the church, which should be the center of resistance to the positivist spirit, had betrayed its trust.

Supporters of the church asked the littérateurs to provide scholarly support for their attacks on the church and to describe the new revelations they had experienced. But Merezhkovsky and his associates would not translate their feelings into accurate historical exposition and rigorously logical philosophy. They considered the demand that they do so to be indicative of the very positivism they rejected. The "Godseekers" posed a fundamental problem of early-twentieth-century Russia and inspired widespread intellectual creativity, but made little impression on the church. On April 5, 1903, the Over Procurator of the Holy Synod, Konstantin P. Pobedonostsev, closed the public meetings. As the Revolution of 1905 approached, discussions continued in social gatherings, books, and journals and became influenced increasingly by political hopes and fears.

The Revolution of 1905 climaxed over two years of increasingly numerous and violent peasant disturbances and worker strikes. Long-time unsatisfied grievances temporarily united peasants, workers, revolutionary activists and terrorists, students, and the well-organized middle class liberals against the bureaucratic government.[1] Rural anarchy most frightened the regime, but the thousands of workers concentrated in St. Petersburg and Moscow acquired decisive importance. Denied trade unions or political organization, they began to move violently against factory owners and government. Revolutionary terrorists, propagandists, and agitators encouraged them, while liberals sought to bring to existence a constitutional political system which would make possible laws to improve the living standards of the poor and grant them civil rights.

Humiliating defeat in the Russo-Japanese War (1904–1905) weakened the government, particularly among moderate groups. Hatred against it was sharpened and concentrated by its bloody dispersal of a peaceful, organized march of workers and peasants in the streets of St. Petersburg on January 9, 1905 (Bloody Sunday). That merciless act increased the tempo of criticism, political organization, peasant depredations, and strikes and culminated in the national general strike of October 1905. The strike brought transportation, communication, and industrial production to a halt and forced the government to capitulate. On October 17, 1905, the czar issued the October Manifesto, which permitted the election of a national legislative assembly, the State Duma, and granted basic civil rights to millions of Russians.

The Moscow Religious-Philosophical Society emerged from the St. Petersburg Religious-Philosophical Meetings as a reaction to the Revolution of 1905. Of those who created it, the students, Vladimir Ern, Valentin P. Sventsitsky, Alexander V. Elchaninov, and Florensky had attended the meetings in St. Petersburg. Its most prestigious founder, Bulgakov, served as an editor on the journals publicizing the ideas of the Merezhkovsky group, *New Path* and *Questions of Life*. Based on the philosophy of Vladimir Soloviev and offering "open courses" on religious-philosophical topics, the Moscow society differed substantially from the St. Petersburg meetings. While discussion of Orthodox Christianity and the Russian church continued to dominate, political demands motivated its leaders.

The Moscow group attacked the church because it sanctioned a despotic regime and its highest officials publicly supported the government's bloody reprisals against workers and peasants in the Revolution of 1905. Through the hastily organized, miniscule Bratstvo Khristianskoi bor'by (Brotherhood of Christian Struggle) they tried to inspire a political movement aimed at establishing a socialist order based on the example of early Christian communities. That effort involved only a limited critique of the church. Ern, Sventsitsky, and Bulgakov rejected the idea of new revelations and the possibility of a "new religious consciousness." The Orthodox church embodied the One and Final Truth and, brought back to its primal purity for an apocalyptical struggle with evil, would capture the world for sanctified man. As the base for a political movement the Moscow Religious-Philosophical Society did not survive the continuing revolutionary violence and government armed repression in 1906–1907. The events of those years had decisive effects on the roles which Bulgakov and Novgorodtsev were to play in Russian life until 1914.

Both Novgorodtsev and Bulgakov had been founders in 1901 of the Liberation Movement, from which the liberal Constitutional Democratic party (Kadets) developed. That party dominated the First Duma (April-July, 1906) and struggled to legislate a land reform bill which was far too radical to be acceptable to the government. When the Duma majority persisted, the government, using powers granted to it by the laws establishing the Duma system, dissolved the assembly. For several reasons, including the enforced absence of the most important Kadet candidates, government interference in the electoral process and the presence of Social Democratic candidates, the Second Duma (March-June 1907) included a much smaller liberal representation. The new assembly clashed with the Stolypin-led government on a variety of issues and was dissolved in June 3, 1907. After that date the czar decreed changes in the electoral laws in order to ensure more conservative dumas. The attempt to establish constitutional government went on, but with much less attention to the economic and social needs of the people and in an atmosphere of harsh government repression.

The dissolution of June 3, 1907, marked the end of any real chance in the immediate future to establish democratic representative government. Continuing peasant and worker violence in 1906–1907, encouraged by the revolutionary parties, led to fierce government reprisals, arrests, exile, shooting, and hanging. Except in the very moderate form espoused by the Octobrists, the leading force in the

59

Third and Fourth dumas, liberalism could not exist in the polarized atmosphere that rapidly developed. Novgorodtsev, a Kadet politician, reacted to the situation with an effort to describe in a scholarly historical framework the kind of liberalism demanded by twentieth-century Russia. Bulgakov became an opponent of Russian liberalism. Even the writers who led the St. Petersburg Religious-Philosophical Meetings of 1901–1903 became "revolutionary" and denounced efforts to introduce Western liberal doctrines and practices in Russia. The new situation also did much to establish the tone of the new Religious-Philosophical Society, established in St. Petersburg in the fall of 1907.

In 1906–1907 the leaders of the Moscow Society fostered and helped organize the St. Petersburg Religious-Philosophical Society. Under heavy pressure from church officials, by 1908 the public discussions in Moscow gave way to intellectual exchanges in various salons and scholarly meetings. St. Petersburg became the scene of widest public participation. In its first sessions, fall and spring, 1907–1908, Merezhkovsky and Ern offered conflicting views on the nature and mission of the Orthodox church, the "new" versus the "old" religious consciousness. Though equally apocalyptic and urging what would have to be a futile attempt to revive "primitive Christian communism," the Moscow thinkers provided a more realistic view of the relation of Orthodox Christianity to Russia, its high culture, and the masses of its people than did Merezhkovsky, Hippius, and Rozanov.

These interchanges, especially the contributions of the Brotherhood, raised sharply the question of the relation of religion to politics. Ern and Sventsitsky's religious revolutionism aroused the oldest fear of European liberalism—indeed, the issue which lay at the basis of the emergence of liberal thought in seventeenth-century England. Novgorodtsev, Struve, and Frank spoke out strongly against the introduction into politics of the intolerance born of religious conviction and enthusiasm. On the other hand, while he did not share fully the views of the Brotherhood, Bulgakov came to believe that only religious politics could be effective in the twentieth-century era of mass politics. The Russian peasants and workers in particular would not respond to appeals to their self-interest, but only to vistas of transfiguration promising justice and freedom based on brotherhood and love.

Throughout 1908 and the first part of 1909 writers like Maxim Gorky, Blok, and Ivanov and Social Democrats such as Plekhanov, Bazarov, and Lunacharsky entered this controversy at the society or in print. By the spring of 1909 the discussion of "religion and politics" at the society had reached an end. If new perspectives on that topic were possible, they would emerge from the substantial controversy inspired by the publication of *Vekhi* (*Landmarks*) in March of that year.[2] The importance of the religious-philosophical societies to society dwindled, and the meetings became largely scholarly colloquia discussing philosophical and religious problems. Even so meetings continued to be held in a salon atmosphere in Moscow and St. Petersburg.

THE ST. PETERSBURG RELIGIOUS-PHILOSOPHICAL MEETINGS OF 1901–1903

The St. Petersburg Religious-Philosophical Meetings of 1901–1903 grew out of social relationships among contributors to *Mir Iskusstva* (*World of Art*). That journal contributed strongly to the spread of new Western trends in art, poetry, and literary criticism in Russia.[3] In it, Merezhkovsky published his best work, *Tolstoi and Dostoevsky*, which contained in its second volume the essence of his religious views. In the winter of 1900 some of its contributors began to meet in the apartments of the Merezhkovskys and Rozanov to discuss such religious ideas, which did not interest the editors and artistic figures dominating the journal.[4] Often present were Dmitry V. Filosofov, Bakst, Alexander N. Benois, Peter P. Pertsov, and Nicholas M. Minsky.

Rozanov brought to the meetings both young priests and scholars of the seminary, such as Anton V. Kartashev, Vladimir V. Uspensky, and Valentin A. Ternavtsev and others with church and religious interests, such as Berdiaev and George I. Chulkov. From these discussions arose the idea of public meetings to bring the church and the intellectuals together on a ground which might instigate spiritual renovation of the church and spiritual transformation of intellectuals. It was hoped that they could unite on the common ground of the unitary nature of man and religious philosophy, in order to combat the evils of Russian life and modern positivism.

Hippius first became dissatisfied with the private meetings of the

61

group. She suggested in print that the issues be discussed in public, where they could engage the interest of society, and she urged that they be connected with the concrete problems facing the Russian people. She insisted that both the material and spiritual needs of the people had to be considered, the hunger of the flesh and of the spirit, and warned that intellectual discussion among a cultured few would be meaningless unless it could become "wider . . . connected with life."[5] Merezhkovsky agreed, and they began to sound out official Russia, with their cause aided by the fact that some members of the church hierarchy had taken part in their discussions and were to a degree sympathetic to their plan.

The most important involved church official was Vasily M. Skvortsov, editor of *Missionerskoe Obozrenie* (*Missionary Review*) and head of the church's missionary activity in Russia. According to Vladimir A. Maevsky, the thirst of the intellectuals for a religious grounding of their perspectives pleased Skvortsov, while their religious ignorance appalled him. He believed that Russian Orthodoxy might benefit from the exchanges, but that illegal private meetings would lead to punitive action by the Minister of the Interior, Dmitry S. Sipiagin.[6] Therefore, after gaining the agreement of Pobedonostsev, he proposed at one of the meetings that they be officially sanctioned by the Holy Synod. The majority accepted the plan, although it ran into some opposition, particularly from the future "revolutionary priest," Grigory Petrov. Skvortsov worked out the rules for such meetings, Pobedonostsev accepted them, and Sipiagin permitted them to take place under the condition that two representatives of the church administration should be present. Metropolitan Anthony (Vadkovsky) designated as his representative Bishop Serge, rector of the St. Petersburg Seminary, and Pobedonostsev chose Skvortsov as his spokesman.

Discussion at these meetings, which went on until April 5, 1903, defined fundamental themes of Russian intellectual life before 1917. They rapidly became fashionable and attracted the crowd of dilettantes, social climbers, and "idea consumers" who are indigenous to all modern cities and associated universities. Yet only a select few acquired the right to read papers or take part in discussions, so that the level of argument remained high and serious.[7] In addition to those of the leaders already mentioned, important contributions came from the poet and philosopher Minsky, the seminary scholars Kartashev and Uspensky, another future "revolutionary priest" Archimandrite Michael (Semenov), and the young minor church official Ternavtsev. Bishop Serge, Archimandrite Serge, Archimandrite Anthony, and Skvortsov spoke for the higher levels of the church administration and the state Censor's Office. Also at the meetings, though not speaking, were the symbolist poet Valery Ya. Briusov and the important religious thinkers Florensky and Elchaninov. Through its participants and audience the meetings inspired deep and wide-ranging consideration of what was surely an inescapable question in early-twentieth-century Russia: the role of Christianity and Russian Orthodoxy in a rapidly changing society.

Widespread comment on the exchanges appeared in the press and thick journals of all persuasions, leading to knowledge and concern about the major themes among the educated public. Public discussion attained substantial proportions in 1903, when the Merezhkovskys and Rozanov began publication of *New Path*, which printed the stenographic reports of the meetings and provided a forum for wider dissemination of their ideas.[8] Between 1903 and 1905 thinkers of the caliber of Ivanov, Berdiaev, Bulgakov, Frank, Serge A. Askoldov, Nicholas O. Lossky, Vasily V. Zenkovsky, Elchaninov, Florensky, Ern, and Volzhsky (A.S. Glinka) published articles on religious, philosophical, and related social topics in the journal and its successor, *Questions of Life*. New, learned, and intelligent perspectives inspired thought on topics too long politicized or neglected, and increased numbers of the educated became conscious of some of the rich possibilities of Russian culture. Perhaps the Owl of Minerva *does* arise only at dusk.

Rozanov, in his religion of sex, presented the most striking and original ideas at the meetings. He attacked the church because of its ascetic attitude toward the state-supported repression of human sexual practices.[9] He called Russian Orthodoxy the religion of death and counterposed to it the "truly" Christian "religion of Bethlehem." The latter celebrated open, unashamed, physical sexual relations and sexually-tempered warm kindness toward animals and inanimate nature. Its temple was to be the family and its deepest, most genuine contact with the Deity, sexual intercourse and orgasm. Rozanov believed that the early twentieth century would witness a great apocalyptical struggle, from which the religion of sex would emerge to unite all earthly life. Rozanov's ideas are very rich and very much

63

involved in basic attitudinal and intellectual changes in twentieth-century European culture. But they had little relation to the development of idealistic liberalism and Christian socialism and will not be examined further in this study.

Merezhkovsky confronted the Russian Orthodox church with two interrelated but separable challenges. Resting on a three-stage interpretation of the course of human history, his apocalyptic grand vision relegated the church to the position of the dominant force in a necessary but outmoded stage in man's experience. Under its second aspect, his thought struck hard at the church's continued unwillingness to grant autonomy to human cultural achievements in art, literature, philosophy, and science. However unconvincing his historiosophical visions might be, his critique of church attitudes toward secular culture were real expressions of the modern world's challenge to Christian culture. But even in that context, despite the complexity of Merezhkovsky's cultural background, he badly weakened his arguments by a curious fixation on black-white dichotomies, such as flesh and spirit, Christ and Antichrist, Tolstoi and Dostoevsky, Peter and Alexis, and mysticism and positivism. The church, a source of much of man's greatest cultural creativity, became unrecognizable in his accusation that it could best be described in terms of an ascetic contempt for beauty and mind. Moreover, his conception of an eternal world of freedom and beauty rested on an aesthetic elitism not unlike that of the thinker who influenced him most, Friedrich Nietzsche.

Following a tradition in Christian thought, Merezhkovsky saw religion evolving through three stages, of which Christianity was one. Formal statement of this conception goes back at least to the twelfth-century Abbot Joachim of Floris.[10] The first stage was that of the Old Testament, of God the Father, the All-Powerful Creator. Like the entire objective world created by God, man was mainly a physical object without personality, for only God had personality. Man submitted himself completely to what he understood to be the Master's law, but in symbolizing this relationship his consciousness could not pass the limits of the externally tangible. As tokens of his worship he carried out such sacrificial acts as circumcision and the ritual slaughter of animals, so that this first form of religion was primarily a religion of the flesh.

The second stage began with the New Testament. It revealed that

God was not only the Creator and Master of the entire objective world, but also that He had given man a free spirit, which sought union with God by following the Word to that state of Absolute Love which was Christ's. The "lower unity" of the first stage was broken up into thesis and antithesis, subject and object, spirit and flesh. At the same time, Christ said, "I and the Father are One." The Old Testament was a revelation of the One in One; the New Testament, of the Two in One.

The third stage would be the final synthesis of subject and object, flesh and spirit. It would be the unity of the first kingdom of the Father and the second of the Son in the third kingdom of the Holy Spirit. In it the flesh would be recognized as holy, by the revelation of the Three in One. Merezhkovsky held that the Russian Orthodox church was God's chosen vehicle for the embodiment of the new revelation. It had suffered the greatest of humiliations, almost complete subjection to the point of providing holy sanction for the power of the state. Its priests and believers seemed to be enveloped in ignorance, mechanical ritual, and a narrow positivistic interpretation of dogma. But God moved in mysterious ways.

The Roman Catholic church had forced powers and principalities to recognize the autonomy of the church in its saving mission. But in the process it had submitted internally to the authoritarianism and legalistic spirit of the state and had itself become a barrier to the development of man as a free spirit. The Russian Orthodox church, deprived of power in the secular world, almost an administrative arm of the state, had preserved in its monks and priests and in the hearts of millions of believers the purity, simplicity, and humility of the true Christian spirit. God's purposes had been fulfilled. A vessel for the preservation of His truth had been maintained until the time arrived for new revelations and a final transfiguration. But the final transformation would produce man active in all his powers, aesthetic, intellectual, sexual, and political.

As it stood, the Russian Orthodox church restricted and distorted itself and man by forcing him into the mold of an outmoded ascetic stage of Christian growth. Merezhkovsky and his associates offered the prescription for the illness of the church: recognize in the salvation of man the creative force of the "flesh," understood as mankind's secular cultural pursuits. Especially, acknowledge the power of *art* to grasp and transmit divine truths in compelling images;

65

approach positively the insights of secular mystical *philosophers* into the nature of man and the world; support the efforts of *natural science* to free man from the embittering spirit-destroying struggle against nature for survival; provide sanction for the struggle for *political* freedom, particularly as this had manifested itself in the nineteenth-century Russian intelligentsia; celebrate the spiritually uplifting nature of *sexuality*, an essential aspect of creativity and a decisive force in the communal unity of men. God had revealed a new world in which man would live in full possession of these, his powers.

Not all spokesmen for the Russian Orthodox church dismissed out of hand the intellectuals' arguments. No doubt, the majority of priests who knew of them shared John of Kronstadt's view that God had appeared on earth once and pointed to the true road to Himself—Christ—and that the speculations of the Godseekers were futile and Satanic.[11] But important church leaders at the meetings, such as Archimandrite Serge and Bishop Serge, listened attentively and responded patiently and courteously to sharp attacks from Merezhkovsky, Rozanov, and Minsky.[12] Moreover, young scholars at the St. Petersburg Seminary, such as Kartashev and Uspensky, while supporting Orthodox Christian views, sided to a large extent with the lay critics. Also playing a large part in the discussions were the lower church official Ternavtsev, and the priests Father Michael and Father S. A. Sollertinsky. While loyal churchmen, they evinced some support of critical views.

Evaluations of the discussions in clerical journals varied greatly in tone. Some churchmen agreed with the sheer idiocy of a writer in *Missionary Review* who asserted that public expression of the Godseekers' views should be forbidden as that of a "free thinker" which contains the number of the Antichrist, "666 (V=2) + (O=70) + (L=30) + (N=50) + (O=70) + (D=4) + (U=400) + (M=40) = 666."[13] But others argued that the clergy should embrace those scientific, philosophical, and artistic insights of modern thought which were not hostile to Christianity.[14] And at least one, Peter P. Kudriavtsev, a professor at the Kiev Theological Academy, offered a philosophical refutation of Merezhkovsky's main points.

On the whole, the responses of church representatives pointed up the inadequacy of the Merezhkovsky critique. Against the intellectuals' central accusation, that Russian Christianity irreparably broke apart spirit and flesh and cast a pall of evil over the latter, a substantial number of priestly spokesmen were able to show that the Christian position was much more complex than that. In fact, in Christian doctrine, especially that of the Eastern church, the Word of God "logosized" both spirit and flesh and continuing faith, works, and sacramental activity by the Christian could keep them together in a unity. This meant that the very activity most suspected and denounced by priests and laymen alike, sex, could be carried on in a way that provided a natural, simple, and passionate experience for the partners.

In the same way, other tenets of the littérateurs' critique could not be accepted without reservation and correction. Church spokesmen encountered no difficulty in showing that it did not hate beauty as such, that the effort to know the world through science was an expression of a deeply Christian desire to know God and that church theologians understood and used some of the greatest of pagan philosophical teachings and were far more careful in their philosophical arguments than were the Merezhkovskys.[15] The meetings involved much more than a simple confrontation between the Merezhkovsky group who celebrated the world and the church which damned it.

Rather, two conceptions of spirit collided. The Merezhkovsky conception sought free reign for the human intelligence to work upon the world, whether this was in the realm of literature, art, music, philosophy, or science. It did not demand liberation of the "flesh" as satisfaction of bodily appetites as much as the freedom of the human spirit as intelligence or mind to direct the body toward more refined conceptions and efficacious satisfactions of its needs. Merezhkovsky's "unitary man" was never quite unitary. This was not Christianity's view of the spirit. Of course, it would be entirely presumptuous to attempt to "define" in a few words the Christian notion of the spirit. But it certainly involved the notion of the work of the Holy Spirit upon the human soul to bring the latter to a state of grace where it can, like Christ, will what God wills. In the Eastern church tradition it points toward the gradual internalization of Christ, the acquisition of his capacity for unqualified love, and the eventual divinization of man. In words familiar to early-twentieth-century Russian religious philosophical thinkers, the Holy Spirit divinizes man as Christ, while the Merezhkovsky spirit would divinize man as superman.

Two ideals confronted one another. That of the church suffered from the disadvantage that it had been alive in human societies for twenty centuries and, as Rozanov said, man's spiritual condition in the early-twentieth-century was little different from what it had been at the time of John the Baptist. It was possible to say, as did Dostoevsky, that Christianity had failed. It had the advantage that it took man largely as he was, heroic and cowardly, compassionate and cruel, comradely and egoistic, noble and mean, a restless searcher for truth and goodness who easily lapsed into squalid self-satisfaction. It did not place its hopes for man on this earth on the assertion that he would be suddenly transformed into an embodiment of all the positive sides of these dualities. The ideals of the church and of Merezhkovsky were both lofty and noble, but it cannot be said that the intellectual's view of an earthly embodiment of his ideal inspires any more confidence than the Christian vision of the Kingdom of God, while the latter, at least, deals directly with the problem.

Merezhkovsky's exalted but vague presentiment and onesided attacks contained real concerns of twentieth-century Russia. Its culture included a religion which had been closely intertwined with the lives of the vast majority of its people for centuries. It could not move forward without a confrontation with that heritage. A society seeking to gain and preserve freedom in a time of threatening social upheavals, it had to look for an understanding of art, philosophy, science, and politics which would preserve their autonomy and employ them in the interests of human liberty. The bureaucratic spirit in church and state and positivist determinism in thought were real threats to a solution to Russian problems which would embody freedom.

The Godseekers offered no acceptable alternative. They sought to unite themselves with the liberal and radical intelligentsia, who disliked their aestheticism and at the same time with the church hierarchy, which detested them as free thinkers. They correctly saw the social and political struggle, the transformation of the church, and the inculcation of high culture among the people as tightly interrelated phenomena. But to believe that the three groups—political, artistic, and religious—could put aside their mutual distrust to fight together was a delusion. But the questions remained and had to be dealt with.

Novgorodtsev offered an idealistic liberal philosophy of change. He remained on the secular level while respecting and preserving Orthodox Christianity as an essential part of men's private lives, far from the marketplace and the political arena. Bulgakov proposed a Christian socialist alternative which would strive for socialist attitudes and institutions within the framework of the real, concrete, but reformed Russian Orthodox church. Both warned against expectations of rapid, final, complete transformation of man's life on this earth. In doing so, they countered not only Merezhkovsky's apocalypticism, but also that which appeared at the Moscow Religious-Philosophical Society in 1905.

THE MOSCOW RELIGIOUS-PHILOSOPHICAL SOCIETY (1905–1908)

The Moscow Religious-Philosophical Society emerged at the time of greatest tension in the disturbances of 1904–1905, "Bloody Sunday." In the fall of 1905, at the time of the general strike and the October Manifesto, it began its public meetings. The St. Petersburg Society was slower to develop, doing so largely on the initiative of the Moscow group in 1907. The religious-philosophical societies furnished platforms for discussion of the fate of Russia. Some hundreds of the most educated and publicly aware citizens of Moscow and St. Petersburg were members and attended the invariably overcrowded meetings. Although faddishness contributed to the "success" of the societies in Moscow and Petersburg social life, they nonetheless provided the serious discussion of Russian culture which one might expect from thinkers of the quality of Berdiaev, Bulgakov, Florensky, Ern, Frank, and Struve. They were a major fruit of the less stringent supervision and censorship of thought characteristic of Russian life from 1905 to 1914.

The societies confronted the ineluctable fact of the deep hostilities and divisions in Russia manifested in the Revolution of 1905. The violent activities of workers and peasants, the implacable hatred of Russian life demonstrated by the revolutionary intelligentsia, the inability of the state to respond except with the most brutal counter measures, the complicity of the Orthodox church in the bloody government reprisals and the activities of the Black Hundreds, and last but not least, the humiliating defeat of Russia in the Russo-Japanese War—these were the concrete facts which lay behind the existence and popularity of the societies. Their members, participants, and interested audience sought a source of unity, a center for a Russian culture, which might make possible necessary changes without utterly destroying their country.

The intellectuals pursued one major topic, the place of the Russian Orthodox Christian religion in the emerging new Russia. They tried to discover the role Orthodoxy played in Russian life and even more, that which it might play in bringing the divided segments of the society together in a culture unified enough to pursue social, economic, and political change without giving free rein to deep-seated hatreds and nihilistic impulses. This theme took several forms in the discussions of the various societies, but they all came down to the same basic question. Had the Russian people internalized the Orthodox religion and, if so, could religious feelings be reawakened in modern intellectuals so that the "people" and the "intellectuals" could inhabit a common ground on which they could transcend their obvious differences and work together for the good of Russia? The participants of the religious-philosophical societies grappled with this topic from many angles and, in so doing, produced a broad spectrum of nonpositivist thought in prerevolutionary Russia.

In the beginning, the Moscow Society pursued a scholarly course. Professors spoke in a learned fashion on topics related to the place of religion in Russian life and history. However, the society originated with a peculiar group of Christian millenarians, whose hatred of existing Russian society matched that of the most extreme revolutionaries and who strove for a return to very early Christian communism. Despite the impracticality of their proposals, these thinkers, Ern, Sventsitsky, Elchaninov, and Florensky, deserve attention. Bulgakov developed his more complex Christian socialism among and to a degree against them. They also provide a striking example of the kind of thought which the idealistic liberal, Novgorodtsev, deeply distrusted.

THE BROTHERHOOD OF CHRISTIAN STRUGGLE

Sventsitsky and Bulgakov, who had arrived in Moscow from Kiev during the summer of 1905, became cochairmen of the Moscow Religious-Philosophical Society. Elchaninov was the secretary, carrying on "primarily invisible, but irreplaceable organizational work."[16] Up to May 1907 the society held 10 public meetings, 5 closed meetings, and 60 public lectures.[17] Its membership grew from 40 to 300, while maximum attendance at its meetings was 600, and minimum 250. In March 1906 it began a "Free Theological University" in which well-known professors presented courses. Professor Maxim M. Tareev lectured on "The Christian Problem and Contemporary Russian Thought," and Professor Nicholas F. Kapterev on "The Schism and the Church." Florensky offered "Philosophical Introduction to Christian Dogmatics," and Ern presented "Socialism and Christianity in their Teachings about Progress." The society gave birth to similar societies in Kiev, St. Petersburg, and Tiflis.

In evaluating the Moscow Society, Elchaninov, as would be expected, called it "one of the most important facts of the religious awakening." With its sister societies, it could become the original point around which religious forces would accumulate, and "more important, the self-conscious organ of the religious movement, so to speak, its brain."[18] He enthusiastically pointed out the heterogeneous nature of its membership and auditors, including student youth, factory workers, office workers, persons of various religious persuasions, and Marxists and other positivists.[19] On the other hand, some highly educated persons objected to the major role played by dilettantish aesthetes, who lent an exotic, playful tone to the proceedings.[20] Officials of the church in Moscow attacked the society as the work of the devil.[21] But to Elchaninov it remained a great "religious thing," where honest searchers discussed religious topics in an air of mutual respect and attention. The society's leaders believed that divergent religious points of view would find unity in Vladimir Soloviev's doctrine of Godmanhood.[22]

Like Merezhkovsky, the Moscow group asserted that Christianity stood at the crossroads. Did it have any constructive role to play in the new historical epoch or should it simply acknowledge its irrelevance and turn over the reins to new historical forces? Russians who could not accept the latter alternative faced a dual task.[23] Cultured men had to go to the people to internalize their simple faith. Yet they could not plunge thoughtlessly into "elementalness," but had to preserve their cultured understanding of man's accomplishments and possibilities, transmit it to the people, and join with them in a revolution greater than any that had yet taken place. Like Bulgakov, Elchaninov, Ern, and Sventsitsky admired Soloviev precisely because they believed that he had successfully combined modern thought

71

from Kant to Nietzsche with deep, religious faith, thus making possible both a scientific understanding of twentieth-century needs and an attitude toward the world which would coincide with that of the emerging masses.

Pursuing that aim, in early 1905, Ern, Elchaninov, Florensky, and Sventsitsky organized the Brotherhood of Christian Struggle. Through it they sought to make the religious approach to Russian problems the center of a large social movement. Ern and Sventsitsky were distinguished from Elchaninov and Florensky by their pugnacity and interest in political polemics. Elchaninov had a strong feeling for the suffering poor and a Christian world view which emphasized its tender, loving aspects and the essential unity of the natural and human worlds. He contributed little to the often hate-tinged polemics associated with the Brotherhood.[24] Florensky, although he was arrested in 1904 for delivering an antichurch and antistate sermon at the Moscow Theological Academy, concentrated mainly on intellectual labors of high complexity and did not involve himself very much in the debased coinage of political polemics.[25] And so the political agitation associated with the Brotherhood was mainly the work of the cold, somewhat arrogant philosopher Ern and the often hysterical, clearly neurotic Sventsitsky.

Sventsitsky's state of mind may be illustrated by the following:

> I saw a mad woman, She was rouged. She wore an enormous hat with a feather, and a bright silk dress, with some kind of stupid train. She had a decolletaged narrow, sick bosom, a wrinkled, aging face, and black teeth. But the rotting body according to fashion was covered in silk and lace.
>   This is your symbol! Behind the silky, glittering, self-satisfied refinement of your life is hidden a mad pitiable mutilated soul, the formlessly grasping claws of the coldest hands, a loathsome monster, the name of which is private property.[26]

A. Golubkina's bust of Ern in the Tretiakov gallery in Moscow suggests the cold and authoritarian manner noted by his classmate Michael Karpovich.

The Brotherhood purveyed an apocalyptic millenarianism alive in Russia at least as far back as the seventeenth century and kept alive in Old Believer sects and individual thinkers until the twentieth century. Among the ideas featuring the mainly underground stream of thought were convictions of Russia's peculiar position as the last imperial center of Christianity, of secular powers and principalities as minions of the devil, and of an approaching apocalyptic end of the the sway of evil over the world. All of these ideas were enunciated and placed in a twentieth-century context by the Brotherhood. They were revivalists, hoping to re-create the past in the present as the basis of a blessed future.[27] They urged the Russian peasants and workers to organize in Christian communitarian ways, thus placing themselves on the side of Christ in the coming apocalyptic struggle against the forces of Antichrist. They tried to do this both as writers and intellectuals and as organizers of a mass political movement. Of course they failed.

Reacting vigorously against January 9, 1905 (Bloody Sunday), the Brotherhood engaged in various types of agitational activity. They distributed inflammatory broadsides in workers' sections of Moscow, tried oral agitation in the factories, toured the provinces speaking to town and village people, and circulated antigovernmental statements in army detachments.[28] To gain supporters among the educated, they published open letters directed at literati, lay society, and officials and priests of the church.[29] Their message was clear and simple: to workers and peasants, refuse to act violently against starving demonstrators from their own ranks; to soldiers, do not fire on the unarmed poor seeking only the possibility of a human life; to lay, literate society, use their relatively safe position to press both church and state to cease murderous activity; to the bishops and priests, refuse to bless state actions which were clearly counter to the Christian conscience. In addition they published eight-kopeck booklets explaining in very simple language the peasants' right to the land and the evils of capitalism.[30]

The political activity of the Brotherhood in 1905 should not be totally denigrated. They spoke for the decency and forbearance badly needed in a period of excessive clerical denunciation, government brutality, and popular suffering. They did so in competition with inflammatory revolutionary agitators in the midst of excited, potentially violent workers and peasants and under the ever-present threat of police action. But they did pursue a futile enterprise. At the same time they accompanied it with a denunciation of capitalist society and statement of revolutionary aims which deserves attention. It shows how the major building blocks of Marxist theory could be built into a Christian revolutionism. At the same time, it manifests the kind of revivalism which locates the golden age in the past rather than the future and often appears in times of revolutionary stress.

In their theoretical and propagandistic statements, the Brotherhood proposed a kind of Christian socialist alternative to Marxism. Unlike that of Bulgakov, their doctrine was revivalist, seeking a way back to an alleged primitive Christian communism. Consciously it shared Marx's (and Herzen's) premodern, romantic revulsion from life infected with the "spirit of property." Unconsciously, perhaps, Ern and Sventsitsky offered a critique of bourgeois society which embodied important Marxist concepts. It may be that certain kinds of Christian denunciation of modernity naturally employ notions similar to those of the great socialist thinker. In any case, they shared another quality with Marx. Both expressed an emotional reaction not only in fevered denunciations of evil, but also in terms of allegedly objective, lawful historical processes leading to the triumph of the good. Marx, of course, claimed to have discovered the scientific "laws of history" making inevitable the appearance of a communistic golden age. The Brotherhood believed in the inevitable transformation of mankind as understood in Christian teachings. Transformed man would live on in a golden age already experienced by a few early Christians.

Ern declared private property of all kinds to be evil and unnatural, because the earth was the joint possession of all men.[31] Nature, the earth, was a living part of God's creation, to be used for the sustenance of the human race, not as something to be marketed, bought, and sold for profit. Factory production offered no exception to the general rule, for it was an extension of nature, from which it obtained all the materials which were worked into useful products. Land and manufacturing plants should belong to the community, to be employed in the community interest, and production should be distributed equally among those who provided useful work for the community.

Private ownership of land and factories embodied an even deeper evil, the possession of men through control of their labor. No man has the right to own the labor of another, for that carries with it control over his life, his thoughts, and his desire and need to be a fully human person by the use of all his faculties and capabilities.[32] Sventsitsky and Ern articulated that same fight for the interest of the *person* as distinct from the individual which featured the idealism of Novgorodtsev and Bulgakov and the religious speculations of the Merezhkovsky circle. However, primitivists and revivalists, they saw the denigration of the person as inherently embedded in modern society and urged its destruction as the only way to reclaim the respect for the person which Christian love required.

The "spirit of property," egoism, had created a civilization in which men barricaded themselves behind a wall with their possessions, seeing everyone else as an enemy who either had what they want or wanted what they had.[33] They noted the irony and danger that while modern capitalism tended to bring people and nations closer together through railroads, telegraph, and other modes of communication, it radically disassociated them by universalizing the spirit of property, hate, and enmity. And to think that an unseen hand would bring universal good from this institutionalized greed was pathetic self-delusion. This line of thought conjures up the Nietzschean question and once again the views of Polanyi introduced above.[34] Was the great productivity and relatively high civility *and* cultural progress characteristic of the bourgeois age the result of deeply implanted religious beliefs working against the untrammeled egoism of public ideology? And when God and His commandments no longer have compelling internal power, can civility continue to go hand in hand with rationalized productivity?

Remaining in a mainstream of nineteenth-century thought, the Brotherhood connected the advance of the "spirit of property" with the exploitation and dehumanization of women. Arguing like Friedrich Engels in the *Origin of the Family*, they noted that in modern society women were largely property, with no independent legal or economic existence of their own.[35] They were brought up from childhood to understand that their sustenance in the world depended upon their ability to please men, so they were taught to be coquettes, to paint themselves, and make their bodies provocative and attractive. Capitalistic societies exploited and dirtied the souls of half of the human race and frustrated God's purpose, that men and women should love one another in tender mutual respect for one another's *person*. Like Engels and later Marxists, the Brotherhood believed that the abolition of private property was the necessary condition for decent man-woman relationships. But unlike Marxists, they held that the "spirit of property" could be overcome only within the framework of a Christian communism in which love would be the guiding star of humanity.

Again like the Marxists, Ern and Sventsitsky saw all areas of modern life ultimately as reflections of the wishes of property owners.[36] Bourgeois masters used science not for the betterment of humanity, but for the production of things to enhance their own pleasure and dominance. The same was true of art, which did not concern itself with simple beauties of line, color, subject matter, and melody that would be satisfying to the great mass of men, but rather, existed to provide amusements for the degenerated tastes of the bourgeois. In this, of course, there is not only a form of Marx's substructure-superstructure theory, but also the ideas of that powerful denunciator of "society," Leo N. Tolstoi.

What was to be done? For a spiritual illness only a spiritual remedy could be effective. The poisonous spirit of property had rushed in to fill the vacuum left in modern man by the loss of Christ. If men could once again take Him into themselves, they would again be "persons" and would turn in disgust from the caricatures which they had become.[37] Only the internalized Christ could be in men a center in which reason, will, and emotion could consolidate to form a "person" capable of acting singlemindedly in the spirit of Christian love. Like Marx's "proletarians," who could grasp reality and the need for a social-communal existence because they had no stake in the exploitative bourgeois order, the Brotherhood's Russians, if they would take the leap back to faith, would become clear-eyed and potent, with a noncontradictory vision of what man needs to be a person. The "spirit of property" was a "false consciousness" to which the believer would not succumb.

And it was later than men thought, for a two-stage revolution was at hand. Ern and Sventsitsky had no doubt that millions throughout the world, suffering in social, political, and economic exploitation, were psychologically prepared to grasp the single truth, the capacity to love which God had placed in all men.[38] Secular socialism, they believed, would surely soon triumph.[39] But, secular socialism was but the last, most progressive form of bourgeois positivism and liberalism, both of which had to be overcome before men could live together in mutual personal respect. It would be nurtured by the spirit of Christ, which it could not acknowledge, and would give way to the truly socialist, communitarian way of life possible only with the free subjection of humanity to the spirit. And Russia would play the catalytic role in this further revolution.

Ern believed that among the Russian peasants, not yet deeply riven by positivism, the spirit of Christian love still had a firm hold.[40] But he urged rapid, strong Christian action for he feared that the peasants would follow the siren song of the socialist propagandists very quickly, for they were desperate and easily deluded by false messages of brotherhood. He also shared the feeling that, despite their wandering among the arid deserts of materialism, the intelligentsia were on the side of Christ, and were seeking the "Future City" in Christian terms, whether they knew it or not. Events, both inside Russia and in the world at large, showed that the time of apocalypse and the New Jerusalem was near. In the meantime, Christians should emulate their forefathers of the catacomb period, practice passive disobedience of evil commands, and spread the Word to increase the army of Christ as much as could be done in a corrupt world. But they must respect the great edifice of European culture, must not "trample on one little flower, which had grown in the sweat and blood of hundreds of generations." With a great many Russian intellectuals including many revolutionaries, Ern shared the fear that a revolution based on peasant feelings and actions would destroy that European culture which the intellectuals deeply valued.

Revivalist movements are common in societies where many feel threatened by rapid modernization. They involve anomic classes or groups brought together by charismatic leaders.[41] Tribes, peasants, even aristocracies can feel the ground being cut out from under them by the rise of new social and economic forces which transform cultures. Time-honored beliefs, feelings, and actions and the social orders in which they find reciprocal satisfactions seem out of place in emerging orders dedicated to different values. Groups threatened in this way seek at the last moment to build something familiar and lasting about themselves, to throw out or, at least, barricade themselves against the new. Ern and Sventsitsky sought to originate a revivalist movement in a Russia undergoing rapid modernization.

The Brotherhood hoped and believed that Russia's peasant class would fight for the revival of ancient Christian communism. The peasants were being buffeted about in bewildering ways by industrialization, population growth, low crop yields, and restrictive institutions. By the beginning of the twentieth century it was clear that their anxieties were driving them to desperate violence. But would they have responded to calls to old Christian modes of egalitarian life even if made by truly "charismatic" leaders? No doubt, many peasants in small religious sects viewed their social-economic plight in religious terms.

But no general belief existed among the peasants that there had been a time in Russia when agriculturalists lived in conditions of freedom, equality, and plenty stemming from religious brotherhood. Nor could they conceive that the Russian Orthodox church could be transformed in terms of such ideals. The Christian religion, its rituals and beliefs, and its ideals of humility, charity, and comradeship were important to many millions. But the idea that the revival of religious, communistic institutions could provide the solution to their social-economic plight had no appeal to them. The peasants' horizons did not extend so far. They desired hardly more than to take back the lands "stolen" by the landlords and to reverse the *barin-muzhik* relationship under which they had lived for so long. Their political attitudes were inchoate, but anarchistic, directed at all principalities and powers (*vlast'*). They sought not to revive blessed states but to acquire a dominant or independent position in rural Russia. In their eyes their enemies were not outside and mysterious as they tend to be for modern millenarian movements, but inside and well known.

The political activities of the Brotherhood continued for no more than three months. Ern, Sventsitsky, Elchaninov, and Florensky then devoted their attentions almost entirely to questions of religious feelings, beliefs, and practice. They entered into direct polemics with Merezhkovsky and other "Godseekers." These exchanges took place at meetings and writings connected with the St. Petersburg Religious-Philosophical Society, formed in the fall of 1907.

THE ST. PETERSBURG RELIGIOUS-PHILOSOPHICAL SOCIETY (1907–1908)

As early as January 1905 the early leaders of the Moscow Society, Sventsitsky and Ern, appeared at the offices of *Questions of Life* in Petersburg. They discussed with former participants in the St. Petersburg Religious-Philosophical Meetings and others the organization of demonstrations and publicity reflecting their Christian approach to Russian life.[42] Like the Brotherhood, the St. Petersburg intellectuals and Metropolitan Anthony (Vadkovsky) reacted negatively to Pobedonostsev's "Message to All Children of the Orthodox

Church,'' which took a harsh accusatory tone toward popular involvement in the demonstrations of 1904-1905.[43] From that time on contacts between the Moscow and St. Petersburg group continued, although those in Petersburg preferred reform activity revolving about the Kadet party and work toward internal church reform to the revolutionary course urged by the short-lived Brotherhood of Christian Struggle. In 1906 major members of the St. Petersburg group published articles applying their religious-philosophical attitudes to the revolutionary situation in Russia. Then in early 1907 representatives of the Moscow Society and leaders in St. Petersburg met and organized the not yet legalized St. Petersburg Religious-Philosophical Society. The meeting of April 8 was devoted to discussion as well as organization.

Bulgakov chaired the April 8 meeting at the Ekaterinskoe hall. Chulkov estimated the attendance at from thirty to forty,[44] to whom V. Rozanov presented a paper on "Why Christianity Is Failing." Rozanov accompanied his usual attack on modern Christianity with praise of revolutionary youth. He was not expressing approval of revolutionary politics, but rather of the idealism and energy displayed by young people as they confronted a frozen religious establishment. Berdiaev, Struve, Askoldov, Kartashev, and the Reverend Constantin M. Aggeev took part in the discussion of his paper.

Following the preliminary meetings and legalization of the society, a final organizational meeting was held by the founding members on September 9, 1907, in the lecture room of the Stoyunin gymnasium. It elected as president Askoldov and as council members the Reverend Aggeev, Ternavtsev, Uspensky, Lossky, Kartashev, and Elchaninov.[45] These officers pointed out that the society pursued the same ends as the Moscow Society organized two years earlier and did not have the "combative character of the old meetings (1901-1903)." Others listed as founders of the society were Berdiaev, Struve, Serge M. Soloviev, Alexander D. Obolensky (former procurator of the Holy Synod), Frank, and Rozanov.

Having been organized and legalized, the society began its official existence with an opening meeting on October 3, 1907.[46] A full crowd was present in the auditorium of the Imperial Geographical Society. Kartashev, as chairman of the meeting, immediately took up the question of the purposes of the society and its relation to its Petersburg and Moscow predecessors.[47] He warned that the society was not a group which would act with a "single voice" to provide an answer to the religious questions troubling Russia at the time. Nor was it as many official church representatives argued, a group of heretics out to develop and proselytize a new form of Christianity in opposition to the official church. He pointed to the wide variation in membership from Frank, "a philosopher-agnostic or at least an adogmatist" to Ternavtsev, "official of the Holy Synod, in whose Orthodoxy it is impossible to doubt." A society with such diverse membership did not and could not seek to establish a single religious attitude and program which it would seek to impress upon the Russian people.

In Kartashev's opinion, such misconceptions on the part of Russian society and the church stemmed from the widespread idea that there was a historical connection between the former religious-philosophical meetings and the new society. In fact, he said that they were connected by a "very thin thread." The true genesis of the post-1905 Petersburg Society was in Moscow, members of whose society had originated it. Its rules were modeled on those of the Moscow group, and "it wants to function nearly the same as that society." Kartashev conceded that it was easy for Petersburg intellectuals to think that the new group would continue the militant attitude toward the official church which had characterized the meetings of 1901–1903, but holders of such a notion failed to note that times had changed.[48]

> That was a time of spring, of general enthusiasm, of some kind of general desire, when all oppositional trends were arising in the intelligentsia, which was not yet differentiated. This opposition itself was rather naive in relation to the Church, thinking that it was possible to change something in it by an open collision. Now these spring time hopes have passed. Indeed, there has emerged a period of disenchantment and those participants in the old religious-philosophical movements who are on the staff of our society no longer desire to collide with the Church. They expect nothing from it.

The members of the new society simply wanted to discuss in conjunction with the interested public the religious and philosophical questions which confronted them.

The St. Petersburg Religious-Philosophical Society quickly became an important forum for the expression of ideas by Russian intellectuals. It emerged in the period of general disenchantment following the collapse of the Revolution of 1905, in an atmosphere of the restrictive suffrage decrees of the summer of 1907. The latter greatly reduced the Duma's capacity to be a truly representative force opposing bureaucratic dominance of Russian life in a time of increasingly harsh repression of recalcitrant workers, peasants, and revolutionaries. To the society's meetings came philosophers, priests, religious thinkers; liberal, revolutionary, conservative, and reactionary political journalists; and interested members of "society." In public they discussed important questions of Russian life from a religious and philosophical point of view.

THE NEW AND THE OLD RELIGIOUS CONSCIOUSNESS

Seven of the first eight meetings of the St. Petersburg Society were devoted to discussions of Merezhkovsky's "heresy," the new religious consciousness. The reports were as follows:[49]

1. October 3, 1907, S. A. Askoldov, "On the Old and the New Religious Consciousness."

2. October 15, 1907, V. V. Rozanov, "About the Need and the Inevitability of a New Religious Consciousness."

3. November 8, 1907, D. S. Merezhkovsky, "On the Future Church."

4. November 21, 1907, V. V. Rozanov, "The Sweetest Jesus and the Sour Fruits of the World."

5. December 21, 1907, N. A. Berdiaev, "Christ and the World."

6. February 3, 1908, V. F. Ern, "On the Idea of Christian Progress."

7. February 14, 1908, Val. P. Sventsitsky, "The World Meaning of Ascetic Christianity."

Merezhkovsky and Rozanov read or submitted papers, but except for a newly discovered belief in political revolution, these added little to the ideas they had expressed in 1901–1903. The Orthodox church, ascetic hater of life, could be the center of the emerging world of goodness, truth, and beauty only if it could come to terms with the spiritualizing aspects of modern culture.[50] To the Moscow thinkers this view of the church and its relation to "high culture" was simply untrue.

Since the Christian revivalists believed that both Orthodox and European culture were *holy*, they had to refute the idea that the Orthodox church was inherently hostile to sexuality, art, philosophy, and science. To that end they attempted to explain the Russian

81

Orthodox church as a living institution, both forming and being formed by the history and characteristics of the Russian people. To them, the Merezhkovskian effort was mainly "literature" and terribly abstract. Into the space marked out by the Petersburg writer's antinomies, the writers of the Brotherhood inserted some degree of historical reality.

Both Merezhkovsky and Ern posited ideals. Merezhkovsky's was a Nietzschean cultural ideal which involved an uncritical denigration of Christianity's ideals in terms of a future transvaluation, while that of the Brotherhood was a Christian ideal, one which Ern found working in himself and assumed to be a widespread Christian experience. Where Merezhkovsky had the conviction of one who claimed to have glimpsed the inevitable course of history, Ern spoke with the assurance of one who believed that his ideal had been realized at least once in the past, in the believers of the first three centuries of Christianity.[51] He asserted that the extant historical record of the first three centuries of Christian life refuted Merezhkovsky's triadal critique of the church: that it hated the world and, hence, culture; that it was ineradicably hostile to human sexuality; and that it was indifferent to the social needs of believers.

The true Christian, past and contemporary, neither hated the "flesh," nor felt a fundamental dichotomy between it and the spirit. Rather, the two God-given parts of his being were inseparably connected and strove for full harmony and peace.[52] They did sometimes answer different calls, but as part of a whole, the reality of which was always felt by the Christian in sacrament and prayer. Most significant, central to Christianity was the early Christian saying on this subject, "we await the spring of our body."[53] The early believers did not seek to escape the body, nor did they wish to subjugate it; they awaited the life, the mingling of natures, the promise of rebirth characteristic of spring. Sure of what they were, where they stood, absolutely honest and clearsighted, the earliest Christians spoke words of love for the flesh and the world which had to be taken as "pure gold."

Ern found the assertion that Christianity considered all sex "unclean" equally inaccurate. Much emphasis was placed on "chastity" by early Christians, but chastity to them did not refer to the marital state or virginity. Chastity referred to a state of the soul, to the feeling of having been reborn characteristic of those who had surrendered to the Father's will. Indeed, it stood out most strongly in those who had left behind a debauched life to enter the Christian community. Although Merezhkovsky was a learned man and religious searcher, in identifying chastity with physical virginity he committed the error of the modern positivist or the ignorant, superstitious peasant.

In Ern's interpretation early (true) Christianity balanced ideal conceptions of earthly beauty and experiences in the world. The early Christians accorded absolute value to beauty in the world and could find nothing demeaning in relations with women, as the most moving earthly manifestations of beauty. Sexual relations could be approached with infinite trust, for in chaste relations with women, the border between the pure and the impure known with such refinement by the early Christians could not be crossed. The images of Christ as bridegroom and church as bride "burned in the hearts of the first Christians" and filled all sexual life with beauty and holiness. Modern men knew little or nothing of this, for what the official, ascetic church had not destroyed, bourgeois civilization had spoiled, but it was a reality, a Christian ideal, which had been lived once and could be again.

In these remarks, Ern approached Merezhkovsky in a way similar to that in which Novgorodtsev confronted Marxists and other secular utopians. He counterposed a complex, tension-ridden dialectic of the soul, which made of life a never-ending struggle on the edge between the pure and the impure, to a historical dialectic which posited great, conflicting stages of mankind's historical development to be eventually reconciled in eternal universal harmony. He saw harmony as an ultimate, deeply overladen "fact" in man's nature, making possible in the world that precious bit of unity which enabled him to survive his own contradictory impulses and the hostility between him and other men without interminable, destructive bitterness. The final harmony could not come on this earth, but men could live in relative peace by seeking out that common ground beyond space and time where all human experience was present and active in each person.

The Ern-Merezhkovsky confrontation highlights important contrasts between the new religious consciousness and Orthodox revivalism as responses to the early-twentieth-century crisis in Russian culture. Both sharply criticized the intertwined Russian state and church for their concrete evil actions; both looked for a reconciliation between Orthodoxy and European culture; both foresaw a radical transformation of man and a swiftly approaching apocalypse. In the same way, each tried to relate its religious message and quest to the allegedly deep religious nature of the mass of Russian peasants and the radical intelligentsia. In much of this they thought as they were, intellectuals, literati, trying to inspire the appearance of what they deeply desired, an understanding of their world which would be both intellectually satisfying and politically humane. They sought a social alternative to both bourgeois dominance and the release of "elemental" destructiveness which they feared would be the midwife and continuing mode of action of a Russian social revolution. But the tone of their indictments and promises differed significantly.

There can be seen in the Ern-Merezhkovsky contrast traces of the oft-noted contradistinction between Moscow and St. Petersburg cultures. Moscow traditionalism, the tendency to look back to find the golden age, whose elements would provide stability in a changing world, confronted the Petersburgian habit of looking toward the novel and experimental, the transformative agent embodied in its name. Moscow's self-image of patriarchal sobriety, seriousness, and restrained manliness contrasted with St. Petersburg's tendency to "let go," to indulge in intellectual and oral self-gratifications, with no fear of the subsequent bitter taste of self-betrayal. Muscovite literal moralism, the calling forth of the wrath of God on evil powers and principalities, stood against the Petersburgers' sophisticated relativism, their attempt to eradicate the sense of sin and guilt in a world of regained innocence. One expressed itself in a wide but cautious use of scripture, while the other employed the often incomprehensible language of mystical symbolism. Equally at variance with the church because they postulated a heaven on earth, Merezhkovsky and Ern embodied and felt a temperamental estrangement not unlike that characteristic of the two capitals over the centuries.

To Ern's defense of Christianity, Merezhkovsky could reply: "Perhaps the ideals of Christianity and the practice of early Christians did not exhibit hatred of the world and suspicious hostility toward sex. But Christianity, from the time that it became an organized, hierarchical religion, and especially since the Middle Ages, deserves these epithets." But Ern, Florensky, and Elchaninov pointed out that the use of the term "Christianity" in this way was still too broad, that what was in question was the Russian Orthodox church. And the Russian Orthodox church had developed among a

84

given people, the Eastern Slavs, and under the environmental and historical impact of the early experience of Russians. It could not be explained or characterized by a few dogmas of the Eastern or Western church, nor even by the actions and beliefs of some of the greatest theologians. It not only acted upon the Russian people, but was acted upon by them as they reacted to the conditions of their lives over time.

RUSSIA, ITS CHURCH, AND ITS PEOPLE

In this spirit Elchaninov, Ern, and Florensky offered in 1908 their book *Pravoslavie* (*Orthodoxy*). Neither a thorough historical nor an authoritative treatment of Russian Christianity, the work stands out, nonetheless, as the only attempt by the various religious intellectuals of the period to provide an empirical base for their conceptions.[54] It should provide some insight into the theoretical and political activities of the Brotherhood, their belief that Christian communism could be reconstructed on the basis of the Russian peasant in his commune, their sharp dislike of bourgeois civilization, their almost "holy fool" attitude toward the state, and their belief in Solovievian mystical conceptions of the onset of the apocalypse and Godmanhood.

In a way which is by now familiar, the authors identified three forces as leading to the peculiarly Russian form of Christianity. These were the *religion of Byzantium*, as brought to Russia by the priests and monks of that empire; *Slavic paganism*, which, while assimilated into Russian Orthodoxy, lived on and deeply affected the Russian people's understanding of Christianity; and the *Russian national character*, which reworked Byzantine Christianity to conform to its own spirit.[55] From Byzantium came two major aspects of the Russian religion: among the clergy respect for philosophy and theology, and among all Russians deep attachment to ancient, correctly carried out ritual. To Russians the latter became more important than the fulfillment of moral commandments.

But the people remained deeply affected by the Slavic pagan religion and preserved feelings inspired by them in their Christianity. Animistic Slavic paganism embodied the feeling that men and animals, plants, and the earth were beings of similar character, who could communicate directly with one another.[56] The most powerful

85

of all these natural forces and the true God of the Slavic pagans was Mother Earth, still worshipped for her fertility in twentieth-century phallic practices. Intimately connected with nature, the Slavs also felt the presence of the dead, the forefathers, in their lives. Communion with ancestors, who were thought of as still being able to affect the fates of their descendants, manifested one of the primary facts of Russian history, the sacrifice of the personality of the individual Russian to the communality of the family, extended to long-dead forebears.

Elements of the Russian national character also contributed to the unique form of Christianity, Russian Orthodoxy. The Brotherhood accepted Kliuchevsky's speculations on how the Russian forests, steppes, and rivers produced a particularly Russian type.[57] He believed that the steppe with its vast horizons had induced in the Eastern Slav a tendency toward distant, imprecise dreams of far-off places, a tendency toward that "broad" Russian nature which so many Russian writers and foreign observers had pointed out. In Christian terms this could be experienced as a longing for the "Future City," far off beyond the horizon, which made ultimately nugatory the calculated struggles of men in this world.

The forest would have an almost opposite effect, disciplining men, arousing in them the sober realism needed to clear the forest, plant, and tend crops in an environment which yielded grudgingly and implacably punished dreaming. In Christian terms this could inspire dedication to a calling and recognition of how much of the peasant's life was directed by higher powers, which he could propitiate, but never control. Finally, Kliuchevsky considered most lasting in their effects the great rivers of Russia. From his travels on the Dnieper, the Don, the Volga, the Kama, and so many others, the Eastern Slav learned the value of comradeship; for there he met those who, like him, were traveling in dangerous solitude. Settlements developed on the rivers in which Russians learned the value and pleasure of trade and peace. From the Christian point of view, the much extolled peasant qualities of brotherhood and compassion, his awareness of the universality of man's fate, could have developed in these places where men of different tribes and nationalities came together in grateful sociality.

The early-twentieth-century peasant had to be viewed as a complex product of human and natural forces acting over many centuries. He believed in God, the church, and the sacraments, but no less firmly in goblins and charms. To protect his soul, he concerned himself more with the proper performance of ritual than with obedience to a rationally expressed moral code, for reason or knowledge meant less to him than prayers, songs, icons, and relics. Feeling largely helpless before his natural drives, the peasant deeply revered those monks and saints who overcame them. Saints, by their association with certain days of the year and certain agricultural tasks, entered directly into the peasant's deepest earthly concerns. As for parish priests, they were valued mainly for their readiness and ability to carry out such sanctifying rituals as baptism, marriage, burial, and prayers in the fields. It could not be denied that some of the ritual and prayer which made up the peasant's religious life was carried out mechanically, but it also seemed true that they had a meaningful, though perhaps largely unconscious, effect on the peasant's soul.

Ritual practices both reflected and formed that strong Orthodox person, to whom so many Russian writers referred with respect. Strict subjugation to church fasts, obligatory attendance at service, prayer before all the affairs of life penetrated the life of the Great Russian and gave him the feelings of being in *his* place, doing the things which had been done by a dozen generations before him.[58] They protected him from the fidgety flightiness of the modern urban dweller and created peace and a certain tenderness in his soul.

In the centuries-long constancy of his life-style lay the peasant's link with Orthodoxy's suspicion of social and political activity. To the Brotherhood both peasant and church rightly understood that social and political activities in themselves could never bring much improvement to the human condition. But they realized that the church was over-ascetic in this matter, seeming to believe that suffering and poverty were necessary to keep men humble and disinclined to disobey God. As a very humane priest, Bishop Serge, said during the most violent days of 1905, "The people are innocent, only wishing to plead with the Tsar for some relief from their suffering. But are the police and the army guilty, knowing no other way to stop disorder than shooting? Terrible, terrible days for Russia, but simply, the punishment of God has been brought down upon us. . . . Master, save the Tsar, save Russia. . . ."[59] Following Soloviev, the Brother-

87

hood sought to overcome this very central Orthodox attitude by showing that the attainment of Christian ends required political action.

In these remarks the basic Orthodoxy of the Brotherhood clearly emerged. They attacked the synodal church as ally of the state and bourgeois society in repression of the people, they proposed political action and a social role which the church would view with utmost suspicion, but they remained within identifiable Christian limits. Through the writings of Elchaninov in particular there flowed the spirit of Christ-like humility and love of men and nature.[60] The Brotherhood also manifested understanding of how little the Christian posture in the world had to do with human reason and how much lacking in understanding were intellectuals who subjected it to rationalistic criticism. In what they took to be Orthodoxy and the Orthodox peasant, they found far superior standards for human behavior than those celebrated in the social, political, and intellectual lives of the "educated."

The Brotherhood also seemed to suggest, though not explicitly, that the cultural influence of the Orthodox church on the peasants may have been as much as was possible under the circumstances of Russia's history. The centuries-long brutalization of the people by harsh environmental and harsher human conditions may have placed limits on the capacity of the peasants to move quickly into the atmosphere of a freer, pluralistic society. The overlords had not permitted the internalization of the respect for culture and personal freedom which had made relative tolerance of partial satisfaction possible among more fortunate peoples.

As far as barriers to explosions of elemental passions existed, they resulted from a popular self-image combining the humility and compassion so persistently brought before the people in the images of Christ and the saints. To accomplish that much, the church had had to tolerate the persistence of pagan magic, sexual license, and orgiastic practices which complicated the complex adjustment which defined the peasant personality. The Brotherhood believed that only the church had so intertwined itself with peasant life and character that it could hold together this volatile mixture. At the same time, they sharply criticized the actions of the twentieth-century church and the living style of its officials and feared for its survival.

After the schism brought about by Nikon's seventeenth-century reforms and the bureaucratization enforced by Peter I, the church lived on in noncanonical form.[61] In a crippled state, increasingly unable to fulfill its mission in the world, it changed little until the period of the Revolution of 1905. That event exposed the degree to which capitalistic economic and social development had torn the fabric of the Orthodox life-style. Class hatreds let loose among a peasant population torn from its roots in the countryside, herded into cities, and finding no spiritual sustenance in its religion, had produced a bitterness in thought and action which showed that Orthodox Christian feelings had been largely eradicated. Cut off from their familial and occupational traditions, from the cyclical agricultural pursuits which had been merged with their Christian beliefs, the worker-peasants had lost their unity and strength. Moreover, their continuing ties with the village accelerated an already developing alienation among their brothers in the countryside.

In addition, the revolution made it clear that the Russian church might now have to pay the price for its use of state force and identification with the state in the popular mind. A mystical faith in the Czar's autocracy had become a central element in Orthodoxy. Therefore, the deep changes in the form of government which had taken place would inevitably call into question the authority of the Orthodox church itself. The mystique of Orthodoxy would have difficulty surviving the destruction of the mystique of autocracy.

These historical, social-psychological conceptions of the Brotherhood strikingly illuminate the contrast between their "old," though anti-establishment, religious consciousness and the "new" perspectives of the Merezhkovsky group. They show what, in the minds of the former, a Russian religious rebirth had to entail. These intellectuals had no doubt that the Russian peasants provided the only base on which a truly Orthodox culture could be built, not only because they made up over 80 percent of the population, but also because they had best preserved true Christian religious feelings. To appeal to that base a Russian religious approach to the world required the sustenance of Christian ritual. As twentieth-century intellectuals, the Brotherhood did believe that enlightened consciousness had to be brought to bear on religious experience, but they understood the intimate involvement of religious belief and feeling with ritual.

The condensed symbols of ritual embody a highly complex set of ideas and interlocked emotions that have meaning for persons, even if not rationalistically articulated. They act to form personalities and guide activities more powerfully than moral maxims and rational thought systems.[62] Moreover, they formed the greatest part of what religion meant to the Russian peasants. Although peasant religion very much needed "consciousness," if it did not lead to conclusions compatible with Christian symbols as expressed in ritual, it could not garner wide and lasting support in Russia.

Built on a base of ritualistic experience, a unifying religious consciousness in Russia would also have to recognize and celebrate the mediating force of nature between God and man. It could not center exclusively on the man-God relationship, for the Russian peasant experienced the work of the Spirit not only in the sacrament, but also in his involvement with the natural world. In his environment, he saw plants and animals who manifested love and hate, joy and sorrow in the same way as the human sons of God. Moreover, he understood God, Christ, and church through his participation in the endless cycle of planting and harvesting, living and dying, characteristic of agricultural life. He would find it difficult to comprehend and take part in the "storming" of nature as a citadel to be overcome.

The church and its rituals, like the earth, was a mother. About both it could be said, "She is the mother because in baptism she bears the new man into holy life, and in anointing, strengthens him in it. She purifies feeling, sanctifies thought, strengthens the will. She is the mother because in the sacrament of penance she forgives sin and in the Eucharist unites with Christ. . . ."[63] To bring community to a torn and hate-filled Russia, then, a religious consciousness had to embody tender, comradely feelings toward nature, for the peasant could not experience as religious the modern exploitative mastering attitude toward the nonhuman world. The people's entire attitude toward the world would be shattered, for if nature did not deserve man's compassion, service, and prayer, neither would other people, earthly powers, and, ultimately, God. There would exist no mother and, hence, no trust.[64] Deprived of its immeasurably complex interconnection of ritual and nature, the strong but compassionate, stern but tender Russian peasant personality would disintegrate and its timeless community dissolve in the thrashing about of a "groundless" existence.

The Brotherhood urged "consciousness" in order to overcome the negative sides of the positive characteristics of Russian peasant religious life. Peasant nature worship easily degenerated into orgiastic, Dionysian modes of celebrating life and fertility. A ritualistic approach to religion carried with it tendencies toward mechanical posturing and repetition of prayer which left the soul untouched. It also bred a contempt for thought and feeling expressed in literature, drama, or philosophy, despite the enrichment of spiritual life embodied in these. Concentration on the most simple and personal relationships with nature and like-thinking men forestalled social, political, and economic progress. The Brotherhood sought to preserve the religious, personal, and social strengths of traditional culture, while intruding into them the enlightened perspectives of those deeply imbued with the most positive values of developed high culture: *a truly redoubtable task, which frustrated and de-energized all those in Russia who tried either to conceptualize it or to do it.*

Measured against the perspectives of the Brotherhood, the link of the Merezhkovsky group to the European intellectuals' "unhappy consciousness" becomes clear. The "new religious consciousness" was not one rooted in an organic unity of peasant Christian ritualism, nature worship, "elementalness," and consciousness, but rather an attempt to cure the wound in the psyche of the over-intellectualized, over aesthetically sensitized urban literati. Its union of flesh and spirit, its "unitary man," even its bows to nature, were not rooted in awareness of undeniable realities of peasant religious life in Russia, but in the yearning for the pastoral, known in Western art and literature at least since the seventeenth century.

Merezhkovsky's new Johannine revelation would not reveal to most men the way of their salvation, but to some men the way of transcending their manness. The artist's awareness of the priority of his creative impulse over the restraining influence of all tables, codes, and folkways would become awareness not of his actual limitations, but of his limitless possibilities. Art, philosophy, and science would become the bearers of a new religious relation to the world, whose adepts would become the new priests, leading the unlettered flock to the destruction of man and the creation of superman.

The discussion of the new religious consciousness led directly to consideration of the topics, "the intelligentsia and the people" and "religion and socialism." Both the Merezhkovsky group and the Brotherhood considered that their speculations would be functional in the social-political dimension of Russian life, though Ern and Sventsitsky considered the Godseekers' efforts to be purely "literary," since they included none of the concrete political action on which the Muscovites embarked. At the same time, the idealistic liberals participating in the religious-philosophical societies found their attitudes toward religion activated by political questions. In the meetings in 1908–1909 and in print they made clear their fundamental difference with Bulgakov: their conviction that, for the sake of both liberating politics and saving religion, the two foci of man's cultural activities had to be kept separate. For his part, Bulgakov, deeply involved in both societies, developed his contrary view that modern politics as mass politics had to be religious.

Chapter IV

SERGE BULGAKOV'S CHRISTIAN SOCIALISM

FACED WITH THE REVOLUTIONARY VIOLENCE of 1904–1905, Bulgakov moved sharply away from his associates in the Liberation Movement. He lost whatever taste he might have had for political action. Party programs, inflammatory speeches, hate-filled slogans, street demonstrations, and armed clashes awakened in him latent fears that Russia might disintegrate without the unifying presence of the czar's ultimately religious authority. When, on October 30, 1905, Russia acquired a partially constitutional, representative government he welcomed the new freedom, but had little confidence in Western-style party government. Even though he was elected to the Second Duma (February 20–June 3, 1907) and worked with Kadet committees on religion and factory legislation, he considered Duma politics to be dangerously incommensurable with the nature of Russia, its peasants, and workers. Between 1904 and 1914, in close contact with the Moscow and St. Petersburg religious-philosophical societies, he sought to lay the groundwork for a Christian socialist movement which would be above the parties. Contemporary social science, aesthetic sensibility, and Schelling's grasp of the oneness of man and nature were to guide a people ultimately inspired by Russian Orthodox loving communitarianism.

In the fall of 1903, Bulgakov became a political editor of Merezhkovsky's journal, *New Path*. The St. Petersburg writer had offered him the post in an effort to bring a concrete progressive political emphasis into the journal. Bulgakov accepted because he found the religious antipositivism of the writers attractive and hoped to introduce the mystical poets to political realities and sophisticated modes of analysis. The partnership influenced poets like Blok, Belyi, Ivanov, Briusov, and Chulkov very little.[1] However, it did accelerate the movement of Bulgakov back to his childhood faith. Close association with the symbolist poets also fortified his attachment to the conviction of Dostoevsky and Soloviev that "Beauty can save the world."

Many late-nineteenth-century thinkers considered the creation of beauty to be man's most progressive achievement. Unlike science or philosophy it appealed to the whole feeling, thinking, and willing man. To some, the experience of artistic evocations of man's condition seemed to guarantee that "softening" of men which would make a world of "sweetness and light" possible. To others, it seemed that, shaped by art, the personality would reject the ugliness of lies, cowardice, mean punitivism, and sentimentality. Nowhere were those feelings stronger than among Russian symbolists. Eternalized in art and deeply felt and understood, beauty would not allow men the self-satisfied mediocrity which was leading them to a stagnant world of herdlike being.

Like Bulgakov, symbolist poets and mystical writers self-consciously opposed positivism. Also, like Bulgakov, they championed a philosophy of life over against abstract metaphysics and arid epistemology.[2] Of course, they went further in that direction than he wished, so that he urged that their basically sound aesthetic intuitions be supplemented by a sizable dose of philosophical rigor.[3] Nonetheless, he assigned autonomous value to art, because it offered great truths about God, man, and the world in images whose appeal could be broader and impact deeper than that of complex rational discourse.[4] Even the sometimes overheated emphasis of the poets on the saving powers of sexuality coincided with his Solovievian view that the sexual drive and feelings exerted a mysterious force helping humanity to attain the highest communitarian levels of which it was possible.[5] Eros, binding man and man and mankind and nature, became a central force in his philosophy.

Early in 1905, Bulgakov, with Sventsitsky and Ern, founded the Moscow Religious-Philosophical Society in the name of Vladimir Soloviev. He opened the pages of *Questions of Life* to the group and in 1906–1907 published a pamphlet and several articles generally supporting their Solovievian critique of church and state. But he could not abide their revivalism, apocalypticism, and political agitation.[6] Denying any value to capitalist activities and offering ancient Christian communities as a model for solution of modern problems, they betrayed their deep ignorance of vitally important social and economic thought. To turn men's eyes toward an allegedly rapidly approaching apocalyptic end to evil in the world indicated a light-headedness akin to that of Bolshevik and Social Revolutionary maximalism. And those who inspired workers and peasants to bloody confrontation with police and army deserted the Christian cause while espousing it. Bulgakov sought to originate his own Christian approach to the political struggle, the "union of Christian Politics." Fundamental to that effort was his own return to faith.

A striking statement of the religious faith and yearnings which became the permanent center of his life during the violence of 1905 appeared in the short-lived newspaper *Narod* (*The People*), which he published in Kiev in 1906. In the Easter issue he prayed, "Be resurrected, Christ, in Your people, lighten by Your Truth the darkness, the bitter hatred of man for man, tribe for tribe. Lay waste the enemies of Your deed, from the ashes of our infirmity and cold indifference, ignite, make our hearts burn with Your Flame. Come, Jesus Christ . . . . "[7] Also in *The People*, Bulgakov published a letter to a correspondent which tells us much about his return to religion and his feelings of inadequacy. In it he told readers how he had been a "Marxist-practical worker," but had experienced a religious crisis, impelling him to search for God.

Bulgakov quickly found rational grounds for believing that man could not prove scientifically that God and the divine world did not exist. At the same time, he knew that he was incapable of the mystical experience which alone could assure him that God *did* exist. "I do not possess this gift. From this comes my despair, the despair of a man waiting in vain for the movement of the water."[8] Bulgakov was to venture into the heady realms of Neoplatonism, but to remain a sober intellectual all of his life. After 1905, as he moved closer and closer to the mystical thinking of Jacob Boehme and Schelling, much of his thinking developed under the impact of the St. Petersburg Religious-Philosophical Society.

THE ST. PETERSBURG RELIGIOUS-
PHILOSOPHICAL SOCIETY (1908–1910)

In the fall of 1908 the Petersburg Society turned from increasingly vague theological disputations to questions of the relation of its religious-philosophical views to Russia's social-political destiny. Events and discussions among the leaders during the preceding summer had brought about this change. One of those events was the return of Merezhkovsky, Hippius, and Filosofov to Petersburg from Paris in July.[9] Under the impact of the Revolution of 1905, they had concluded that both the Russian state and its "religious arm," the Orthodox church, barred the way to Christian communism and the third, final form of human existence. The church could not be transformed while the state existed.[10] If the intellectuals were to guide change in terms of their religious-philosophical ideas, they would have to attune them to the revolutionary drives of the Russian people.

Remarks by the student of religion Alexander A. Meier on October 22, 1908, demonstrated that other members of the society wished to turn to the question of "religion and communality." Noting that the society was about to open its fall sessions, he pointed out that it stood at the crossroads.[11] If it continued to pursue highly abstruse discussions about the nature of Christianity, it would become more and more a "private circle." Meier urged the leaders to consider wider topics of Russian social-cultural and intellectual life, admitting to its meetings "all who are adrift in modern Russian society." He wanted to invite intellectuals who were not necessarily religious thinkers, but who wished to discuss themes connecting Russian social-political life with religion.

When the leaders of the society accepted the new course urged by Meier and Merezhkovsky, dissension emerged. Early in February 1909, Rozanov publicly in *Novoe Vremya* (*New Times*) resigned from the council of the society so that he would not "bear responsibility for the change from its former good and necessary aims!"[12] By this he meant concentration on religious themes and efforts to influence the clergy. He argued that the political direction of 1908 had resulted from the entrance of Merezhkovsky and Filosofov into the society. But the society's council pointed out that on October 23, 1908, the membership had voted not to "resurrect in the society the tendencies of the old society meetings, not to establish as the first task of the society the effort to seek the participation of the Church.''[13] Though the decision to take the new course had not been unanimous, it accepted "full responsibility for the direction of the society's activity." This letter was signed by I. Andreev, chairman; Merezhkovsky, associate chairman; Askoldov, Lossky, Uspensky, and Filosofov, members of the council. This, however, did not end the discussion of the aims of the society.

On March 12, 1909, those who desired a more narrowly religious focus for the society succeeded in splitting it into two parts. One, a "Christian section," took as its task the "investigation and working out of religious-philosophical questions on the basis of the Christian religion.''[14] This section held its first meeting on April 15, 1909, when Aggeev presented a report on "Individualism in Christianity." It had thirty-nine active and fifty-four participating members. Askoldov was its chairman until November 22 when he was replaced by Ivanov, and its secretary was S. P. Kablukov. In 1909 it held five meetings at which papers were read by Aggeev, Rozanov, Ivanov, and Filosofov.

The larger, or main section, counted a membership of 712, of whom 87 were active and 625 discussants. On November 29, Filosofov replaced Andreev as chairman with Merezhkovsky remaining as associate chairman. In 1909, twelve meetings were held at which Bazarov, Blok, Rozanov, Meier, Ivanov, Ternavtsev, Struve, Merezhkovsky, A. A. Kamensky, and Serge I. Gessen presented reports. At these meetings the following papers were read and discussed.[15]

1. November 13, 1908, G.A. Baronov, "Russia and the Intelligentsia," and A.A. Blok, "On the 'Confession' of Gorky."

2. November 25, 1908, V.V. Rozanov, "On the People as God."

3. December 12, 1908, A.A. Blok, "Russia and Intelligentsia," at the *St. Petersburg Literary Society* chaired by Vladimir G. Korolenko.

4. December 16, 1908, A.A. Meier, "Religion and Culture," a joint meeting of the Religious-Philosophical Society and the Literary Society.

5. December 30, 1908, A.A. Blok, "*Stikhii* and Culture," and V. Ivanov, "The Russian Idea."

6. January 2, 1909, Kornei I. Chukovsky, "Nat Pinkerton and Contemporary Literature," at the *St. Petersburg Literary Society.*

7. January 9, 1909, V.A. Bazarov, "God-building and God-seeking" at the *St. Petersburg Literary Society.*

8. January 16, 1909, St. Ivanovich, "The New Intelligentsia," at the *St. Petersburg Literary Society.*

9. January 20, 1909, D.V. Filosofov, "God-building and God-seeking."

10. February 6, 1909, B. Stolpner, "F.M. Dostoevsky and the Intelligentsia," at the *St. Petersburg Literary Society.*

11. February 6, 1909, N.A. Berdiaev, "Attempt at a Philosophical Foundation of Christianity."

12. March 6, 1909, S.F. Godlevsky, "Revolution and Religion."

13. March 18, 1909, P.B. Struve, "Socialism and Religion."

14. April 21, 1909, D.S. Merezhkovsky and D.V. Filosofov on *Vekhi.*

Discussions of these topics aroused the greatest public interest in the society and led to numerous publications on the "relationship between the intelligentsia and the people" and "religion and socialism." It also activated the police, who, throughout 1908 and 1909, harassed the society.[16] They forbade some meetings, closed others to any but active members, and disallowed discussion of papers whenever it seemed that "seditious" words might be spoken.

Three points of view dominated discussion. The poet Alexander Blok raised the old question of the "relation between the intelligentsia and the people." He denounced the participants in the societies for indulging themselves in delusive talk and feelings about the needs and desires of the "people." Blok prophesied that the freezing, hungry millions would pursue their true needs and in the process utterly destroy all but a tiny handful of the intellectuals.[17] Casting themselves in the role of those close to the people, the Social Democratic "Empiriomonists" Lunacharsky and Bazarov and the writer Maxim Gorky argued that socialism was the final, most inclusive form of religion.[18] Mankind was God, gradually reaching self-realization on earth through the labor of the millions. Revolutionary intellectuals were its priests and martyrs.

The religious question held the attention of the Russian Social Democratic colony in Paris for over two months in 1908. Lunacharsky made a major speech on socialism as a religion at the large hall on the Rue Cadet. Another Social Democrat, Egorov (E.J. Levin), reported that while doing propaganda among workers during the general strike, he found that they were "genuinely religious." George S. Khrustalev-Nosar called Orthodox Russian Marxism "too dry

. . . too pseudo-scientific," and said that it required that active pursuance of ideals which was the "essence of religion." The Menshevik leader Julius I. Martov took the view that the religious searchings going on in Russia at that time were genuine and demonstrated that the revolution was still dominated by the bourgeois, who as revolutionaries were moved "more by religious feeling than reason. The more the proletariat participates, the less there will be of religion. Religion will disappear." As for Lenin, his abusive denunciation of Social Democratic "God-building," *Materializm i Empiriomonizm*, is well known.

Against the vague intuitions of Blok and the romantic interpretation of Marxism offered by Lunacharsky, liberals like Novgorodtsev and Peter Struve spoke out. They vigorously warned of the dangers of bringing the ultimate commitments and resulting zealotry of religious feelings into political thought and action. In these highly charged intellectual interchanges, Bulgakov developed his own Christian socialist view of Russia's early-twentieth-century needs. This belief grew out of the open conflict with the liberals, Novgorodtsev, Struve, and Frank, which had begun in 1906.

BULGAKOV AND RUSSIAN LIBERALISM

The conflict between Bulgakov and the Russian liberals concerned the early-twentieth-century arrival of the masses on the political stage. It also concerned the contrast between the natures of the *person* and the *individual*. While mass politics posed a threat to all European liberals, it especially endangered the very small, economically weak liberal movement in Russia. Even though the liberal Constitutional Democratic party included major land reform and factory legislation in its program, it would find it difficult to compete with the parties of the left for popular support. The politics of representative government and gradual reform on the basis of compromise among interest groups might seem mysterious or trivial to Russia's largely illiterate and desperate peasants and workers. These were realities to which Bulgakov addressed himself.

Bulgakov argued that the vast majority of Russia's people would reject the liberal party. They would do so not only because they would find the Kadet program uninspiring but also because of the rationalistic individualism which characterized the assumptions and

99

personalities of its leaders. These late individualistic humanists would arouse contempt from a Russian peasantry which could not conceive of a world without God and the warmth and brotherhood of a living Christian community. Bulgakov concluded that everywhere in Europe, but especially in Russia, mass politics was religious politics.

Protesting a report of a St. Petersburg telegraph agency which listed him a member of the Kadet party, Bulgakov wrote that "Christian socialism" might best describe his position.[19] He would join neither the Kadets nor any other party in the Second Duma. However, he noted that the Kadets stood for the "right" principles, were unquestionably on the side of political freedom, cultural growth, and necessary social and economic reform. Moreover, in making room in their ranks for most people who supported the general principles of liberation they made it possible to overcome the poisonous suspicion, jealousy, and intolerance which had kept Russian antigovernmental forces isolated in small circles and unable to further their common cause.[20] Bulgakov discerned the crucial weakness of the Kadet party in that very pluralism.

Kadet pluralism reflected its urban upper middle class base and the predominance of intellectuals among its leaders and most articulate supporters. Their great watchwords were tolerance and compromise, without which liberal politics could not function. But not only high principles lay behind liberal tolerance. Urban populations whose members held many different religious faiths and world views developed at least a surface tolerance, because otherwise the tensions bred of proximity would make civilized life impossible. Political parties embracing diverse urban groups could not be compounds, but only conglomerates, which could exist only as long as their members feared strife more than they valued their particularities. They enshrined particularity in the name of tolerance, while avoiding it in life and action. From this point of view liberal parties rested on the uneasiness of the middle class urbanite. At the same time, the ability to transform that uneasiness into humane liberating action rested on social and economic security.

Though he implied it, Bulgakov did go on to discuss the role of security in the success of European liberalism in the nineteenth century. Confident and secure, liberal leaders transcended the weakness of their instruments. Particularly in England, they were a small minority of men of high and similar education, of a strong sense of duty to serve their country in the most rational way possible, of unusual sustained integrity and dedication to freedom for all as they understood it. Their weakness was that they could function politically only among men as tolerant, as willing to compromise, as attentive to the voice of reason as they. And only people as secure as they, as free from the embittering experience of poverty and humiliation, as similar in family, school, and university background as they, could react to political, social, and economic tensions and problems as "liberally" as they.

Confronted with universal suffrage and the massed organized workers their policies brought into being, the gentlemen-liberals very soon found it difficult to function and entered their period of decline. One of the several tragedies for Russia was that, by the time it developed a minority of dedicated politically active men of this liberal persuasion, its problems were of a kind (millions of highly concentrated, miserable workers; desperate peasantry; parasitic noble class; entrenched bureaucracy; revolutionary socialist ideologues and organizers) that placed almost insoluble problems before their rational politics. Bulgakov understood the sharpness of this problem for early-twentieth-century Russia.

Bulgakov believed that the game of mutual reduction of tension through exchange of dependencies and goods could not appeal to the masses of Russian workers and peasants. In the first place, these classes knew no other stratum except as an external enemy or friend. Internal differences posed no problem, since common ways of life and common tradition developed common political behavior and belief. They felt no need or inclination to embrace pluralism as a program while denying it in practice. Simple people with straightforward, pressing wants needed to feel part of something greater than themselves in order to feel loyalty and hope. A party which could not offer monolithic unity because of its need to embrace persons of many particular convictions could not appeal to them.

Beyond politics, in the religion of humanity, Bulgakov found the fatal error of liberal humanism. Blinded by the light emanating from the godlike man of their hopes and dreams, individualistic humanists could not see the Russian need for religious community. They were the final product of the historical process which had begun when men of the Renaissance and Reformation pitted their aesthetic, intellectual, and volitional powers against the medieval church.[21] They had broken out of the mold forced upon them by a religious authority which had sought to create the Kingdom of God on earth by repressing human modes of creativity. Once liberated from *theocracy*, creative humanity had greatly enriched all aspects of human life. But good would not outweigh evil if the individual search for beauty, wealth, and power were to remain the dominant source of human endeavors.

Egoistic individuals with no understanding of goals beyond humanity itself had brought human culture to sterility. Science had become a godless religion—delusive scientism, philosophy—empty epistemology, art—degrading naturalism and eroticism, and everyday life—"the decay of the spirit, flabbiness, routine, and enslavement to the body."[22] Political and economic forces, unrestrained by objective values, exploited and enslaved men in the name of their material well-being and freedom. All of these were signs that individualistic humanism had reached the end of the road. Mankind stood on the edge of an abyss, faced with the prospect of toppling over the edge individually, one by one, but increasingly moved by a vague feeling that only religious communality could provide a bridge over which they could advance toward peace and plenty. Bulgakov concluded that the eternal Christian church, manifested in the twentieth century by Russian Orthodoxy, provided the only bearer of saving, forward movement.

Much of Bulgakov's critique of liberalism hinged on his concern for the *person* and distrust of the *individual*. In his theory, the person contrasted with the natural man.[23] The person was part of the world-soul, therefore holy and outside space and time. It could be neither circumscribed by forces in the world subject to the laws of mechanics nor identified with reason. Rather, its identifying feature was life, the true life implanted in nature and man by God, the life struggling upward from primeval chaos to reunion with Him. Bulgakov attacked individualistic humanism and its political expression, liberalism, because it encouraged, indeed sanctified that egoistic individualism which stood in the way of human personhood and, hence, salvation. Christian Socialism would give mankind a chance to turn to its true path.

Nothing frightened or aroused liberals more than the introduction of religious belief and attitudes into political movements. Novgorodtsev wrote a large volume in an endeavor to show the dangers of "religious politics." Other liberals, such as Struve, Frank, E. Trubetskoi, N. Ezersky, S. Lur'e, and Alexander S. Izgoev (Lande), spoke fervently against "religious socialism" in the religious-philosophical societies and related literature.[24] Most of these considered an ultimate religious faith necessary for a politics dedicated to the freedom of the person and the existence of absolute ideals. Yet, any mode of thought and action which brought religious passion into politics or political relativism into religion worried them.

They shared the feeling which had given birth to liberal attitudes in England in the seventeenth century. Frightened by the hatred and destruction which had featured the English civil war and attributing these to the identification of political positions with religious attitudes, the English had endeavored to separate the two realms. Distrust of "enthusiasm" in politics permeated the definitive writings of John Locke and remained a liberal shibboleth. It was particularly strong among Russian liberals because of their exposed position between the power of the bureaucratic state and the backward, silent peasant majority. In the early-twentieth-century the state consciously sought to mobilize peasant religious passion against liberals.

Writing in *Russkaia Mysl'* (*Russian Thought*), of which Struve had become editor in 1907, N. Ezersky made a systematic attempt to specify the areas of politics and religion and to show the dangers of confounding them.[25] Stated generally, the differences came down to those of the absolute and relative, ends and means, persuasion and force. Religion demanded of man that he give his entire being to the Absolute Truth which would make him free, but that in pursuit of the Blessed Kingdom, he use persuasion, the only means compatible with that end.

Politics dealt always with the relativity inherent in concrete problems and followed the policy of "least evil" in a given historical situation. The political actor could not avoid using impure means in pursuit of contingent ends, for he had to deal with men as they were. Though he might prefer persuasion, he had to be ready to employ force against the relatively evil in the interests of the relatively good. A religiously motivated political leader would either destroy freedom because of his commitment to the true or be impotent because of his rejection of the use of force.[26] And so it seemed to Russian liberals that Bulgakov's proposed Union of Christian Politics pursued a dangerous course that negated the exalted ends he proclaimed.

103

Peter Struve entered the lists against his old polemical opponent, Bulgakov. As he demonstrated in several contributions to the Religious-Philosophical Society and in his editorial comments in *Poliarnaia Zvezda* (*Polar Star*), he did not believe that the church was the religious base for a liberating politics.[27] Although "all politics and political systems in the last analysis rested on certain religious ideas," they could not be restrained by the dogmas of the church.[28] Bulgakov believed wrongly that the religious structure supporting politics had to be a church which defined an "objectively ordered system of beliefs" to which all members of a party or movement had to assent. Struve attributed this error to the "dogmatic tenor" of Bulgakov's mind, which made it impossible for him to accept "subjective religiosity" as the proper conviction with which to approach life and politics.

Christians, atheists, idealists, and positivists could all experience subjective religiosity. Struve never defined this term carefully, but certainly meant some kind of faith that man's struggle for the triumph of the good, the true, and the beautiful in the world was in tune with an impersonal divine plan. The liberal Constitutional Democratic approach to politics rested on this premise, the only true and safe way to view the relation of religion to politics. Struve believed that this urban intellectual's approach to religion mirrored the state of the mass mind, that the "people" responded more to a generalized "truth of God" than to the liturgies, rituals, and priestly ministrations of the Orthodox church. In the hearts of men from all churchly bodies and walks of life lay the true religious attitudes, deep concern for "the supreme meaning of religious values."[29] In making statements like these, Struve spoke dogmatically, for he had no way of knowing the nature of peasant religious attitudes.

Struve's "subjective religiosity" was dubious religion. First, the term is meaningless, for it is impossible to designate what particular subjective states might be termed "religiosity." The candidates are innumerable. Probably little is gained by attaching the term "religiosity" to the state Struve described. It might be better to consider it the linking together of symbols lending rationality to the world for men to whom religiosity had become impossible. Not new, all great religions had confronted it and denied that it was sufficient to induce a religious state. Rationalistic metaphysics could inspire aesthetically based feelings of reverence and even awe, but lacked the ritually supported communion with men and God which the great religions included.

Religiosity has to do with feelings of communion with other men through mutual identification with a living reality of unique power. A religion has a specific God, with specific liturgies, prayers, and rituals, which arouse immediate unexamined feelings of participation in the destinies of man and the world. It establishes an experienced connection between man and God. The religiosity celebrated by Struve is that of the modern intellectual, embarrassed by that Being and those rituals, and arrogant enough to label "mechanical," even nonreligious, the observances of premodern social strata like the Russian peasants. By concepts such as "subjective religiosity," liberals in particular attempted to appropriate religion to a mental set which found religion intolerable. When he turned to the alleged internal link between religion and socialism, Struve dealt with a topic more congenial to his customary historical and ideological approach.

Struve tried to draw a firm and accurate line between religion and socialism. He directed his arguments mainly to Lunacharsky and other Marxist "God-builders," but he also attacked Bulgakov's Christian socialism. He expressed the fundamental idealist position that deterministic Marxism could not consistently support the struggle for freedom. Like Bulgakov, he attributed socialism's nineteenth-century hold over men's minds to the surrogate religion it seemed to offer.[30] He also shared Bulgakov's view that as a political and economic force it would triumph soon. But, unlike Bulgakov, he did not believe that the socialistic religious enthusiasm which moved so many to seek freedom and justice could be once again united with the Christian church. The religious spirit was immortal and would be resurrected in the midst of new ideas to lead mankind further on its progressive path—but not in the framework of an authoritative church. In 1914, Struve resigned from the governing board of the St. Petersburg Society because of its continuing attempt to mix politics with religion.

This confrontation between Bulgakov and the liberals raised tragic issues. Much truth resided on both sides, but they could not exist together. As political developments in Europe after World War I were to show, populations responded excitedly to those who offered something more captivating than the rationality and utilitarian considerations on which liberal parties sought support. Slogans based on race or class hatred, promises of action against clearly designated "enemies," and the excitement and self-loss of mass political rituals proved much more attractive than quiet, dignified pursuit of agreement to postpone satisfaction. In Russia, of course, the number of those who would seek the middle was particularly small, while the problems it faced between 1900 and 1917 were particularly threatening. However disheartening the recognition and however impractical Bulgakov's proposals, he understood something about the emerging political struggles in Europe and Russia which late-nineteenth-century liberals, by their very nature, could not fully grasp.

At the same time, the liberal distrust of religious feeling in political matters rested on a true perception. Binding people together with religious ties and feelings in pursuit of absolute political ends would produce an environment in which liberalism could not survive. And with the demise of liberalism there would disappear a potent force toward decency in politics, toward the preservation of individual rights, toward a society able to pursue broad-gauged progress in human culture. The practice of liberal politics proved to be inordinately difficult in the twentieth century and was perhaps impossible in Russia. But to forego it for "mass politics" was to make difficult or impossible the attainment of human values which socialism, as well as liberalism, sought. Rejection of liberalism pushed Bulgakov in the direction of the other political force with which he had been associated, Marxist socialism. But, where its approach to Russian politics and social problems impressed him as superior to that of the Kadets, its positivistic philosophy could no more support a move for liberation in the modern world than could individualistic humanism.

CHRISTIAN SOCIALISM AND SOCIAL DEMOCRACY

In the complexities of Russian society and progressive Russian politics, Bulgakov saw health and Apollonian light in the Kadets, but an attractive and more realistic Dionysian force in Social Democracy. On the secular level the Russian Marxists would win. Kadets might scorn their philosophical naïveté and carefully point out in "sober, serious learned . . . analysis" the errors of their economic programs, but this had no effect on mass politics. Indeed, the earnestness of Kadet efforts in this direction showed their misunderstanding of the Russian people.

Calls for the immediate overthrow of an enslaving social order would arouse more response than reasonable Kadet gradualism. The majority of the peasants would follow the Social Democrats, only a small minority, the "economist-muzhiks, calculating hoarders," being interested in Kadet appeals to free enterprise and the business spirit. Moreover, Bulgakov believed that Social Democratic propaganda was not only more effective, but also more realistic. It offered a vision of a *sobornal* future, a "union in love and freedom," which corresponded to age-old yearnings of Russia's people. The Kadets were healthy and "right," but pathetically out of touch with the realities of Russian politics. The Social Democrats were theoretically wrong and unhealthy, but very much in touch with a good Russian reality.

Bulgakov noted approvingly that Social Democracy and its priceless socialist spirit moved the Russian radical intelligentsia. Like his associates among the "ex-Marxists," he had once viewed that social group with dislike and condescension, labeling them self-destructive romanticists and vapid theorists who did more harm than good to the cause of freedom. However, his drift away from idealistic rationalism and liberalism to Christian socialism had awakened in him a more ambivalent feeling toward them. He now saw them as "idealistic to the last little finger," unconsciously Christian heroes. When Western positivism had triumphed in Russian thought, the intelligentsia had embraced it but had brought into it a creative, religious force which it lacked in the works of the widely read, influential materialist thinkers, Ludwig Büchner, Karl Vogt, and Jacob Moleschott.[31] When Western social democracy had degenerated to the bourgeois search for material plenty of Bernsteinism, they had kept alive its quality of a religious brotherhood, pursuing the City of the Righteous. They were the "salt of the earth" whom he hoped to recruit by convincing them to become openly and consciously what they were unconsciously, strugglers for the Kingdom of God on Earth. But short of that transformation, socialism, socialist parties, trade unions, and labor movements could offer no productive escape from the dilemmas of individualistic humanism.

Socialists shared with liberals the mistaken belief that "natural man" could be free. Noble men, pursuing basically sanctified ends, could seek but external freedoms, which perished as fathers and sons followed each other in an endless cycle of imagined human greatness and recognition of impotence.[32] They might base their life activities

107

on love for humanity, being ready to sacrifice their comforts, careers, even their lives for the well-being, present or future, of the "humiliated and the injured." But their natural egoism and willfulness made it very difficult for them to pursue the good of others consistently and without the use of means which made ultimate ends of freedom and justice unattainable.

Because of its opposition to the unbearable evils born of ancient political oppression and modern capitalistic greed, socialism would surely triumph in the near future.[33] But it could do nothing to overcome the reification which had reduced man to a slave of his own creations. Social Democracy, for all its healthy communitarianism, was itself a reification, a concept whose reality in the external world was mocked by the gap between its pretensions and its possibilities. It promised man a secular utopia which it could not produce. Already, recognition of that fact had broken the unity of the movement. Many Russians had accepted what Bulgakov despised, Bernsteinism. Others continued to raise the banner of a transformed man in a society of brothers, but used political means which could not possibly lead to that end. His dissatisfaction with liberalism and fear of Russian Marxism led Bulgakov to offer his own Christian socialist doctrines.

During 1906 and on into 1907, Bulgakov hoped with some optimism that a Christian socialist movement might emerge from the Revolution of 1905. He believed that the great majority of Russians would unite with a Christian force struggling for enlightened social and economic reform. The Russian Orthodox church would be that force if, rather than damning or ignoring modern secular institutions, it would acquire a social-scientific understanding of them. It even seemed possible that the revolutionary intelligentsia could be brought to exercise its heroism in a positive, not nihilistic way, if it accepted the basically religious nature of its quest. Bulgakov planned to establish a center at Kiev and published the newspaper *The People* to make known the existence of the new movement.[34] He envisaged collaborators in the major cities and the publication of booklets for the mass audience. Bulgakov hoped to inspire, if not a Christian Socialist party, at least its spirit, capable of influencing Russian leaders toward socially just and economically productive politics.

As the government reaction and clerical intransigence deepened after mid-1907, Bulgakov abandoned organizational efforts. As early as 1905 the Russian church aroused in him mingled anger, shame, and compassion as it arrested and silenced priests who expressed liberal or moderate socialist views and proved helpless to assert itself against state authority.[35] He served in the Third and Fourth Dumas, though he viewed with great disgust government manipulation of the elections and the radical use of the assemblies as platforms for inflammatory revolutionary propaganda.[36] It also sharpened his contempt for the Russian noble landlords, about whom he wrote, "Akh, this estate! . . . When you see with your own eyes the degeneration united with arrogance, pretensions, and, at the same time cynicism . . . you fear terribly for the *vlast'*, which stubbornly bases its power on this element." As the prewar decade wore on, he became progressively more disgusted with official church action, particularly with regard to Rasputin.[37] He despairingly concluded that the church could not carry out its saving function without further political change in Russia. Even the Orthodox people remained deaf to church authority. From 1908 to 1914, Bulgakov turned to the philosophy of Schelling to express his increasingly mystical views on the link between men, nature, the economy, and God.

The polemics of 1905–1906 brought to the surface Bulgakov's conviction that only the church, the bearer of universal love, could save humanity. For it alone embodied the synthesis of personal and *sobornal* principles which were the aim of God through history. Vague "religiosity" was not enough. An individual could not be a religious person, could not experience religion outside the church, for the church and religion were one. Isolated personal faith and love of God could not be a true religious experience. On these grounds, Bulgakov rejected the current writings of his former idealistic comrades, Struve and Frank, whom he accused of sowing the greatest possible confusion with their expressions of religious individualism.[38] But he insisted that only a greatly modified Russian Orthodox church could bring man into the true church and to a new life.

As Soloviev had argued, secular struggles for the liberation of men from political despotism and grinding poverty did God's work. The church should seek to solve these problems as a necessary means to raise men's spritual nature to the level from which they could respond to the message of Christian love.[39] This entailed a positive attitude toward modern science, including that social science which showed that the organization of societies for the well-being of all could be achieved. Priests should be taught social sciences so that they could understand the problems of their time and safeguard their people from the blandishments of atheistic socialists.[40] If necessary, they should seek political office and actively support acceptable candidates for the Duma in the post-1905 constitutional order.

The church should replace the asceticism of "bridling the flesh" and pious mendicancy by true asceticism, the realistic understanding that evil was present in all human actions. To be ascetic meant to forego the pleasure arising from the childish fantasies of a solely human road to purity.[41] Serious study of the social sciences by the clergy would weaken the force of inhuman asceticism, while making it possible for them to combat utopianism. But Bulgakov felt strongly that the potentially productive scholarly social sciences could not serve the interests of the church and man until their university practitioners eliminated from them certain harmful aspects.

Social science had been infected from its nineteenth-century beginnings with *hubris* and utilitarianism. The social scientists' undue pride lay in their oft-repeated claims that they understood the "laws" of social development, and could show the way to a perfect society.[42] To this "scientism" was appended a fixation on social and economic engineering at the behest of its early patrons, states and businesses.[43] Following German thinkers like Rickert and Max Weber, Bulgakov held that social sciences were not exact theoretical sciences, but applied sciences, like medicine. But neither were they mere technologies, useful only to implement the policies of political and economic leaders; they should originate policies for the benefit of all.

However, social scientific thought took place in the university, and that great institution had surrendered to the spirit of the times. There, where men should, many had, and a few still did pursue truth, unentangled with political and social ideologies and modes of action, the "party spirit" had taken hold.[44] Professors had become political agitators, about whom truth-destroying political passions clustered. Most students responded to political excitement and ignored the fact that it mocked daily and hourly their right to the most sincere pursuit of truth by their professors. A true *trahison des clercs* had taken place which endangered not only Russia, but all civilization.

In opposition to politicized social science, Bulgakov sought to describe a Christian political economy that would include major aspects of Marxism, which remained unchallenged as an analysis of the interrelations of natural forces, technology, and industrial and social-political development in the modern world. But it would reject Marxist and any positivist claim to have discovered "laws" of human development and any assertion that such "laws" could be unearthed. The social sciences depended for their raw material on the events recorded by history. But historians could not provide a body of data from which laws could be formulated, for the "facts" they unearthed were too many and pointed in too many directions. Reflecting the multifaceted particularities of man's existence and the unpredictable nature of his choices, historical accounts were selective and relative to the time and place of their authors. But although the positivist effort to replace the manifold of history with reductive law could not succeed, history had to be transcended in some way if men were to progress against the weight of its monumental character.[45] Therein lay the role in social science of Schelling's Christian philosophy.[46] It showed why and how man's economic activity aimed at the "spiritualization of nature."

In *Filosofiia khoziaistva* (*Philosophy of Economics*), Bulgakov signaled his acceptance of Schelling's idealism as the philosophical base. He found it most compatible with his religious views of the world and the only adequate ground for any economic theory which would make possible a world in which work for all, high production, reasonable equality of consumption, and a nonhedonistic and hence humanly worthwhile approach to life could be combined. He also attempted to give his work a Kantian flavor by describing his effort as that of finding the transcendental point of view from which economics as a fact would be possible. To complete his bow to German idealism he suggested in a Hegelian vein that he wanted to "understand the world as an object of laboring economic influence . . . and (at the same) time define the philosophy of the world as a philosophy of economics." None of these tasks could be accomplished unless all were subsumed under the ultimate truth, Christianity.

God demanded, men required, and the church should cease to oppose economic progress, the expenditure of human effort in pursuit of material abundance. However, private property, once necessary to that purpose, increasingly thwarted it. It siphoned off unjustifiable amounts of the social product for the few, and condemned the many to miserable, often bestial lives incommensurable with further material and spiritual progress.[47] Moreover, the "spirit of property" infected almost everyone, from top to bottom of society, presenting a powerful psychological barrier to spiritualization.[48] Bulgakov deeply feared man's propensity to bury his spiritual longings under the weight of squalid material satisfactions. In a self-revelatory remark, he said, "Not all progress is desirable and good from the Christian point of view. To the perversion of high and refined culture it is proper sometimes to prefer patriarchal coarseness with its parsimonious and salutary forces." So he established both his contempt for the high life of the Russian nobility and the limits of his socialism. It was to provide for the *necessities* of all people, not for ever higher levels of consumption.

Although these comments expressed a moral critique of capitalism, Bulgakov strongly insisted that the approach of moral damnation by itself would avail little. Thundering denunciation of an industrialized society by Tolstoi and Carlyle, the call for a return to an alleged primitive Christian communism by the Brotherhood, Fourierist attempts to set up islands of communal living in a capitalist sea, or the endeavors of humanitarian industrialists to share the wealth or turn factories over to workers would not help. Nor would a violent revolution made in the name of the equal distribution of goods.

Human control of nature had reached a level from which men could begin to plan for an economic order pointed toward equal distribution of an abundance of goods.[49] But that state of things required high productivity. Fulfilling their historical role, capitalistic entrepreneurs provided the plant and organized the labor force which brought it about. Private property should not be abolished until an alternative workable method of production and distribution was possible.[50] Certainly Russia, with its technologically and morally backward millions and underdeveloped industry and agriculture could not consider taking that step. Efforts to increase production took precedence over all moralizing ideology and all "sorcery and quackery" promising a rapid transformation of man's condition.[51] Typically, however, he praised the moralizers, Carlyle and Tolstoi, because they proposed active, practical Christianity, not abstract contemplation. Christians should support the socialist parties, the most correct and morally worthwhile of all political forces existing in the early twentieth century. But they should do so realistically, striving stubbornly and intelligently against poverty and injustice, while remembering that any final solution to man's problems would take place under a new heaven and on a new earth.

In his accent on productivity, Bulgakov pointed very accurately at a serious failing in the economic views of Russian socialists. In their long-held concentration on means of improving the material well-being of the Russian peasants and workers, they focused too much on a fairer *distribution of goods* and too little on the true basis of progressive improvement, *increased production*.[52] And he correctly traced this to the prejudices of the intellectuals, producers of ringing phrases and little else, who could not see the irreplaceable value of plain, sober hard work in the organization and carrying out of industrial and agricultural projects. They poured scorn on those who sought to energize initiative and a sense of responsibility in Russian life, seeking to discredit them as "bourgeois" or self-interested lackeys of capitalism trying to deceive the workers.

Bulgakov criticized one of the truly harmful effects of the influence of some literary intellectuals in the modern world. In the Russia of his time these often *did* use their literary skills to inculcate the idea that their activities were "higher, nobler, more worthy" than the mundane pursuits of economic life. It is not necessary to accept Bulgakov's assertion that they exhibited a lower "quality of human personality," to agree that they lacked the "stubborn will and clear-sighted gaze" needed to bring about economic and attendant social progress.[53] And, perhaps justly, he complained that the retreat from concrete, productive tasks by this sizable portion of Russia's tiny minority of educated people and the degree of influence they exerted on the general attitudes of educated society contributed something to the developing "economic conquest of Russia by foreigners." Nonetheless, Bulgakov knew that many Russian Marxists were neither salon socialists nor proponents of immediate transformation of Russia into a socialist society.

Mensheviks approached Russian politics in a thoughtful, realistic way, but even they would eventually become despotic rulers. They held that Russia had yet to experience a successful "bourgeois revolution." They argued that when that should occur, socialists should employ the civil rights and political democracy characteristic of a capitalist regime to organize and raise the political consciousness of the ever increasing industrial proletariat. Revolution would come after the bourgeois had established an economy of abundance and after that economy developed the inherent contradictions between its mode of production and its social order. Bulgakov thought along these lines, but believed that a socialist society arrived at by these means would itself become repressive or collapse because its leaders would lack respect for the free human personality. Leaving aside individual subjective desires, in which he had little confidence, Bulgakov argued that economic growth itself would be thwarted. Political leaders would inevitably grow impatient with the failure of *persons* consistently to pursue goals which the leaders "knew" to be the "inevitable" result of the historical process. The self-disciplined, responsible and, at the same time, social man Russia needed could flourish only in a society resting on a broadly humane philosophical and ultimately religious world view.

Bulgakov admitted that his doctrine confronted any individual with a serious dilemma. He would have to accept this world and its often evil economic relations, help create it and support it by his labor, but he could never become reconciled to it. He had to judge it harshly, particularly in terms of the presence or absence in it of Christian love, but he had to avoid mesmerization by words, the Idols of the Market Place, false symbols of good and evil, like "capitalist" and "worker." Zealot cries of "opportunist" or "hypocrite" would sting and hurt, but were ultimately beyond the mark, for the true Christian lived outside of these designations; his role as a social animal did not determine the nature of his person.

In these arguments and proposals, Bulgakov confronted his liberal and socialist opponents with realities and possibilities in early-twentieth-century Russia. Struve's "subjective religiosity" could not act as the barrier to individualistic competition and its social fruits. The hope that the church could transform its relation to everyday life through exposure to modern education was not totally illusory. In view of the thousand-year heritage of Orthodox Christianity in Russia, it was not foolish to believe that the peasants of Russia might respond to its basic spirit if it was presented to them in terms of their concrete everyday needs. Bulgakov correctly pointed out the damage done to scholarship and education by the politicization of the university. It was not absurd to deny what was taught by so many professors, whether in Comtian, Spencerian, or Marxist form, the existence of "laws" governing the development of mankind in history.

Finally, Bulgakov was not simply a "reactionary" when he suggested that increased production of goods, rather than egalitarian distribution of existing products should be the goal of those who wished the best for Russia and its people. All of these statements could be discussed. Empirical evidence and logical rigor could have been fruitfully brought to bear on them, even in the presence of ideological commitments. But the degree to which discussion concerning these points could go on depended on the willingness of the government, the church, the intellectuals, and the people to accept a reasonably stable and progressive political order. It became clear, particularly after 1910, that a minimal level of agreement and search for ordered change scarcely existed. Reflecting the feeling of impending confrontation apparent in the last years before 1914, Bulgakov, while not rejecting his concrete proposals, began to seek solutions in the wider, mystical aspects of Schelling's philosophy.

If men were to relate communally and ethically toward one another, it seemed to nineteenth-century philosophers as it had to pagan and Christian mystics that they must be connected in some direct way to the world of nature and to other men. As long as men were not united with the world they would be unable to know it and, if unable to know it, incapable of acting rationally in their relations with it. They could know nature and other men only as objects to obey or dominate. In either case, men would remain unfulfilled and alienated from nature, from other men, and also from themselves; for since they were embedded in the world, they could know themselves only insofar as they knew the world. The only true knowledge was complete knowledge, and the only complete knowledge was that which the united subject-object could have of itself.

Subject-object unity, an age-old aim of religious mystics, called forth the prodigious labors of early-nineteenth-century German thinkers. As Goethe said, ''Here we come face to face with our real difficulty . . . that between the idea and the experience there seems to be a certain gulf fixed; we exert all our strength to cross it, in vain. In spite of this, we strive constantly to overcome this gap by means of reason, understanding, imagination, faith, feeling, madness, and, if nothing else will serve, with absurdity.''[54] Hegel, Goethe, and Schelling attempted to cross this gap, by placing themselves '' . . . in the middle between personal existence and the existence of the world.''[55] Hegel's vision of unity through the historical spirit, with the ''cunning of reason'' making good or evil as seen from the limited human view equally servants of progress, was perpetuated, but transformed by Marx in his doctrine of historical materialism.

Bulgakov did not accept either Hegelian panlogism or Marxist materialism as suitable ways to unite subject and object. Marx did believe that man acted through labor to change the world to suit his needs and in the process changed himself, proceeding in a dialectical fashion to the point where men would see themselves and act as a brotherhood. But although man created progressive political, economic, and cultural institutions for himself, he still found the world and other men mysterious enemies to be conquered. Marx believed that only social equality, socialism, the end of the class struggle could bring this sad drama to an end. Even though Bulgakov accepted Marx's hostility to class government, he asserted that the needs of the war with nature would ever again turn institutions into a "second nature," an enslaving force. As long as men pursued almost entirely materialistic satisfactions they would remain alien to and hence ignorant of nature. In contrast to his successor Marx, Hegel had been right to see that spirit had to be the driving force behind unity and knowledge. But he had been wrong to see that spirit as a logical, rational force.

Love, not mind, formed the essence of spirit. It was love born of an original identity as postulated by Christianity and by Schelling. Bulgakov attempted to use Schelling's philosophy of identity to explain the inevitability of a union of subject and object in a transfigured world. Originally united in the Godhead, man and nature strove with the same purpose, to recapture that unity. And love was the world force which worked to bring them back to united participation in the whole. So Bulgakov moved away from Hegel's philosophy of universal reason toward the mystical pole whose metaphor is love. Schelling's philosophy was not the deciding factor, but rather the form in which Bulgakov presented his ideas to secular intellectuals. The deciding factor was the Neoplatonic Christianity which he shared with both Schelling and Soloviev.

In his Christian socialism, Bulgakov attempted to safeguard the *person* against "rationalization" while providing a basis for community. In doing so, he sought to rescue the human subject from subservience to putative objective laws of social development and to assert human freedom of choice under objective ethical law. To him, despite its great technological value, Marxism stood forth as the exact negation of the truth. It was *objective* where it should be *subjective*, in its views on man's place in social progress in history, and *subjective* where it should be *objective*, in its relativizing of ethical choice. Bulgakov held that to assert, objectively, that the technological, social, and economic development of mankind would inevitably culminate in a community embodying freedom and justice could not be done objectively. History provided no real evidence for such a claim, while the major characteristics of the Marxist doctrine, mainly its fixation on equal distribution of material things, were not compatible with its exalted aim.

The Marxists asked men to surrender their essence as persons, their capacity to make free choices, to an "iron law of necessity" which was not an objective truth, but a subjective faith. Bulgakov agreed that the advent of socialist institutions was an objective necessity in that it would inevitably take place, but not that it resulted from the so-called laws of economic materialism. Rather, it would result from the multitudinous choices of men in historical situations as they acted to improve their lot on this earth. As far as there were deeper ends conterminous with human history, they would not be reached by the working out of mystical social-economic "laws," but by the spiritual development of man, revealed by God and demonstrated in the highest material and cultural accomplishments of men in history.

If history had a purpose, *actual infinity* demanded that there had to be a governing principle outside historical process itself. To base a theory of communism almost entirely on the materialistic drives of men as they appeared on this earth was to fall into the toils of potential infinity. Fallen men could make no secure progress toward the communal existence of which Marxist theorists dreamed.

Marxist subjective ethics also fit poorly with high hopes. Marxism claimed to speak for a unified humanity, but it proselytized a "class ethics." Of course, its expositors argued that the ethics of the proletariat, because of its freedom from the false consciousness inspired by the ownership of property other than labor, was or would be universal. Once the bearers of the selfish, competitive, and acquisitive approach to life had been consigned to the ash bin of history, all men would accept the fraternal ethics which was natural to the proletariat. But this remained a purely logical construction, for which no evidence could be adduced from the empirical world. It was a faith that if certain social-economic conditions were destroyed, a new, unified humanity built around the undistorted ethical convictions of the proletariat would emerge. But in the meantime, its supporters preached a relativistic, divisive ethics which appealed to some of man's least attractive qualities.

Men were urged to hate class enemies, to covet their property, and to view human aims in exclusively materialistic terms. Bulgakov believed that these characteristics of Marxist teachings made a mockery of Marxist ideals. They simply perpetuated the spirit of property and the acquisitive drive under the guise of eliminating it. Under socialist institutions men, whose world view had been developed in this way, would continue to view others as competitors for material possessions and would continue to take a selfish, relativistic ethical position, if any at all. Communal existence, which Bulgakov thought necessary, could only exist if there were a real universal ethic, positively grasped and acted upon by all and not based upon the presumed negative lack of involvement. Not the negative lack of property, but the positive concern for the well-being of others would make socialism possible. And only Christianity could universalize that attitude.

To Marxism seen in this way, Bulgakov opposed his *Christian socialism*. He saw history not as a realm governed by the iron laws of social-economic determinism, but as one in which men made free choices in the pursuit of their freely decided purposes. Good worked in the world and it would inevitably conquer, but at each single, isolated confrontation between men and the world, the person had the God-given capacity to choose freely. Human subjectivity was a fact of the world. Bulgakov would not deny that there were economic and social forces impinging on man, constituting restraints on his freedom of choice. But there were "good" social forces and "bad" social forces, and men as "persons" could choose to serve the good and oppose the bad. Moreover, Christian ethics, as opposed to Marxist "class ethics" provided an objective standard by which the "good" and the "bad" could be separated.

The objective standards had been approximately stated in religious tables and idealistic philosophy, but their true expression was the fact of Christ. Christ not only provided an objective standard of goodness, but He also provided the way by which the fallen man could acquire some capacity to do good. To observe simply, from faith, the injunctions of the Sermon on the Mount would have a salutary, though not a saving power. But in becoming one with Christ through faith, prayer, and sacrament, a man could acquire the possibility to do objective good in the world. The Christian ethic was the universal ethic which could make the communal life possible.

When Bulgakov went on to aspire to the ground of being, total unity, or subject-object identity, whether in the vocabulary of Plotinus, Boehme, Schelling, or Soloviev, he spoke as a subjective idealist or religious mystic. Most men have felt that these terms describe states toward which humans on this earth could not realistically aspire. As Struve said, subject-object identity is a characteristic of sainthood, while in Freud's language, an "oceanic feeling" may be its true base. It may well be that all humans have an ultimate desire to return to the feeling of warmth, security, utter belongingness characteristic of their experiences in the womb, but it is doubtful that even the most thoroughly successful practitioner of *hesychasm* reaches that state.

Moreover, making the desire to re-create primal unity on the higher plane of complete consciousness a criterion of worthy or unworthy action in the world would doom all choices to almost equal nullity. The standard is so infinite that, as far as human reckoning can go, an enormous number of concrete actions would be equally distant from it. To determine Bulgakov's degree of success in bringing the world and Neoplatonist conceptions to some kind of commensurability would require an exhaustive study of the sophiological philosophy he developed after 1917. In the period before 1917, he escaped, however illogically, some of the traps of sophiological mysticism by combining it with a more common-sense Christian religious view of the world.

Bulgakov did not succumb to the "oceanic feeling," nor did he seek the ego dominance of the world which so attracted some German romanticists. He taught sober, empirically-based courses in political economy at Moscow University, the Moscow Commercial Institute, and in Shanyavsky University, the only private institution of higher learning in Russia.[56] In all the circles in which he traveled before 1917, he gave the impression of sobriety, solidity, a certain distrust of imaginative flights, a tendency, as Struve said, to seek out objective institutionalized forms about which to build his thought.

As he himself lamented, his feet were on the ground. This, of course, was one of the great strengths of Christianity. Though its heart and soul were in the heavens, it did not escape or, except in the case of the most inspired mystics, really seek to escape the ground.

So it was with Bulgakov. Though he entered the mystical worlds of Schelling's subject-object identity and Soloviev's total unity, he maintained his direct connection with the manifold of relativistic events and relationships of human life. In this world he tried to maintain an objective standard of judgment by referring actions to the traditional everyday Christian values and Christ as a model for just action in personal life and in social-economic relationships.

Christ was the genuine, ultimately irresistible love which men had experienced and which they struggled to understand and internalize. Materialistic action in the world as understood by Marxists prepared man for liberation by freeing him from his long, embittering, and spiritually exhausting struggle for physical survival. As secular struggles lessened poverty and injustice, his spirit could respond to God's call, grace could work upon him, and he could accept the demands which love placed upon him. Secular culture, great philosophies of the spirit like Hegel's, raised men to a level of consciousness where they could draw sustenance from the spirit of love. But, in the end, the basis of victory transcended material progress and the power of reason. It was Eros, a world-uniting sexual force; but it transcended Eros as Agape, an unconditional love for God. Christ had shown man what that love was, and the church as the Body of Christ stood ready to accept man once again into His loving embrace. The choice stood before men, the wrong one leading to a swinish existence and an eternity without hope, the right one to a warm and loving relationship and eternal union with God.

Could *love* be one of the positivities of the human condition? Men throughout history have rightly discounted the power of love to induce decent behavior of men toward one another in social, political, and economic matters. It has seemed better, on the record, to try to attain cohesion through the mutual appeals of men to self-interest. Yet love of neighbor, love of country, love of wisdom, love of principles, love of God have in all places and in all times been celebrated as men's highest achievements. No doubt this is because they manifest themselves so rarely. But man's love for his mother, rooted in his life in the womb and in infancy, continually draws him toward personal and social relationships in which that warmth and unity might be re-experienced. The mystic's cry for unity in an erotically tinged, but selfless unity with all may express for all mankind the ultimate force that holds these creatures of asocial sociability in any lasting mutual relationship. And however romantic and unrealistic, the call for the mobilization of love in each man may be the only call which could activate any of the utopias, from Plato's to Marx's and beyond, of which men have ever dreamed.

The idealistic liberal Novgorodtsev ignored or denied the efficacy of love in bringing about lasting social cohesion. He believed that permanent contradiction and struggle between men were not only facts, but ultimately progressive facts. They provided the true basis for that degree of human universalism attainable for man on this earth. Human conflicts brought about not only the economic progress which would eliminate much human suffering but also the political developments leading to human solidarity. Conflict would gradually, but never completely, teach the lesson that, when it tried to establish unitary communities on this earth, every church, nation, state, or party would inevitably repress and constrict people. Like Bulgakov, Novgorodtsev offered an alternative to Russian Marxism which he hoped would safeguard the autonomy of the person. Unlike the religious thinker, he insisted upon stubborn concentration on that person, rather than institutionalized modes of community, and counted on time and the spread and deepening of humanistic culture to bring men within sight of the *social ideal*.

Chapter V

NOVGORODTSEV'S IDEALISTIC LIBERALISM

With a sense of great liberal victory between 1904 and 1907 and sharp, but not despairing, disappointment during the years of reaction, Paul Novgorodtsev worked in politics and education and continued to develop his idealistic liberal theory. As liberal organization, worker and peasant demonstrations, and revolutionary activity developed throughout Russia, he became a leader of the academic unions in the Union of Unions formed in May 1905. Composed of members of the Union of Liberation, zemstvo liberals, unions of lawyers, doctors, engineers, accountants, and others, that organization urged the election of a constituent assembly chosen by universal suffrage and secret, direct, and equal vote. In July 1905, the Union of Unions and representatives of the zemstvos began to organize a liberal political party. In connection with this, Novgorodtsev sharply criticized D. Shipov and the moderate zemstvo group, which was willing to accept a less democratic assembly and a more restricted political program than that desired by more radical liberals. He labeled them twentieth-century Slavophiles, who wished to hold on to old perspectives when only new, fresh, bold policies could set Russia on the right track.

Novgorodtsev defended his Westernism against zemstvo liberal attacks. Conceding that importations could not be grafted on to deep, fundamental aspects of any culture, he claimed that legal forms were among the most adaptable, least dangerous of foreign elements.[1] He went further to argue that borrowing was a positive force, breaking down national insularity and leading to universalism. Against Dmitry

Shipov he demanded that Russia jettison its punitive bureaucratic government and replace it by a legal government capable of safeguarding the natural rights of men. Against both zemstvo liberalism and radical socialism, Novgorodtsev asserted that the only mode of organization available for that purpose was representative democracy. When the czar issued the manifesto of October 17, 1905, the various liberal groups formed their legal party, the Constitutional Democrats (Kadets). Novgorodtsev played a major role in drafting the Kadet program, which demanded a full parliamentary regime, the constitution of which was to be established by the national legislative assembly, the State Duma. The Kadets also announced their commitment to wide-ranging economic and social reforms.

During the following few months, Novgorodtsev campaigned in Ekaterinoslav for election to the Duma. In his speeches, he admitted that a partial relaxation of bureaucratic control might encourage much violence, destruction, and even bestiality, but he remained optimistic.[2] Whatever might happen, the day of arbitrary bureaucratic government, the privileged noble estate, and legal barriers placed before the rise of peasants and workers was over. More positively, he urged a political program based on every man's right to "a worthwhile human existence," and accented for liberals his belief that this required major economic reforms so that the poor could exercise rights they would acquire in the new order. Novgorodtsev entered the First Duma on April 27, 1906, as a major Kadet planner, a member of several committees, and an occasional spokesman in the Duma.[3] To him, the most important task of the Duma was to establish laws safeguarding the inviolability of the person, whose rights were "sacred and natural." All hope for continuing popular freedom in Russia depended on the enactment into law of these and other Kadet proposals.

Novgorodtsev supported the Kadets' agrarian program, the proposal to transfer land to peasants by expropriating large estates with compensation to their owners. He considered this action necessary not only to protect the economy but also to preserve and advance whatever elements of culture existed in the countryside. In this context, "culture" meant a principled respect for persons, law, and higher values that the peasantry could not acquire while exhausted and embittered from an endless struggle to survive. In urging this kind of national legislation, Novgorodtsev also strongly supported the decentralization of government and an increase of democratic control of local concerns.

The strongest bar to cooperation between Duma and government was the agrarian program, which representatives of the government dismissed as "totally inadmissable."[4] To soften Kadet radicalism, bureaucratic leaders sought to bring the liberals into the government by appointment to ministerial posts, but the effort foundered on Kadet intransigence and basic governmental hostility to constitutional government. Bitter wrangling and irreconcilable differences led on July 9, 1906, to the dissolution of the Duma. Within a few days, 120 Kadets joined other leftists to proclaim the Vyborg (Finland) Manifesto. It urged the people not to pay taxes or accept military draft until the lawful Duma was reinstalled. Novgorodtsev was an important signer of that document.

The Vyborg Manifesto had no effect on the people, but Novgorodtsev and other participants were imprisoned for three months and then forbidden to take seats in future Dumas. Novgorodtsev remained a leading member of the Kadet planning committee in the period of the Dumas (1906–1916) and in the Provisional Government after the revolution of March, 1917.[5] After the Bolshevik seizure of power in November, 1917, he was in great danger. He fled Moscow to avoid arrest in May, 1918, and, very ill, left Russia in the fall of 1919. Freed from day-to-day participation in politics, he sought between 1906 and 1914 to provide an intellectual statement of liberal attitudes and principles which could be effective in early-twentieth-century Russia.

NOVGORODTSEV AS A RUSSIAN LIBERAL

Novgorodtsev produced a very complicated liberal doctrine. He tried to synthesize those elements of nineteenth-century liberal thought which had not been negated by Western European political experience. But it cannot be said that a clear and convincing liberal doctrine resulted. It proved impossible to avoid conflicting positions in a social philosophy based on selective use of the writings of Bentham, Kant, Alexis de Tocqueville, William von Humboldt, J.S. Mill, Schleiermacher, and others. Even the less complex English and French "new liberalism," which sought to soften the economic struggle so that as many people as possible would find self-fulfillment, embodied contradictions difficult to reconcile in a liberal approach to the twentieth century.

Novgorodtsev sought a philosophical underpinning for political action which would safeguard freedom and encourage equality in liberal countries and help create them in twentieth-century Russia. But his commitment to Orthodox Christianity, to Kant's cognitive epistemology and rationalistic ethics, and to romantic notions of the wider needs of persons introduced unavoidable tension into his work. At the same time, the strains in his social doctrine reflected not only his personal loyalties and assumptions, but also inherent characteristics of liberalism.

The liberal philosopher stands forever against the deeply implanted, perhaps innate, tendency of humans to bifurcate reality. Against those who would say that "purity of heart is to will one thing," he would assume that compromise is always necessary and possible, given time and good will.[6] Adjustment of views can always be carried out, and a partial and acceptable consensus found. The same conviction lies behind the effort of liberals to update liberal doctrine to fit new circumstances. Novgorodtsev sought to outline the tradition of liberal thought, to show the modifications made in it in response to nineteenth-century problems, and to point out the further adjustments necessary if liberalism were to be a positive force in the twentieth century. His work in twentieth-century Russia can be compared usefully to that of his famous liberal predecessor, J. S. Mill, in mid-nineteenth-century England.

Novgorodtsev resembled a Mill out of time and place. Where Mill had sought to update a successful liberal philosophy and politics by the infusion of romantic notions of the demands of the personality, Novgorodtsev attempted the same for a liberalism which had not yet found embodiment in Russian life.[7] Where Mill had tried to rid liberalism of its tie to the utilitarian view of the nature of man, Novgorodtsev tried to destroy the credit of a utilitarian ethics which had not yet carried out its productive work of economic and social advancement. These anachronisms illustrate an important factor in early-twentieth-century Russian political life.

Russia had some of the "advantages of the latecomer" in economic life. Its leaders could have used the experience and newest methods of industrialization and business in Britain, France, and Germany. In *economics*, with some modification, the newest would be the best.

But the concomitant receptivity of political opponents of the regime to the most "advanced" political ideas and actions could be destructive. The lure of the most up-to-date tempted even nonrevolutionary liberals to seek changes which could be brought about only by the destruction of the monarchical regime, and which the great majority of population did not understand or desire. Excessive rationalism could lead them to a "no enemies to the left" position which would aid forces who aimed at the destruction of liberalism. Too much faith in rationally worked out doctrine might inspire an elitist attitude toward the Russian masses that would make a mockery of liberal democratic promises. Novgorodtsev understood these impediments to liberal change in Russia and tried to avoid them, but he did not always succeed.

Like so many intellectuals of the *fin de siècle* period, Novgorodtsev felt deeply that Russia faced a crisis and that it might provide a solution to world-wide social-political problems "before anywhere else."[8] He urged governments to guarantee to each person the right of a "worthy human life," but he rejected revolutionary demands for rapid, concrete satisfaction of that right. He cautioned his readers that government should provide the conditions in which all men could *exercise* their right, not that it should *give* men all the elements of worthy existence. As Vladimir Soloviev had said, "every man should have sufficient food, clothing, shelter, and rest" so that he could pursue spiritual advancement.

On the other hand, to the liberal exponents of complete laissez faire, Novgorodtsev pointed out that laws could and should be established to elevate every person to a material position from which he might be able to succeed.[9] No man of normal sensitivity could deny material help to the hundred million barely-surviving Russian poor. But it was also necessary to give the weak and defenseless the consciousness that the law stood behind their efforts to raise themselves. Without that feeling, the masses of Russia, sunk in ignorance and hopelessness, did not represent the kind of human material from which a free or even a stable authoritarian society could be constructed. Self-interest alone should induce the government to pass such laws. Without their preparatory work a liberal society could scarcely exist.

Novgorodtsev professed an updated liberalism which was unlikely to appeal to those forces in Russian society who would support a liberal approach to government. He started from conceptions which had scarcely existed in Russia, the *legal state*, the doctrine of the *general will*, its economic counterpart the *unseen hand*, and the widespread faith in *secular progress* to perfection. He then showed the modifications brought into these by European experience of the nineteenth century. The economic base, social structure, political order, and conceptions of personality and its legitimate claims had changed. Novgorodtsev espoused a "new liberalism," which represented an ideal for liberal West European men in the early twentieth century, but its relevance to Russia was questionable.

Many of Novgorodtsev's theoretical proposals could have provided good guidelines for Russian liberal political activity. But at the same time certain claims and much of the general tone of his liberalism reflected what one might call the desire for the "revolution of sensibility," rather than the political revolution which Russia had not yet experienced. It put forth those demands for the satisfaction of the needs of the "whole personality" which well-fed, mid-twentieth-century social strata have placed upon government and society, but which no Russian government or society of Novgorodtsev's time could have satisfied. Indeed, despite his own effort to move beyond individualistic rationalism to a broader based personalism, he well knew that no government or society would do so much for man.

Novgorodtsev developed his Russian liberal doctrine in three steps. First, he pointed out the basic error on which liberal doctrine of the nineteenth century rested, the idea—which he attributed to Rousseau—that a state of complete social harmony could be established among men on this earth. He attempted to show how this conviction had vitiated liberal theory and practice. Then, he examined the idea of social harmony from the standpoint of what is perhaps the fundamental question of social philosophy, the relation between the individual and authority, be it state, society, or culture. Concluding that the claims of the two could never be completely reconciled, he sought a means of reconciling individual freedom and the need for community. He found it in a *social ideal* toward which all men and societies could strive and which could be a standard for judgment of concrete actions.

Throughout, Novgorodtsev remained a sober restrained thinker, taking man's asocial sociability as a fact whose influence could be greatly reduced, but never eliminated from human affairs. And his Orthodox faith, which remained largely undiscussed in his political polemics, engendered tolerance for human failings, modesty with regard to man's capacity to master the world intellectually, and a deeply rooted conviction that a truly civilized order must be a universal one. Novgorodtsev wrote entirely as a legal philosopher and historian of ideas, very seldom alluding in his major books and articles to the Russian political and ideological struggles of his day. But in what follows, the various aspects of his doctrines can and will be related to the fate of liberalism in Russia.

THE LOST ILLUSION OF SOCIAL HARMONY

One of the legacies of the eighteenth century had been the idea that the state could establish and safeguard social harmony. The idea of social harmony attracted Novgorodtsev's sharpest attacks, whether it appeared in a liberal, a Comtian, a "Godseeking," or Marxist form. Its main characteristics were enunciated in the *Social Contract*, where Jean-Jacques Rousseau stated that, "the problem is to find a form of association which will defend and protect with the whole common force the persons and goods of each associate and in which each, while uniting himself with all, may still obey himself alone and remain as free as before."[10] Stemming from that "Bible of the nineteenth century," this conception had developed in two directions. The first reflected Rousseau's anthropology, his feeling that men could become fully moral only in the civil organization. The second embodied his idea that the state and the law could be morally justified only if they emerged from the popular will. Only in the state and under its law could men attain the morality which made social learning possible, but only if the state and its law were created by the people. Emphasis on the first of these led toward Kant's philosophy of right and German idealist philosophy in its political aspect, while concentration on the second brought about the Western search for institutions to make the popular will effective.

Kant, by emphasizing Rousseau's idea of civil man as moral man, established the frame of reference for much nineteenth-century German political thought. He claimed that the *legal state*, resting on legal principles equally binding on all citizens, would be the political order in which men could live moral lives.[11] If both the state and the individuals making up the society would act in terms of the categorical imperative, something like social harmony might result, though its full manifestation in the kingdom of ends might be beyond human capacity. Novgorodtsev found two aspects of this unacceptable. To Kant, rational laws could not arise from the agreement of all, for he pessimistically doubted the capacity of men to reach national agreement.[12] Rather, law need only reflect the spirit of the people as understood by rationally operating leaders. Secondly, the relationship Kant specified was to exist between the state and the atomized individual, abstracted from the social matrix in which he lived. Novgorodtsev concluded that this extension of Rousseau's thought led to an idea of politics which was neither democratic nor lodged in the concrete experiences of men in society. Moreover, it suffered from the undue formalism of the categorical imperative.

Novgorodtsev argued that Kant's great successor Hegel overcame the formal individualism of Kant's political theory, but not its antidemocratic features. For Hegel laws arose out of the concrete struggles of social and national groups and at any one time reflected interwoven empirical and ideal realities.[13] In the irrational, often bloody struggles which so dispirited Kant, man, a social creature, worked toward the triumph of the absolute in history. But in attaching man's moral impulses to his social life, Hegel, more than the Königsberg philosopher, placed him under the dominance of a higher power, the state. Of course, Hegel saw the state in its relation to the absolute, but in practice, it very often embodied the principle of "Might makes Right" and repressed man.[14] Succeeding attempts to rescue the doctrine of the legal state from Kantian formal individualism or Hegelian statism had failed.[15] By the beginning of the twentieth century, the conception could not satisfy the growing numbers, who held that the enactment of just laws required popular participation.

As a guarantor of social harmony, Rousseau's demand for popular sovereignty had fared no better. The efforts of the English, American, and French representative states to devise mechanisms for making democratic rule a reality had foundered on the rock of human social and personal inequalities.[16] As Rousseau had realized and the French Revolution had demonstrated, direct democracy could not exist in modern large societies.[17] This set the stage for representation, then political parties and mechanisms like proportional representation, referendum, and recall; but none of these made it possible for the majority to determine government policy. Political parties fell under control of party committees and these under the direction of dynamic leaders, such as prime ministers and presidents. Recognition of that reality and the development of wide-ranging communication had led liberal theorists to claim that democracy rested on public opinion, the final arbiter on political matters.

Novgorodtsev denied that "public opinion" was general enough or clear enough to determine public policy. It was an elite concept, which in practice meant the opinions of the educated and the powerful in select newspapers and journals.[18] Even as such, public opinion spoke with many voices. In the end, it was made, rather than found, by leaders who for a time grasped a general need or desire of society and through the spoken and written word engendered it in politically active groups. The legal state could not show how laws "in the spirit of the people" could emerge, but the representative democracies could not show how the people could make laws in their own spirit.

Novgorodtsev saw major nineteenth-century legal philosophies as efforts to deal with the inevitable failure of European states to reach the illusory goal of social harmony. Rather than justifying laws, positivistic theories recognized the failure to find their legitimacy in the spirit or the will of the people.[19] Historical jurisprudence, with its effort to ground law in the historical growth of organic totalities, ended in utter relativism. It made impossible any general theory of just law, and in the end provided one more form of an ultimately mystical belief in established orders. Legal positivism simply defined law as the statute of a legally constitutional government, thus giving up the philosophical effort to demarcate the boundaries of just law. Again, no sanction to which people could appeal against injustice existed.

To Novgorodtsev, historical jurisprudence and legal positivism were methods for the study of existent law, not philosophies of the right.[20] Both included the healthy principle that law should be studied using all the resources of modern psychology, sociology, and history. Against both, he argued that moral principles must be present in the making and implementation of law.[21] Any given system of law represented the collision of the moral idea of law with its temporary manifestations. Able to choose the right by employment of his practical reason, Kant's noumenal person provided the ultimate base for the involvement of morality in law. But, to supply a base for just law, twentieth-century thinkers had to go beyond Kantian formalism to show how the categorical imperative could be embodied in positive law. As late as 1903, Novgorodtsev believed that the Neo-Kantians, Stammler, Natorp, and Windelband, had accomplished that task. But in the years 1908–1914, as reaction deepened in Russia and world war approached, he rejected their thought as itself subjectivistic and relativistic.

Novgorodtsev attributed great importance to Rousseau's claim that under the general will the individual could be both free and subject to community authority. He asserted that the *Social Contract* inspired and provided theoretical underpinning for nineteenth-century attempts to establish social harmony by means of both the legal state and the popular sovereignty. The most important nineteenth-century political and legal doctrines could be best understood as efforts to restore hope to thinkers and politicians deeply shaken by the inevitable failure to establish what Rousseau had promised. It may be said that Novgorodtsev misunderstood Rousseau's claims.

After all, Rousseau introduced qualifications into his doctrine of the general will which may have absolved it of the error of excessive utopianism. He held that only a very small population of relatively equal small property owners could govern themselves in terms of the general will, and he may have already forestalled the accusation that the disappointment arising from pursuit of his unreal goals was a major source of the modern malaise. One reply to that would be that, whatever Rousseau's caveat, his promise of freedom and equality had inspired extravagant hopes and destructive political action in the large societies of nineteenth-century Europe. However, Novgorodtsev's argument struck directly at Rousseau "properly understood"—to him, the limited size and social homogeneity which might make Rousseau's doctrine functional was also what would make it, to use the modern term, totalitarian.

He pointed out that small size and isolation featured most utopias, from Plato's *Republic* to Fourier's phalansteries. They could be interpreted as the refuges of humans who could not stand the tensions of life among individuals and groups of conflicting interests and points of view. Those of modern times might be seen as an extension of the premodern rural mentality into the complex, unsettling world of industrial civilization built on the division of labor. Utopias either tried to fix the economic activities in eternal estates or to fix a social order in which men could undertake a variety of simple tasks in the name of the full flowering of the personality. In either case, it was the uncertainty, the abrasiveness, the open-endedness of modern life in large, pluralistic societies which they could not bear. Novgorodtsev's liberal theory centered on the notion that differences and conflict are unavoidable and, in fact, the spice of life. Indeed, they provided the necessary conditions for individual development as a many-sided person. This meant that the subjective illusion of the uncontested free will could not be sustained, but men who attained high productivity and freedom by attention to the reality principle would pay that price. Novgorodtsev erred not in misunderstanding Rousseau, but in approaching nineteenth-century history from an overly idealistic point of view.

To Novgorodtsev, the legal state and the representative democracy were unsatisfactory compromises arrived at by men striving for social harmony. But Marxists asserted that these political orders were mere superstructures, created to maintain and legitimize the control of the material means of production by the middle class. And others could well question whether the representative systems progressed in pursuit of lofty utopian ends. Perhaps they could be described better as the kind of political order which would evolve as several necessary and strong groups sought to maintain political control over the majority and at least a continually shifting equilibrium among themselves. It is difficult to imagine Lord Henry Palmerston, François Guizot, Adolphe Thiers, or Otto von Bismarck and the classes or bureaucracies which supported them striving to establish social harmony as understood by Rousseau. Novgorodtsev's idealism betrayed him at this point, but his perspective sharply highlighted crucial points of conflict between Marxism and liberalism.

Obvious economic injustice and growing social hatreds had sharply reduced confidence in nineteenth-century liberal theories and institutions. Conservatives used the resultant disorder to buttress their contention that the partial destruction of the old order connected with the French Revolution and the attempt to base social cohesion on reason and democracy had been nearly fatal to civilization. Socialists cited the crisis of the late nineteenth and early twentieth centuries as proof that the entire individualistic political and economic order of modern Europe had to be jettisoned for a socialist system.

Where could the liberal idealist turn? Could he accept the consequences of his pessimistic findings and drop the idea of popular sovereignty and the legal state, join the search for other modes of political organization? Novgorodtsev, at least, could not do so. The idea of popular sovereignty had been one of the healthiest to emerge in modern politics; under its banner great progressive ideas had been and could be spread, and great social victories had been and could be won. Even though the true idea of class struggle had arisen from the experience of the nineteenth century, the very existence of society demanded a supraclass consensus.

Novgorodtsev's exposure of the root fallacy in the "Rousseauan base" of nineteenth-century liberalism can be seen as a reaction to liberal experience in the ill-fated First and Second Dumas. No one who had experienced the government's arrogant determination from the beginning to dissolve the First Duma could believe that cooperation between the bureaucracy and society, much less social harmony, was likely to emerge in the near future. In the Second Duma government intransigence found itself confronted with Social Democrats, who used the parliamentary platform to disrupt legislative processes and to arouse the violent actions of workers and peasants.[22] To this the bureaucracy responded with a second dissolution, destruction of the democratic franchise, and brutal repression of mass disorder. The government and the revolutionaries were rapidly eroding whatever basis for mutual accommodation existed in Russia. Novgorodtsev warned liberals not to expect too much too soon. He urged them to discard lingering utopian dreams and to turn to patient, protracted work for reform. In order to inspire realism and sobriety in liberal politics, he focused attention on a root liberal concern: individualism and the relation between the individual and society. Novgorodtsev tried to show that the two could never be reconciled, although political and cultural orders which would vastly increase the satisfactions of the individual could be created.

Nineteenth-century problems and temporary setbacks did not negate the validity of Enlightenment dreams of freedom. The basic eighteenth-century principle that rational men could shape their own destinies had been shaken, but not overturned. The general will, which legislation and action rightly sought to reflect, remained a vital concept if understood as an ideal to be pursued, rather than as the product of any particular mechanism for eliciting popular consent.[23]

And despite its limitations when confronted with the ideal of democratic freedom, representative government was "the inevitable state of all cultured people at a certain stage in their development."[24] As a budding legal state, Russia needed it very badly. But where it existed it posed for man, society, and the social philosopher much deeper and more intractable problems than those involved in the construction of an apparatus to make a partial reality of popular sovereignty.

Novgorodtsev's liberal theory can be approached profitably as an attempt to deal with the problem of wholes and parts. Stated most generally, the point at issue is whether wholes are something more than the sum of their parts.[25] This poses an inherent and ancient dilemma in social philosophy, and, indeed in all areas of human thought. In pursuing this line of inquiry in social philosophy, Novgorodtsev conceptualized and confronted a series of dichotomies, each on a higher level of generality than its predecessor. First directing himself to the polarity in the context of the failure of Enlightenment views on the state and popular sovereignty to hold up under nineteenth-century experience, he framed it in political terms, *the state and the citizen.* Once having reached a position which seemed to preserve the autonomy of both part (citizen) and whole (state), he immediately found himself face to face with a higher level disjunction.

If the modern liberal-democratic state were possible, it would inevitably bring to the surface the contradiction between the *society and the individual.* Efforts to deal with this social question in theory and practice (the "New Liberalism") brought into the center of the stage a still more general struggle, that between *culture and the personality.* Novgorodtsev was a liberal theorist precisely because he refused to accept a final solution to any of the three dichotomies, whether it were a Merezhkovskian union of flesh and spirit, the religious union of subject and object posited by Bulgakov, or the unity promised by secular utopias. All his "solutions" were forever partial.

THE STATE AND THE CITIZEN

To overcome the limitations of the legal state, Novgorodtsev posited an organic relation of state and citizen. He explained in organismic terms the failure of popular sovereignty to arise, despite the many mechanisms invented and tried in the late nineteenth century to make it a reality. Like Herbert Spencer he accented the universality of hierarchical order in organic structures and drew the conclusion that however democratic in form, representative states would be directed by men of greater than ordinary energy, will to power, and intelligence. But inherent in each member of the organism, ruler or ruled, there yet lay the judge of the state, the individual moral consciousness. The latter sought a kingdom of ends, where each would be treated as an end, never as a means. A state which failed signally to pursue that goal would arouse popular opposition, for, being its subject as well as its object, the people would experience deviation as moral culpability.[26] Since Novgorodtsev believed that this would inevitably happen, struggle between state and citizen would be a permanent fact of human life.

The citizen could react with some surety; for upon taking thought, he had before himself the natural law, norms to which the state was subject.[27] As 1914 approached, Novgorodtsev turned back from Neo-Kantian perspectives on natural law to the platonic principles which provided the foundation for his thought. He labeled Stammler's idea of "natural law with a changing content" contradictory, a bankrupt idea, an eclectic attempt to reconcile Plato's ancient insights with the data of empirical history.[28] By bringing into it the limited perspectives of churches, peoples, states, and classes, the Neo-Kantians made subjective a principle which was the very essence of objectivity. Novgorodtsev asserted that Hugo Grotius and Kant had made the correct modern statement on natural law.[29] Human nature demands a peaceful and well-organized society. Reason shows that the minimal conditions for such an order are "good faith, substantial justice, and the sanctity of covenants." These conclusions are natural laws in the sense that they are deductions from human nature, the nature of things, and the nature of law.

Novgorodtsev accepted Grotius' claim that the principles of natural law were guaranteed by their clearness, simplicity, and self-evidence. Men could proceed like mathematicians to develop irrefutable conclusions from rightly understood axioms. This idealistic principle was very important to Novgorodtsev, because it enabled him to construct his theory without reference to his religious beliefs and attitudes. Natural law did not mean an "unchanging system of laws . . . but an unchanging idea or principle of law," which like platonic forms, always existed. When such principles seemed to be absent, they were simply hidden from view by human ignorance or ill-will. Human laws, even social movements like socialism and anarchism, acquired moral sanction to the degree that they were consistent with them. Natural law would guide men eternally as they sought happiness and virtue in lives which would forever place formidable obstacles in their paths.

Recognition of natural law could bring citizen and state together in a constructive enterprise. Since natural laws derived from man's *social* nature, they made morality more than a private matter between an individual and his conscience. Providing an escape from formalism which Kant had not developed, Novgorodtsev held that morality would have a political dimension, serving the citizen as a way to approach the state critically, and the state as a means of softening and broadening the application of law. It would make possible what might be called Novgorodtsev's "minimum program" for Russia. Recognizing natural law, the czar and the bureaucracy would admit limits to their arbitrary power other than those set by counterforce. The Russian state and the people could live on as an organism, in which the former could legitimately ask citizens to sacrifice personal interests to the whole, while remaining permanently subject to popular judgments. The citizen would enjoy real, but always limited and always threatened freedom.

But Novgorodtsev wanted much more for the Russian people than a twentieth-century *Rechtsstaat*. He struggled for democracy. Unfortunately, experience in Western representative democracies seemed to show that they gave birth to a new and broader dichotomy, the *society and the individual*. As the greatest of nineteenth-century liberals, John Stuart Mill, had shown, democracies embodied the ever present threat of the "tyranny of the majority." Safe from the despotism of the state as long as he remained alert and moral, the individual could find himself submerged, deprived of his need for self-fulfillment by the force of socially intolerant opinion. Novgorodtsev found that just as they had failed to safeguard the citizen's freedom from the state, the Enlightenment thinkers, especially Kant and Bentham, had not understood the individual in a way that would safeguard him from social leveling.[30]

Both the Rousseauan tradition as modified by Kant and the utilitarianism of the English economic liberals seemed to provide a strong basis for individualism. But in attempting to show how individuals could live together in a permanent state of harmony, they had sacrificed the very individualism they had sought to defend.

THE INDIVIDUAL AND THE SOCIETY

For Kant, men would be most human, most united, and most fulfilled when most rational. In English utilitarianism, men could find personal satisfaction and social justice by approaching all areas of life in ways analogous to the "free" exchange of goods and services in the marketplace. Novgorodtsev held that these views ignored all that made man unique, his most personal aspirations and hopes and those affective aspects of his personality which made him different from other men. Both Kant's "rational man" and Bentham's "economic man" schematized and oversimplified man. Adapting these points of view, society overtly oppressed the occasional rebel and covertly repressed most nineteenth-century men. It distorted and impoverished personalities and aroused the anxious fidgetiness of modern men.

But again, Novgorodtsev found a kind of balance between whole and parts, this time in the perspectives of nineteenth-century romanticists. They had brought into the open the claims of many-sided man, his demand that his emotions should find expression and weight in the world, that society should provide room for the expression of his feelings as he sought a broader and deeper self-fulfillment.[31] Stated most brilliantly by Goethe and the German romantics, Schleiermacher, Friedrich Schlegel, Novalis (Friedrich von Hardenberg), and to a degree, Hegel, this declaration of the rights of sensibility also surfaced in the camp of individualistic political theorists in the writings of Benjamin Constant, Tocqueville, Humboldt, and J. S. Mill. The most impressive statement came at the beginning of the century from the universal genius, Goethe. In *Faust*, he presented the picture of modern man, restlessly pursuing his completion in a broad life of scholarship, sensuality, aesthetic experience, and political and social pursuits.[32]

Goethe pursued the question of man's relation to the world beyond the cognitive answers offered by Kant. He directed the understanding toward the concrete, qualitative aspects in which men were unique and irreplaceable. Negatively speaking, this might appear to ask the impossible, that men should value in other men internal, scarcely communicable, subjective states. But Goethe urged men to be consciously and positively unique, to view their personalities as objective, active realities, works of art to be constructed in the world. Though this implied conflict in the world and frustration for the individual, it did not destroy unity, for to Goethe there was but one nature. By affirming and developing their own characteristics, men contributed to the exposure and knowledge of the infinite richness of the whole. Goethe seemed to reconcile individualism and universalism in a way that the "Unseen Hand" of Adam Smith and the categorical imperative of Kant did not. To the immensely important insights of the great pagan, Schleiermacher added an ethical element arising from his deeply Christian religious consciousness.

Schleiermacher, a more typical German romantic than the many-sided Goethe, celebrated that "feeling," so undervalued by Kant and Bentham.[33] Feeling became man's most direct experience of the world, a split-second individual perception which changed almost instantaneously into conscious thought, a transformation which entailed an irreplaceable loss of direct, immediate knowledge. Unique to each individual, feeling was not merely subjective, but also man's most objective experience of the world. It was the very essence of Goethe's individualism, which made of the world the harmonized personalities of its elements. For Schleiermacher the primary principle of morality became the right of the person to fulfill himself not only by understanding the rational law of duty, but much more by externalizing his "feeling" in the world. Whatever infringed upon that individual contribution to world unity became the immoral, so that the moral judgment of men on their fellows became more living, but infinitely more difficult. The focus shifted from "good" or "bad" acts to an attempt to understand the circumstances, reasons, and motives behind the acts.[34]

Man became a much more complex, a richer creature, about whom much had to be known before moral judgment could be offered. Universal moral ideals were to be learned through the ever widening and deepening experience of men with one another. The ultimate aim to be approached was the idea of a loving union among independent personalities—"Humanity," which each man expressed and bore in his life experiences. Just as Herder defined the ideal as the most luxurious flowering of as many cultures as possible, so Schleier-

138

macher saw it as the development of as much spiritual richness in each person as could be achieved. Novgorodtsev believed that these conceptions of the person and morality supplemented Kantianism to provide the basis for a successful twentieth-century liberal philosophy.

If this romantic conception of man could permeate society, fear of the "tyranny of the majority" might turn out to be groundless and democratic individualism possible. But, of course, it had not done so by Novgorodtsev's time. Individuals seeking fulfillment beyond "rationalism" and the "market" had to do so in ways having little to do with Novgorodtsev's democratic aims. Actively Promethean, some would make far greater demands on society for attention to their wants than the legal state or a majoritarian society would be likely to give.[35] Pessimistically convinced that society could do little to solve their most real problems, others would urge the return to nature and passive resistance to evil[36]—thus the aristocratic and ultimately suicidal individualism of Nietzsche and the radical individual moralism of Tolstoi and Carlyle.

Novgorodtsev did not share Nietzsche's omnivorous appetite for unmasking and self-laceration and, firmly convinced that social institutions played a large role in forming men and their path to the ideal, he could not accept Tolstoi's attempt to simplify life radically. Rather, he saw signs that the idea of the new man had penetrated society deeply enough to produce forces which sought to overcome the society-individual dichotomy in constructive ways. Novgorodtsev greatly admired the subtle thinker, Georg Simmel, who in a Goethean vein argued that modern society rested on the interactivity of qualitatively different individuals. But he also found a basis for hope in the concrete political programs and actions which, in the advanced liberal societies, England and France, went under the name of the "New Liberalism."

Novgorodtsev called Simmel the "most contemporary" of all twentieth-century social theorists and praised his thought as the "most refined." The German sociologist deeply concerned himself with the problem of the "individual and society" and had concluded that the terms did not express a true dichotomy.[37] Rather, under the influence of the division of labor, the factors appeared to be mutually reinforcing. Simmel showed that concentration on the simple opposition "individual and society" necessarily limited and distorted

139

thought. He pointed out that society appeared in different guises to different people, in fact, in several different guises to each individual. Even on the individual level a person had numerous loyalties—to a family, to an occupation, to a political group, to a stamp club, to friends—which meant that his personality was not formed and restricted by any one force. Instead, pulled in several different directions at all times, the person had to sacrifice the values of one role to another in terms of some set of shifting priorities. And Simmel was cautiously optimistic that, whatever degree of objectification social forms should reach, there might always be room for expressions of individualism embodying the modes of actions of both the Kantian and the Goethean persons.

Novgorodtsev could not accept Mill's pessimism, Nietzsche's scorn of mass man, Tolstoi's moralism, or Simmel's optimism. Was the modern world moving inexorably toward the stagnation of culture and the halting of individual development, toward inert mediocrity? Evidence seemed to show that Mill had been wrong, that "instead of the downfall of individualism, Europe in recent times has experienced its flowering."[38] Were the masses of the people simply a herd, resenting excellence in any form and inevitably making creativity impossible? Study of the development of culture in history did not seem to bear out this harsh judgment. Novgorodtsev said, "The greatness and beauty of the moral world is maintained not only by isolated individuals, but also in the collective creativity of the masses. Social inspiration and social building, establishments and morals have their own harmony and beauty and also serve as a source of moral culture."[39] Moreover, men knew no truly isolated individuals, for the personality inevitably had both an individual and a social character. By the same token the social could not be external, lifeless, and soulless. These beliefs would appear to set the stage for some optimism that a reasonably harmonious relationship between individual and society was probable. Yet, while he believed in progress and the positing of ideals, Novgorodtsev refused to follow Simmel in a flatly optimistic statement.

Simmel did not pay sufficient attention to the fact that growing, interrelated, "rationalized" societies, while they did provide new opportunities for the expression of individuality, also constricted the functioning of these individual qualities. Indeed, in his study of the modern big city, Simmel provided arguments in that direction.[40] For the persons who built them they became purely objective, represented such an overpowering profusion of crystallized impersonal spirit that the personality easily became impotent. To resist loss of spirit and preserve individuality required exceptional originality and personal strength. To the degree that the development of the modern world created urbanism, freedom remained problematic and tension-filled, for society offered the person opportunities with the one hand that it took away with the other. What theories and programs had liberalism devised to help provide reconciliation and coexistence for these eternal demands of humanity?

Novgorodtsev found hopes for reconciliation in the "New Liberalism." In both the form supported by George Russell, Herbert Asquith, Herbert Samuel, Albert Dicey, and Leonard Hobhouse in England and in that of the *Solidaristes*, Charles Renouvier, Henri Michel, Célestin Bouglé, Dominique Parodi, and Emile Faguet in France, it took a much wider view of the needs of the poor which required state attention than had the older liberalism.[41] While retaining their healthy respect for initiative, energy, and competition as a goad to progress, the English liberals argued for state efforts to improve the health, education, and welfare of the masses so that they might have a fairer chance to fulfill themselves and contribute to national wealth.[42] The French solidarists correctly noted the degree to which modern societies brought individuals together interactively and placed great emphasis on the use of modern means of communication to educate the poor so that they could pursue individual fulfillment in nondestructive, culturally elevated ways.[43]

In both the English and the French updated liberalism, Novgorodtsev saw threats to the society and the individual which he sought to overcome in his liberalism. In the English case, he feared that the move toward the welfare state might discourage the initiative of the gifted and soften too much the competition which provided the motor of material and spiritual progress. He thus stated a principle which summed up a century of ideological struggle between liberals and socialists. "A greater national product, even if unjustly distributed, is better for all classes than a smaller one, justly distributed."[44] In French solidarity he suspected a certain doctrinaire quality, an impatience with human foibles, a Rousseauan tendency to demand *too much* in the name of a united national culture.[45] But with mingled sadness and approval, he noted that human egoistic feelings and self-interested aspirations presented a tough, infertile soil to ideas of subjection or even worthwhile sacrifice to the whole. Life was ever-resistant to human logical plans.

Consideration of the pitfalls of solidarism brought Novgorodtsev face to face with a problem that no late-nineteenth-century Russian liberal or revolutionary could escape, the relation between the intellectuals and the people. Spoken or unspoken, the fear of a peasant "tyranny of the majority" runs through the productions of almost all of those who struggled for freedom and justice in Russia. Whether viewed as "noble child" or "elemental force of darkness," the peasant seemed indifferent or hostile to the rights of the individual and rational thought as these were understood by nineteenth-century liberals and socialists.

Russia had long produced thinkers who found a counter to Western overemphasis on the cognitive in an allegedly integral Russian peasant approach to life. As we have seen, Bulgakov espoused this view in opposition to Kadet liberal thought and politics. Perhaps the most striking critique of this kind of idealization of Russia and its peasants had been offered by the liberal novelist Ivan S. Turgenev. He had pictured that attitude as a rationalization indulged in by both revolutionaries and reactionaries to escape the truth of the superiority of Western science and technology, sobriety, and hard work.[46] In his social theory before 1917, Novgorodtsev carried on the tradition of Turgenev, though his Russian Orthodox attitudes introduced complexity into this area of his thought as it did in others. After the First World War and the Revolution of 1917, he was to burst forth in an almost Dostoevskian expression of the superiority of the simple Orthodox soul of the Russians to men molded by overdeveloped Western rationalistic, analytical thinking.[47]

But in the years before 1914, Novgorodtsev cautioned fellow Russian liberals that even the unlikely full implementation of the Kadet program would not rapidly secure the individual's freedom from society's authority. Only modernization, urbanization, the division of labor, and a truly pluralist society would bring that about. And he reminded his readers that even then the individual's freedom would always remain limited and threatened. Men forever objectified their creations, including social institutions and usages, and there would always be some which represented the basic agreements of large majorities. These the individual could flout only with grave danger.

Only prolonged education and experience could bring the Russian peasants to the point where they would objectify institutions and practices which would not attack those things which Russia's educated minority felt to be inalienable rights.

CULTURE, PERSONALITY, AND THE SOCIAL IDEAL

In England, France, and Russia cultural education would play the basic role in bringing the masses onto the political stage without endangering freedom.[48] Herein lay the emergence of the most inclusive of the dichotomies perceived by Novgorodtsev, that of *culture* and *personality*. At this point he struggled with the problem of *wholes* and *parts* on its broadest level. Culture was broader than both the state and the society and the *person* was the sanctuary of man's most genuine identity, more connected with his ultimate needs than his role as citizen and his individualism. If the whole could be seen here as more than the sum of its parts, yet the part could maintain its ultimate worth, the problem of a free, yet deeply social man would be solved. And if it could not be solved here, then it would have to be recognized as insoluble, and men would have to seek another path to self-realization.

Novgorodtsev saw the problem in stark terms. To avoid great social cataclysms and a catastrophic destruction of civilization, the poor, hungry, untutored masses had to be brought rapidly up to a cultural level where they could recognize, internalize, and respect the highest values of man.[49] For the individual, this meant the internal structuring of a *person*, who would be able to pursue human aims—truth, goodness, beauty—common to all men. The process would be self-powered. Cultural training leading to recognition of higher values would bring about an objectified sociability directed at the general aims. This would help form the character of a given generation which would build further on the basis of its already real, but limited approach to humanistic ideals. To Novgorodtsev, always alert to wholes-parts contingencies, this was a necessary, but dangerous course.

A real threat to the autonomy of the person inhered in the concrete process of culturalization. Every human person, however poor, ignorant, or brutalized, was of equal value and had an equal right to pursue his own self-development in terms of his unique qualities.

True, the great values of culture had to be made available to them, but each should subscribe to those values personally, freely, and uniquely, embodying them in the degree possible to him and in his own way. There existed a great danger that the bearers of culture might force it on the multitudes in the form of mere verbal formulas, external trappings, without roots in the person, and hence without deep civilizing effect.

Along with this threat went another, that backed by political power, the intellectual leaders would demand that men subscribe to some particular, concrete manifestation of culture, some nation, state, or church.[50] They would lose sight of the true issue, that men had to be brought to recognize the primacy of the great cultural values themselves. And so while the personality required culture to be in fact a personality, the person had to maintain its autonomous rights as over against culture so that it could be in fact, a person. Culture remained a whole which, while it had no ego other than that of the individual egos of collective humanity, yet was more than the sum of its parts.[51] The personality remained a part, which, while necessarily surrendering to the autonomy of the great cultural ideals of truth, beauty, and goodness, yet preserved a center of utter inviolability. What hope, then, could men have that they could live together in permanent, undisturbed harmony?

To recapture hope man had first to discard the infantile demand for untroubled, eternal harmony. Experience showed that every attempt to construct, in theory or practice, an earthly paradise ended in the despotism of a self-declared group of the select.[52] All utopias, Plato's *Republic*, various islands, colonies, phalansteries, St. Simonian brotherhoods, and back-to-nature movements bore the marks of forcible, sectarian, and stubborn conservatism. And though they seemed more realistic than timeless utopias, the great nineteenth-century efforts to show how human harmony would inevitably emerge from struggle and bloodshed contained the same error. Marxism particularly dissolved the person in society.[53] Whether in a Comtian, Hegelian, Marxian, or Spencerian form, they all posited a point at which the "nightmare" of history would cease, and a blessed state would begin. Though each claimed scientific status, none was scientific, for science knew no leaps or interruptions in the causal series of phenomena.[54] Evolution's basic law was constant changeability, variation, so that by its own principle it could not exercise Faust's choice, "Stop, the moment is so beautiful."

Realistic hope for man lay in the pursuit of the absolute in a world of relativity. The struggle of the spirit with itself in the breast of man was unending and, in fact, necessary and good. To escape both their present war of all against all and the possibility of their degeneration to beasts of the field, men had to seek unceasingly the embodiment of ideals in political and economic activity and philosophical thought. And success demanded the realization that *all men* contributed to relative progress—the multitudes in their mostly unconscious collective thought and labor, as well as the elite in their conscious strivings and leadership. Moreover, unintended consequences posed a stubborn problem, for social relations were so complex that men could never be sure that a given act would serve their ideals.[55] All could pursue the *social ideal* and the pursuit was a socializing and personalizing activity, even though ultimate existence of the ideal in life remained thinkable only within a religious framework, in the transformation of man. Man, as he would be constituted as long as he was simple man, could not live in the "higher realms where the pure forms dwell."

The social ideal included two fundamental characteristics: that it be abstract and that it take the nature of the human personality as its basis.[56] The ideal could neither contain historically relative elements like wealth, power, and happiness, nor find full embodiment in states, churches, God-selected peoples, or progressive social classes. It had to remain a pure ideal, toward which men could and should strive, and it could include only elements inherent in the nature of the personality and mankind as a whole. These were first, the *freedom* and *equality* which the very definition of the personality implied. An individual would not be a personality unless he were free, and he could not be free unless each benefited from at least reasonably equal access to nourishment, health, and education. But secondly, the ideal pointed beyond the individual to the union of families and nations, and above them, of all mankind. It had to contain the principles of *unity* and *solidarity*, which demanded the active force of love among men. A relation among men including freedom, equality, solidarity, and union is what Novgorodtsev meant by the social ideal, and by the absolute toward which men strove. It could be called free universalism.

As noted before, Novgorodtsev, though a devout Christian, said little about religion. But he believed that beyond the social ideal, there stood a religious dimension to life which alone made possible its full comprehension and manifestation. The social ideal made it possible to judge social forms, to point the direction of progress, but as "miracle or mystery" it could not be the subject of social philosophy. In order to say more about the ideal than philosophy could say, men had to enter the field of religious ideals of transformation, complete harmony, and union of men with God, all of which could only be gifts of a blessed higher power. Moreover, men had a need to do so because of human consciousness of man's weakness, inadequacy, and contradiction.[57] Socially, men sought to overcome their limitations in institutions, which always to a degree objectified those limitations and repressed the freedom of the personality—the ultimate gift of God to man.

Novgorodtsev's "alternative to Marxism" posited enduring tension between the nature of man and the force of things. It contrasted human hopes with the often unintended consequences of efforts to attain them in complex relationships among men and between man and nature. Though he postulated a social ideal of freedom, equality, and a "worthy life" for all in a universal city of man, he doubted the efficacy of the practical or theoretical ventures in that direction which modern European culture had developed. On the one hand, Rousseau, Kant, and Hegel and on the other the French Revolution, Bentham, Mill, and Anglo-American constitutionalism seemed to have simultaneously pointed the way to the social ideal and exposed the limitations of human effort to attain it. From the largely political point of view, twentieth-century European man seemed suspended somewhere between the legal state, with its embodiment of the formal conditions for a moral life, and popular sovereignty, with its demand for the active participation of all in political life. From the more generally social point of view, men appeared to reach with one hand for the freedom which destroyed equality and with the other for the equality which threatened freedom.

Of course, these are deeply rooted antinomies of Western life, which have for centuries aroused anxiety and attempts to overarch them with some kind of communal principle. In the context of this study, both Marxists and the Christian thinker, Bulgakov, thought to show the way to the release of tension, one by making it the mainspring of an inevitable path to progress, the other by putting it at the service of Eros and the return of man to oneness with God. But the modern liberal, Novgorodtsev, welcomed unresolved tension. Perhaps because deeply impregnated with the need to achieve, modern men demand obstacles and fear the consequences of their boundless energy if deprived of an external object. Dostoevsky may have well understood modern man as a creature who, if presented *gratis* with the most secure and materially satisfying social order, would destroy it simply out of restless energy and perverse pride. In any case, Novgorodtsev considered tension indigenous to man, one of the manifestations of the dualism which ruled the world.

Corresponding to the poles between which Novgorodtsev placed man in his sociopolitical aspect stood related, but clearly separable modes of thought. To the legal state there responded *idealistic philosophy*, which could define the purposes of man as a free-unfree creature and keep before him ideals, their rational formulation, and the conditions of mind and society in which they might be realized. Popular sovereignty also had its philosophy, really a philosophical evaluation of the history of men's long and arduous struggle to escape their deeply entrenched propensity for master-subordinate relationships. History seemed to manifest a trial-and-error process by which men had gradually learned what political-social structures best protected popular sovereignty. Somewhere between philosophical ideals and historical lessons, stood Novgorodtsev's straining man.

The unsuccessful eclecticism of Novgorodtsev's ethical position also replicated a political duality—freedom and equality. However much he sought to modify his Kantianism, Novgorodtsev associated freedom first with the Kantian individual, rationally pursuing the call of duty. The norm of personal freedom became the man of exceptional will and rationality who denied in the name of the categorical imperative even his own affectivity and ability to control events. But when Novgorodtsev extended morality beyond the formalism of the categorical imperative, he entered the realm of *feeling* which extended the area of man's legitimate responses to and demands on the world. In the political and social, if not the aesthetic vocabulary, feeling, understood as a direct, unstructured coming to grips with reality, correlated with *equality*. Even more than the possession of rationality, modern men consider feeling to be that which makes

147

every man at the same time equal and unique. It is certainly significant that, when asked for an opinion on something, moderns almost invariably begin their response with "I feel . . . ," not "I think . . . ," or "I believe . . . ." Somewhere between the categorical imperative and the claims of sensitivity stand Novgorodtsev's freely choosing men.

Novgorodtsev's reaction to *Vekhi* (*Landmarks*) showed his commitment to ever-present tension.[58] Eliciting great response from Russian educated society, that collection of essays meant many things to many people, but its fundamental points were clear. Politically interested Russian intellectuals should drop their adamant revolutionary stance toward the government; should welcome artistic, literary, and philosophical creativity for their own sake; and should seek to engender in the Russian people the respect for culture which had made modern civilization possible. Adept as always in finding the dichotomous line between sets of ideas, Novgorodtsev focused on the polemic between Struve and Miliukov as the essential aspect of the controversy surrounding *Landmarks*.

He agreed with Struve, who denounced the dominance of politics over all other activities and accented the Fichtean view that spiritual life was "the positive work of man on himself."[59] But he rejected the position that internal self-fulfillment rather than external construction of institutions should be placed at the foundation of politics. Moreover, it seemed to him that Struve was still too politically minded, that he believed that personal fulfillment should be pursued because a progressive politics could be built in that way. Novgorodtsev countered that the fulfillment of the personality should be sought precisely because it was something that stood *outside* of politics.

But Miliukov, in his reply to *Landmarks*, "The intelligentsia and historical tradition," made the opposite error, when he argued that free political institutions were basic to the education of persons.[60] Miliukov would make no distinction between moral education and liberal political activity, seeing participation in politics as a necessary ethically formative agent for the fulfillment of the personality. Novgorodtsev believed that education had its own independent moral task, not dependent on a particular political framework. Political reform had to be pursued, but not with the aim of the moral education of the person; while the moral education of the person had to be sought, but not for the purpose of making free institutions possible in

Russia. In other words, tension between the inner needs of men and the forms and activities of politics could not be eliminated. Men could not retreat to the cultivation of their inner selves, thus ensuring future freedom, nor could they hope that participation in free political activity would provide the kind of education that men needed to develop free universalism.

Men being what they were, those in control of even democratic political institutions would use them to indoctrinate and dominate. And men being what they were, those who claimed to educate for freedom while holding free political institutions in abeyance, would find reason for indefinite postponement of the political freedom toward which they ostensibly aimed. The dilemma was inescapable, and Novgorodtsev provided no clear exit from it, except on the principle of *on s'engage, puis on voit*. Russians should struggle for representative institutions based on full suffrage and complete freedom of expression. They should improve and expand Russian education so that the personalistic values of Western culture and Christian belief could come together. But, Novgorodtsev cautioned, they should not expect freedom and harmony from the new political institutions and should not use education to tell people what to do and how to do it. Let history and philosophy work together in an atmosphere of hope and sober pessimism.

Torn as it was between irreconcilable opposites, Novgorodtsev's idealistic liberalism represented a mood more than a systematic philosophy. He viewed with sharp critical gaze the debris from the wreckage of eighteenth-century hopes and nineteenth-century experiences. Picking amidst the rubble he sought those bits and pieces which he tried to put together to form a productive liberal philosophy for the twentieth century. Yet his Kantianism with its noble rigor sacrificed to the pressing demands of inclination, and his Hegelianism, with its imposing architectonics leveled by the need for democratic participation, could not be combined in a coherent philosophy. Kant had radically split subject and object; and the basic strength of his scientific and ethical doctrine, as Novgorodtsev well knew, depended on their separation. Hegel had made a supreme effort to reunite subject and object in thought and being. In his social-political theory, Novgorodtsev wished to maintain the Kantian dualism as between *individual* and *society*, while bringing the two together as mutual, but nondetermined, pursuers of the absolute. The ash can of eighteenth- and nineteenth-century ideas and experiences contained no bright, shining key, with which he could simultaneously open the door to universalism while leaving ajar the escape hatch to individualism.

Novgorodtsev sought to join together a largely platonic and a partly organic hypothesis. Working in the first direction, he built up a picture of the world from a base of "persons," and from the second, he saw them joined together in the absolute. Unlike Hegel, he would not accept that the absolute had been or could be fully embodied in any historical form, be it nation, state, or church. Only abstract and largely moral norms (forms) could fully embody the absolute, while nations, states, and churches were living historical phenomena. They could not express the idea of the universal solidarity of personalities. Nonetheless, Novgorodtsev held that there was something in the world besides individual instances, and it was not a static, timeless form, but something with a life of its own. In thought and action individuals manifested it. The fundamental truth had been uttered by Socrates, "Do you think that outside you there is nothing natural? You know the relativity of matter, that it is infinite and in you there is only the smallest part of it. So, is it possible that reason is located by accident in you only and nowhere besides you?"[61] Did Novgorodtsev mean a "consciousness in general?"

Novgorodtsev did believe in an absolute, from which emanated the spirit, which struggled with itself in man to realize itself in free universalism. Yet the individual personality remained an ultimate for him. No manifestation of spirit might infringe upon its autonomy, and there existed no necessary, determined linear or dialectical path to unity. Man's asocial sociability was ineradicable; free universalism remained a lofty aim and a regulative principle. What kind of an absolute was it whose spirit could not work its will on its atomized parts? While severely criticizing Rousseau's conception of natural harmony between individuals and collectivities, Novgorodtsev found himself, after a long detour through Kant, Fichte, Hegel, Humboldt, Mill, and the Neo-Kantians, as well as the experience of the nineteenth century, back face to face with the French thinker's problem: how could man acquire his freedom while giving it up? To it he could give no answer.

And so Novgorodtsev's idealistic liberalism embodied a mood. The mood was Kantian and Simmelian, one of recognition of eternal contradictions, of unpassable limits. It took a realistic view of man's proclivities for aggressiveness and selfishness and of the small possibilities of eradicating these through institutional forms. It prized sobriety and suspected enthusiasm. It eternalized struggle. Yet it insisted on the certainty of some moral progress, to take place by the stubborn dedication of each to freedom, equality, solidarity, and universalism. It was very much a liberalism of its rapidly reached elder years, a liberalism which had come to terms with the stubborn refractory contradictions of human life, a liberalism which strongly suspected that it had done its job, that its heroic, heaven-storming days, to the degree that they existed, were past. It seemed to feel that the best for which it could hope was that its respect for human dignity and the creative spirit in man would have taken deep enough root so that, whatever future steps European man might take, these would remain as his permanent possessions. But it was a liberalism intended for a country, Russia, which in the great mass of its population and in the essence of its political-social organization had not tasted the fruits of youthful liberalism. And thereby hangs the tale.

Chapter VI

THE PRIEST AND THE PROFESSOR

BULGAKOV AND NOVGORODTSEV brought European-wide perspectives to bear on Russian problems. Many European political, economic, and intellectual leaders of the early twentieth century glimpsed a frightening future. Signs proliferated that the internal structure and international order which had appeared to make the nineteenth century progressive and relatively stable would collapse. In economics and politics, by creating new institutions or refurbishing old, active men hoped to combine increasing productivity with political and social arrangements which would be solid and, in some cases, free. Intellectuals of many varieties sought a new, secure basis in thought to replace the apparently exhausted capital of seventeenth-century rationalism and empiricism.[1] And in all European societies some thinkers tried to find an explanation of their world which would simultaneously provide a philosophy for the twentieth century and a theory and program of liberating politics.

Novgorodtsev and Bulgakov offered a philosophical and religious critique of Marxism. In doing so, they confronted Russian thought and institutions with modes of thought which, though not dominant, had wide currency in Western Europe between 1870 and 1914. In England Hobhouse and in France the Neo-Kantian Renouvier proposed idealistic liberalism in terms similar to those of Novgorodtsev.[2] Their "new liberalism" expressed the emerging frame of mind of important liberal politicians and public opinion. This was not the case in Novgorodtsev's Russia. At the same time, he did not share the predominant secularism which marked Western European liberal thought. But he stopped short of a Christian political theory.

Bulgakov emphasized his kinship with European Christian socialism. Strongly influenced by the ideas of William Morris, that doctrine spread widely in Western Europe during the last half of the nineteenth century.[3] For Roman Catholics, Christian socialist ideas and movements received strong impetus from the social teachings of Pope Leo XIII in his encyclical, *Rerum novarum* (1891). Bulgakov could not accept the latter's justification of economic equality, nor, for that matter, the very idea that the pope could make pronouncements binding on all Christians. At the same time he rejected much of the medievalism of movements based on the ideas of Morris.

Both Russian thinkers had emotional-intellectual commitments to Russian Orthodoxy, which, in its institutional and theological positions, differed in important ways from the Christian churches of the late-nineteenth-century West. Moreover, they developed their thought in the midst of the Russian religious-philosophical societies and meetings of the early twentieth century. In those societies, concepts and language—the God-bearing people, the selfless intelligentsia, the *sobornal* church, holy Russia, religious Marxism—played roles to which no close counterpart could be found in the West. Neither Novgorodtsev nor Bulgakov would involve himself in the too often frivolous controversies aroused in the societies.

They addressed themselves very little to the religious ideas which aroused most public excitement. Among these were Merezhkovsky's "new religious consciousness," Sventsitsky's sharp, but hysterical denunciation of property, Blok's intuitive indictment of the intelligentsia, and Lunacharsky's attempt to combine Marx and Mach as founders of "religious socialism." But in those largely cerebral visions of allegedly religious roads to the salvation of modern man, real issues in Russian life stood out. They provided challenges in reaction to which Bulgakov worked out his own brand of Christian socialism. For Novgorodtsev, they represented the kinds of ideas and urged the kind of action that no person truly interested in freedom should pursue.

However, both Novgorodtsev and Bulgakov shared with most leaders of the religious-philosophical societies and a strong current of European and American thought an important turn-of-the-century attitude, *personalism*, or *personal idealism*.[4] Novgorodtsev, Bulgakov, Berdiaev, Struve, Ern, Merezhkovsky, Belyi, Ivanov, and several others held that the ultimate worth and irreducibility of the person should form the basic principle of philosophy. They sought to show that the person could act freely in a world of egoistic individuals and could be fulfilled and productive in social orders resting on idealistic or religious principles. Efforts to support those propositions characterized the thought of Bulgakov and Novgorodtsev much more than any defense or expression of class interest.

Marxist "scientific class analysis" of ideas has never been either scientific or, for that matter, analytic. And assertions that the thought of Novgorodtsev and Bulgakov represents the interests of early-twentieth-century Russian landowners and the commercial and industrial middle classes cannot be sustained by empirical evidence. Novgorodtsev expressed a partially nonacquisitive "ethical" welfare liberalism which, on the whole, was unacceptable to and not in the interests of the rising Russian middle class. Bulgakov's social and political plans called for the nationalization of industry and the expropriation of the landlords and was expressed in a religious philosophy which would be as difficult for most landowners and middle class persons to accept then as it is now. Marxist contentions that the idealistic liberal or the Christian socialist spoke for those classes "dialectically" or "objectively" simply deny straightforward statements of intent in the name of alleged knowledge of what the thinkers "really meant." Leaving aside the occasionally brilliant insight of a George Lukacs, Herbert Marcuse, or Arnold Hauser, there is no evidence to suggest that application of Marxist categories to the analysis of ideas provides that kind of understanding.

It is more constructive to view Novgorodtsev and Bulgakov as expressing the claims of major institutions to the moral leadership of Russia. Novgorodtsev spoke for the secular educational system, from the universities on down, as its spokesmen sought to place at the center of a rapidly modernizing Russia a conception of man, culture, society, and the state resting on *individualistic humanism*. Novgorodtsev held nothing more firmly than the view that the future of Russia depended on the internalization of the humanistic value system by Russia's millions of peasants and workers. Bulgakov argued for the unifying and liberating essence of the Orthodox church especially in its transformative rituals. These divergent institutional commitments entailed different views in regard to which segment of the population would play the dominant role in a new Russia.

Bulgakov appealed directly to the people to choose unity in love and freedom by the full participation in Christian life which major reforms of the Russian church would make possible. But Russia's deeply demoralized millions would find it difficult to respond to his ultimately mystical plea. As for Novgorodtsev, though he consistently expressed democratic ideas, he could not turn to the people and expect support. Only prolonged education in humanistic cultural values would induce them to follow his counsels. Leaving aside individuals of all classes, he could appeal only to the traditional supporters of humanistic culture and political liberalism—the variegated urban middle class. But his "new liberalism" could appeal to only a minority, even among the "ethical liberals" of the professions. Examination of the doctrines of Novgorodtsev and Bulgakov suggests that neither was likely to find solid support in the social groups to which they had to turn. Therefore, their ideas should not be discussed as political programs, but rather in terms of the questions they raise and insights they offer regarding the necessary conditions for a free and just Russian order.

MODERNIZATION AND THE FREE PERSON

Twentieth-century Russian reality confronted the philosophies of Novgorodtsev and Bulgakov with a potent modern dilemma. Each was utterly committed to the defense of the "person" against modern rationalization. But at the same time, they firmly supported the social and economic modernization which accompanied the shift from the traditional repressive authority of the czars to the freedom and legal authority for which they struggled. This involved both in a contradictory relationship to the vast majority of the Russian people. Much in the lives of those people which a personalist doctrine would be concerned to protect was incompatible with the emergence of a rational politics and its necessary accompaniment, a modernized social and economic order. This problem posed more difficulty for Novgorodtsev than Bulgakov, but both faced it and failed to solve it. From the standpoint of the person, the question may be insoluble—perhaps the world is moving inexorably toward greater and greater rationalization, with the free "person" an inevitable casualty. In any case, the Russian thinkers tried to overcome the dilemma by suspending man in a realm where personhood and rationalization could live in continual tension.

Each in his own way sought an objective basis for safeguarding the claims of the autonomous person. Bulgakov offered the Christian concept of the timeless holy personality, while Novgorodtsev articulated a complex mix of Kantian, Goethean, and Christian notions of the unique, many-sided, free person. Both attempted to describe an essence which remained after the determining effects of the many roles played by an individual in modern society had been considered.[5] Unlike Russian Machists, such as Lunacharsky, Bogdanov, and Bazarov, they would not accept the notion that there was nothing substantial, no center in man.[6] Moreover, in their view, the doctrines of Karl Marx and his Russian followers identified man with his social roles even while promising fulfillment of the needs of the whole man. Novgorodtsev and Bulgakov sought to point a way to economic and political modernization in Russia while safeguarding the person from rationalization. Their concomitant realization that Russia's peasant-worker millions required a heavy dose of rationality in their approaches to family, work, and politics complicated their effort. But both were sure that Marxism could not help.

Novgorodtsev and Bulgakov attacked Marxist philosophy, its social-economic prescriptions, and its utopian promises. They showed convincingly the *logical* incompatibility of positivist determinism with the setting and pursuit of ideals. Both, though in different ways, placed high economic productivity above attempted equal distribution as a precondition for a free Russia. Each laid powerful emphasis on the threat of Marxism to the person, predicting that a Marxist government would inevitably become repressive as it found its vision mocked by the realities of life. Neither sought a return to the past or even a solidification of existing orders—they criticized Marxism in terms of alternative paths to the freedom and material and spiritual betterment of all men. Novgorodtsev and Bulgakov argued that Marxism would perpetuate "mystical-dogmatic" authority in Russia. Its leaders would pursue Russian economic development by mechanisms having different names than those of czarist times, but a similar spirit.[7] The people would find themselves confronted as of old by rulers who would present them with decrees based on mysterious authoritative doctrine.

The idealistic liberal and the Christian socialist pointed toward a "rational-critical" order, where Russians would choose leaders and programs by open, institutionalized means safeguarded by basic civil rights. Of course, the idealistic liberal assigned central importance in the attainment and preservation of freedom to the mechanisms of parliamentary government in a pluralistic society. The Christian socialist sought the free expression of the Russian popular will in a unified religious conscience. But each sought, Bulgakov no less than Novgorodtsev, to preserve the *person* against the modern threat to its autonomy.

Modernization meant industrialization and Westernization.[8] In Russia at the end of the nineteenth century it represented the effort of the government to overcome economic, military, and diplomatic inferiority to Western European countries. For Russian entrepreneurs it meant rapidly increasing chances to amass productive power, wealth, and influence. For the educated, inside and outside the government bureaucracy, it meant careers and decision-making powers commensurate with learning, energy, and ability. Most members of these social groups had internalized values and aims associated with their counterparts in the West and approached Russian problems and other strata in the population in that spirit. However, the peasants and most factory workers had not become cognitively or emotionally attuned to the modernization of Russia.

In its broadest sense modernization can be described as a process of rationalization. At least since the seventeenth century, European rulers, bureaucrats, and entrepreneurs had systematized and regulated more and more areas of life in search of rational control of natural and human resources.[9] The process pressed ruthlessly on traditional habits and customs which stood in the way of rational utilitarian decisions. It jeopardized the leeway given to people to view their world in "enchanted" ways—to people it with gods and spirits deeply bound up in their daily lives. It refused to sanction behavior which symbolized inner feelings that hierarchies of authority and ritualized approaches to work linked the person with an often incomprehensible world. Though they urged industrialization and shared attitudes of highly Westernized intellectuals, Novgorodtsev and Bulgakov were, at the very least, ambivalent toward rationalization and spoke against it for men.

In different ways, Novgorodtsev's idealistic liberalism and Bulgakov's Christian socialism embodied a problematic relationship to

Russian culture in both its modernizing and its traditional forms. To different degrees opponents of rationalization and equally fervent defenders of the person, they yet could not support the continuance of old Russian peasant attitudes toward nature, human productivity, political authority, and the Christian religion. Even while arguing for democracy, Novgorodtsev argued that most of peasant culture had to be replaced by modern humanism if a tolerably free and equal Russia were to emerge. And, though Bulgakov believed that Orthodox Christian culture held the key to Russian salvation and that peasants best represented that culture, he denounced much of the behavior of the Russian church and people. Defenses of the person by Novgorodtsev and Bulgakov referred to a different order of being than that manifested in the daily lives of Russia's millions.

To employ a phrase used by Paul Novgorodtsev (and Michael Foucault), the alternatives to Marxism sought a fortress for the person somewhere between positive science and eschatology.[10] The Marxist individual begins in positivistic determinism and ends, inexplicably, in eschatology—the *Zusammenbruch* and the leap from necessity to freedom. Neither Novgorodtsev nor Bulgakov denied the restrictive impact on men of the "force of things," the imperatives of the world in which they must seek food, clothing, and shelter. Nor did they see human experience as an endless struggle, a Faustian commitment to eternal striving. The Christian socialist and the idealistic liberal believed in progress in history in terms of political freedom, social justice, economic abundance, and personal fulfillment. Both were sure that progress both entailed struggle between nations, classes, and individuals and moved toward the elimination of those struggles. But each believed that struggles would remain part of human life, ending only at a point of religious transformation.

But Novgorodtsev approached *this world* in the spirit of idealistic liberalism, thought to be sufficient to deal with man's problems. Bulgakov considered that only the introduction of the church in the entangled problems of man could lead from despotism, privilege, and poverty to lasting freedom, justice, and abundance. This fundamental difference brought about variance in the way that their shared beliefs would be understood. In relation to existing classes, institutions, and intellectual currents in the Russia of their time, these engendered different alternatives to Marxism.

Approaching Bulgakov and Novgorodtsev on the level of institu-tions—church, academy, state—provides important insights into the meaning of their doctrines. In a very real sense they represented the claims of church and academy against each other and the claim of both against the state for moral leadership in an emerging new Russia. Largely won by the religious and educational forces in the West, freedom of church and academy from direction and interference by the state was still a part of the general struggle for freedom in early-twentieth-century Russia.

As for church and academy, their respective claims to provide the basic institution and world view for society had featured nineteenth-century European life. The secular educators had won, but in Russia the issue had not yet been fought out. Nor was it entirely certain what the outcome would be. Bulgakov unequivocally stood for a partially modernized culture constructed around Russian Orthodox Christian-ity. Though himself a committed Orthodox Christian, Novgorodtsev clearly believed that the greatest force for freedom in a modernizing Russian society would be the academy, the citadel of individualistic humanism.

Bulgakov believed that Christian socialism could flourish around a refurbished Russian Orthodox church. Despite bureaucratization and the subservience of the Russian church to the state, Orthodox Chris-tianity held the understanding of man on which freedom and commu-nion could be based, and the church remained the vehicle of Christian truth.[11] Quickly, it had to recognize that the struggle for the material well-being and political freedom of the masses fostered the growth of the spirit. Priests deeply needed training in the ways of modern economics and sociology, so that in their approach to the people they could combine Christian communion and an understanding of mod-ernization. Bulgakov was sure that, even where apparently thrust aside by secular revolutionary belief and action, Orthodox Christian-ity still maintained its hold on the Russian peasant soul. If the church would consent to play the role he assigned to it, the people would respond. Was Bulgakov right on either count?

Few reasonably detached observers would deny that the external state of the Russian Orthodox church at the beginning of the twentieth century was unhealthy. Most of its high officials identified their religious task with the task of maintaining a nonpluralistic, obedient population.[12] Undereducated and underpaid, the majority of the parish priests could not transmit faithfully the Christian message of peace, love, and salvation. Indeed, throughout the Russian countryside the clergy's mode of life and their material demands on the peasants aroused hostility and contempt. A conservative, apolitical priest, S. Shchukin, said that the people's faith was deeply rooted in "the beauty of the world and the goodness of God," but that "they hate us, have contempt for us, are cynical about us . . . and not only the clergy, but also the Church . . . What if they just stop coming to us?"[13] In the early twentieth century it appeared to many that only the secular power restrained mass desertion of the church, that the church might collapse if deprived of government force.

Many argued, then and now, that the *internal* life of the Russian church had basic strengths.[14] Among the peasants in particular there existed an internalized need for church rituals to give meaning and hope to their lives. Great saints and ascetic monks manifested a Christian humility, brotherly love, and compassion to which millions of Russians responded. Monasteries became the goal of thousands of pilgrimages and focal points from which examples of Christian dedication spread throughout the country. Although much idealized by literary intellectuals, many Russian peasants did seem to be simple, strong, pious Christian personalities. It may be that the very qualities that Bulgakov and others attributed to the effect of Orthodoxy on the peasants were barriers against political expression. At the same time the kinds of effects mobilized by the church in Russian history may be one of those cultural facts to which an idealistic liberal or a Marxist force had to adapt.

Many upper and middle class Russians, urban and rural, shared Orthodox Christian commitment. Strong Christian personalities were numerous in the Russian nobility. Literature, music, and art presented religious ideas and feelings to which educated Russians responded. Millions found Christian truth and sustenance in the beauty and magnificence of the Orthodox liturgy. Much of the religious thought of the turn of the century represented the efforts of intellectuals to confront the synodal church with the Christian perspectives of its saints and monks and those of intellectuals like Gogol, Dostoevsky, and Vladimir Soloviev. Bulgakov sought to vitalize the eternal inner strength of the church and the drive for social, economic, and political change in Russia by bringing them together in the communal essence of the former.

To place the church at the center of a liberating socialist movement required that the church undertake some modernization of its view toward the secular world. The dominant forces in the church, the bureaucrats of the holy synod and many of its appointees were not disposed to undertake such a task.[15] Between 1904 and 1914 an active reform element within the church struggled with some success for freedom from the state and more internal democracy. But their attitude toward the political order was more often moderately liberal than Christian socialist. If the church were to play an important role in twentieth-century Russian social life, it probably would have done so by adapting some of the liberal mentality and modes of action of the modern world. Indeed, the very changes which Bulgakov thought so important—involvement in political actions and training in social sciences for priests—might have begun the transformation of the Russian church along the lines of the Protestant churches he (and Kierkegaard) so much disliked. It may have been possible to reform the church along the lines Bulgakov suggested, but probably not to make it the kind of social-political force he envisioned.

Novgorodtsev's prescription for change found its institutional focus in the academy. The universities were the originating point and the continuing purveyors of individualistic humanism in Russia. Like his friend, colleague, and fellow idealistic liberal, Serge Trubetskoi, Novgorodtsev considered the restoration of academic autonomy to Moscow University on August 27, 1905, to be a "moral victory for the university, but also a triumph for Russian society."[16] Of course, Novgorodtsev sought to rest his thought on both secular and Orthodox Christian principles, but idealistic liberalism would stand or fall with the spread of individualistic humanism. And in Russia the latter required a government which would support the academy as it usurped the educational position so long held by the church. It was very much a professor's doctrine, which, in the university setting, aimed to accomplish what the religious intellectuals sought with regard to the church—confront the bureaucratic leadership with the true university's need for freedom to seek knowledge crucial to the stability, growth, and power of Russia.

Just as the Russian Orthodox church appeared as a bearer of truth perverted by its involvement with the state, so the academy seemed to be diverted from its true purpose, the advancement of knowledge, by governmental control. The academy, the great universities at St. Petersburg, Moscow, and Kiev, and the preparatory gymnasiums, suffered under the Statute of 1884 which, in the vigorously stated opinion of many faculty members and students, made teaching, learning, and research impossible.[17] Both groups carried on their academic careers in an atmosphere where liberal reforms establishing basic civil liberties seemed to be absolutely necessary.

In the 1890s, amid the general unrest developing as the twentieth century approached, student and faculty unrest became increasingly overt and threatening. Students formed illegal associations, numerous mass student demonstrations with some faculty participation took place, and many expulsions failed to stem the tide. Student and faculty challenges to the bureaucratic authorities continued at an increasing pace until 1905, when in the general revolutionary turbulence of that year, the universities regained academic autonomy and new rules permitted students to form voluntary associations.[18] These concessions led to the variegated intellectual life of free discussion and writing, of which the religious-philosophical meetings were a major part. But after 1907, when the reaction set in all areas of Russian life, the Ministry of Education began once again to keep a wary eye on the academy and to restrict its freedom. Nonetheless, though the university's autonomy remained shaky and its central position in a modernizing Russia unacknowledged, it was strong. Russians looked upon it with justifiable pride, and its powerful role in further progress was assured.

Novgorodtsev and Bulgakov both spoke for the *autonomy* of the person, and both were committed Orthodox Christians. But their emphases were different.[19] The liberal wished the Orthodox church to form personalities and ultimately guide actions, but not to provide the language, concepts, and institutional structure by which secular affairs would be conducted. Otherwise, the person's inner Christian fortress would be infiltrated and overcome by the very forces it thought it controlled. The Christian socialist believed that the church must be a direct, visible, authoritative force in secular affairs, with rituals symbolizing and solidifying the personhood and sociability of its members. This church confronted the growing forces of apparently healthy militant individualism, particularly in the academy.

Individualism dominates the world view of the professional of the academy. Whatever self-image he may have or ideology he may profess, in the great majority of the cases he provides a perhaps purer example of nineteenth-century Manchesterism than most appearing in twentieth-century economic life. He may well be the last of the "entrepreneurs," egoistically selling his goods and services, subject to and accepting the law of the market, and confident that the unseen hand will bring general good out of his private endeavors. Idealistic liberals, all of whom were academics, would push for individualism, particularly in those areas in which the cultural development of the person and personal creativity were involved. But could Novgorodtsev's philosophy garner support from other Russian social forces which would seem susceptible to individualistic liberalism?

Bulgakov, who committed himself to and increasingly approached occupational identification with Christianity, would view the needs of the time differently. He would seek communitarian solutions, would feel that personal egoism had no saving unseen hand, but would perpetrate the disorder and wilfullness which barred men's return to union with his fellow men and God. He would sharply distrust largely rational approaches to human problems, would seek rather the light of the Spirit to fill the whole being with the love that binds. Institutionally, he would seek a church, rather than an aggregate of self-interested competitors for worldly goods and honors, no matter how rational that self-interest might claim to be and no matter how democratic it might consider itself. But, was a church-directed society possible in twentieth-century Russia?

Both church and academy lived uncomfortably with the early-twentieth-century Russian bureaucratic state. The idealistic liberal and the Christian socialist deeply deplored state despotism, cruelty, corruption, and obscurantism. Though Novgorodtsev and Bulgakov favored democracy, their philosophies embodied some dangers with regard to the emergence of such a polity. Novgorodtsev's conception of a liberal Russia contained a bias toward government by an educated elite which, whatever the intentions of individual participants, could freeze class lines erected by human natural inequalities, access to education, and resultant accrued wealth. On the other hand, oriented as it was to an authoritarian church necessarily institutionalized in bishops, priests, and buildings, Bulgakov's political view would have a strong tendency toward theocracy. Would the Christian socialist state find the response in the deepest feelings of the people which Bulgakov thought to exist? Some argued that it would not, and that an Orthodox state would then force obedience on Russia.

THE STATE AND THE PEOPLE

Both Novgorodtsev and Bulgakov worked for the end of the bureaucratic state in Russia. There can be no doubt about what political order the liberal desired—a full-scale parliamentary government like that of England, in which ministers and bureaucrats would be answerable to a representative assembly, full civil rights would exist, and the czar would have no arbitrary power. Bulgakov did not specify the form of state he sought for Russia. Up to 1906 he held a political view close to that of the liberals of the Liberation Movement. But, after that time, he came to dislike deeply the practice of parliamentary politics and believed that the czar had to retain enough authority to act as the mystical center of the Russian nation. He did not turn against democracy; indeed, he served in the Dumas and wished them to be more truly representative. But he became progressively more pessimistic about the chances for political reform and developed a religious theory which some believed to commit him to a theocracy.

To Novgorodtsev, the state was a necessity growing out of the "objective principles of history." It was a rational institution which united and reconciled different faiths, political views, peoples, and languages in an organic unit having a definable spirit and calling in the world.[20] The true state was never despotic. Its ultimate nature and call on man's loyalties were not rational, but rooted in natural and universal human ties; a native land-mother, which would treat all of its children equally; a fatherland-family, in which all would be brothers, differentiated not by religion, class, or wealth, but by natural gifts and personal merits.[21]

Novgorodtsev considered that the Russian intelligentsia had sinned most grievously in its completely negative relation to the state. More dangerous still was the degree to which society as a whole agreed with that position. Even among members of Russian educated society who did not truly share that hostility, many remained silent because of the intelligentsia's long history of struggle and martyrdom for the helpless people. They wished to be thought "progressive" and to withhold any sign of support for bureaucratic despotism. It appeared by 1917 that rejection of the state dominated in "society," where state ideals should be articulated, while anarchistic impulses held sway among the masses. Russia could not long survive in that condition.

In considering the nature of the state, Novgorodtsev expressed one of his most fundamental conflicts with Marxism. He showed himself to be related to the "state-historical" interpreters of Russian history, with their correct emphasis on the role of the state in directing Russia's destiny.[22] The modern state existed to apply laws which reconciled the interests and other claims of as many of Russia's conflicting social groups as possible. The state wielded force, because reason, sympathy, or even self-interested compromise could not settle all disputes. In order to fulfill its function, the state had to seek sovereignty, in which its authority and force would be greater than those of any struggling group in society.

The state did not reflect the interests of a particular social class. It became the center about which there developed another class, a *governing class*—in Russia, the bureaucracy and the military. That class had lasting interests of its own. Of course, in order to survive it formed unions with the strongest social class at any given time. But, to maintain a certain divisiveness in society and with the forethought that today's weaker might become tomorrow's stronger social group, it also cooperated with weaker classes. In order to maintain authority along with its power, the governing class accepted norms limiting its own freedom of action. Though self-preservation might be the origin of such self-restraints, over time they created moral obligations and fostered the sense of morality in the dominant group. To the degree that this happened, the state exercised legitimate power, though the danger of tyranny remained strong as long as popular participation in lawmaking did not exist.

Novgorodtsev believed that no state could be democratic in the sense that the people would determine its ongoing policies. Not even the representative systems of the United States, England, or France had been able to function in that way. How much more the case for Russia! If a constitutional regime were to be established, the educated, particularly the professional, business, and industrial middle class, would rule for an undetermined period of time. That would be unavoidable, despite the selection of representatives by universal

165

suffrage. Would the middle class elite agree to direct a society in which the choice of leaders ultimately resided in a very large culturally backward majority? And would that majority understand and accept the kind of policies a patiently developing liberal order would require?

Practically, Novgorodtsev's new liberalism demanded sizable social strata willing to trust majoritarianism as a general principle and to devote substantial portions of the national product to partially equalizing the economic struggle. There were no such strata outside the academy in early-twentieth-century Russia. Urbanized, educated people, from anarchists to monarchists, were not willing to place their fates in the hands of the Russian peasant. Landlord liberals like Shipov wanted only moderate change in the direction of a consultative assembly and civil rights. Bourgeois liberals, of whom Guchkov may be taken as an example, demanded representation for their group, were largely satisfied by the Manifesto of 1905, and would not restrict economic acquisitiveness and increase taxation to support welfare programs.

Leading Kadet liberals demanded universal suffrage, trade unions, and factory legislation, and land for the peasants with compensation to the landlords. But the Kadets did not represent a sizable social group committed to the new liberalism. And for general support of their program, Kadets had to compete with reform socialists. The failure of the new liberalism even in England's much more hospitable environment resulted in large part from its ambiguities in the face of socialism's promises of democracy, social reform, and a gradually attainable brotherhood of man. As an idealistic liberal, Novgorodtsev supported these aims, but also social elements which opposed them, and always with a strong feeling for the limits of their attainability by self-interested man. Yet he put forth his own perhaps unrealizable demands as well, those required to satisfy the needs of the romantic person.

On the other hand, it could not be expected that Russia's millions would be willing to postpone satisfaction in the way Novgorodtsev's theory demanded. Though they might seem to those on their left as ideological defenders of a dying social system, idealistic liberals were actually, in their Russia, intellectually "too adventurous." The urbanized university-centered intellectual believed in the person, in ratiocination to fulfill the formal laws of duty, and in refined feeling to establish affective relations among persons with widely variegated needs. There was too great an intellectual and cultural distance between him and the mentality and feeling of most of the Russian people. The transformation of the latter into the idealistic liberals' kind of democratically functioning citizens could not take place in the time available before it would be overtaken by resort to "spontaneous" action directed against the entire structure of Russian society.

Turning from Novgorodtsev, we enter the realm of the "mystical authority" of the czar and holy Russia. Before 1917, Bulgakov believed that Marx's insights into modern social and political life remained true, despite the errors of his deterministic materialism. Therefore, he saw the early-twentieth-century Russian state as serving the interests of the landowners and, to a lesser degree, commercial and industrial entrepreneurs. At the same time, he recognized the independent role of the bureaucracy in Russian politics.[23] His own experience campaigning for the Second and Third Dumas alerted him to the bureaucracy's determination to gain control of the emerging new system. Through propaganda, denying individuals the right to run, using force at the polling places, and putting up candidates allegedly representing certain constituencies, but actually handpicked by them, they sought to control the Dumas. In short, there was a state organization in Russia trying to maintain its power, whatever the political institutions. But, after 1907, Bulgakov said nothing about the specific state forms which would safeguard freedom, economic progress, and civil rights. It seemed to liberal opponents that his belief in the Orthodox church, mystical Russia, and the God-bearing people committed him to a theocracy.

Bulgakov did not suffer from the illusion that the czar ruled or could rule Russia, and he believed in dismantling the repressive, corrupt bureaucracy. But he held that Russia, with its many nationalities, numerous conflicting religious groups, and especially sharp class hatreds needed one symbol of community, a center of blessed authority, around which all could unite.[24] The parliamentary politics associated with the first three Dumas so disgusted him that in 1909 he became a "monarchist," but he continued to support civil rights, nationalization of industry, and eventual expropriation of the landlords.[25] He thought that the czar and his government were committing suicide by resting his power on force and the black hundreds. Bulgakov simply did not know where to turn. He loved the czar, scorned Duma "democracy," and dreamed of a state pursuing socialist policies and resting on the "elemental feeling of the Russian people" for religious authority.

Novgorodtsev accused Bulgakov of proposing a vision of life on this earth in which the Word would become law and the church would perform state functions. But Bulgakov denounced the theocracy which he believed had destroyed the unity of the Roman Catholic church in Europe. Bulgakov's idea of political authority on *this* earth was not theocratic. He did not renounce his position of 1905–1907 that, even before reform of the Orthodox church could be undertaken, at least the legal state had to be established. He urged those who desired freedom, Christian or secular, to engage in the political-social struggle using political means: publication of programs for a mass audience, political and economic education, worker organization, voting, and representation. And the first act of a government elected under conditions of political freedom should be the complete separation of church and state.

Bulgakov proposed a Union of Christian Politics to take part in the struggle for freedom, so that the political freedom and economic equality so needed by the church would not be acquired solely by the efforts of its enemies. But he accented his conviction that the Union would not be a *clerical* party. In practice, clericalism either simply reflected the self-interest of the clergy or sought to capture political power in order to force one religious belief on a society. The church was the guardian of the one true faith, and God intended that all humanity should live it, but not necessarily in the city of man, and certainly not through oppressive political activity by the church or any clerical party which might claim to represent her interests. The reformed church would seek freedom and justice for all because these were rights of man and because the triumph of Christianity required free men. And so in the social struggles in the twentieth-century world toward which Bulgakov directed his attention, he could find no place for a theocracy. Yet there were elements in Bulgakov's view of politics which could threaten Russia's millions with theocratic control.

He insisted that the political struggle going on in early-twentieth-century Russia was no mere contest of parties, but a war to the death between two religions, Christian and secular socialism. Bulgakov believed that the truth had to triumph, in the short run, in the victory of Christian socialism over Feuerbachian worship of man, and in the end in the routing of the Antichrist as pictured in the Revelation of John. But in the short run, it was unlikely that the truth of which Bulgakov spoke could be experienced by the millions of Russian peasants and workers. Ill-fed, ill-housed, and ill-clothed, filled with hatred born of centuries of exploitation and with desperate confusion arising from the rapid economic, social, and political changes in their environment at the turn of the century, they would find it difficult to demonstrate love for their enemies.

It was more likely that, once unloosed, the masses would proceed, not toward the Christian truth, but toward that of this world as they understood it. They would perpetrate physical violence against those who had so long dominated them. They would seize the land they considered rightfully theirs and the factories, whose production, they were encouraged to believe, resulted almost entirely from their labor. Bulgakov's regime would have confronted what Lenin confronted in 1918. As a *movement*, bearing the ultimate truth about man's condition, would it not have been obliged to insist upon and, if necessary, enforce obedience? This, of course, was the specter which liberals saw hovering behind Bulgakov's wish to introduce a religious movement into a political struggle.

Bulgakov's willingness to allow the people to delude themselves about the temporal attainability of ideal goals would compound the problem. Though he believed and wrote many times that, in history and for an indeterminable period of time, men would earn their bread in the sweat of their brows and suffer the egoistic sinfulness, pain, and death of natural man, he nonetheless thought it advantageous to leave intact the people's ''faith in the limited nature of the historical horizon.''[26] They needed such a faith to prod them into continuing work to change themselves and their world so that their return unto God could become possible. Bulgakov knew that faith to be an ''optical illusion,'' a myth, yet believed that it should be employed to facilitate God's purposes. Of course, this was the way of Marxists and other socialist utopians, and its consequences are evident.

When Bulgakov announced his Christian conviction he came under attack not only from liberals of a positivist bent and Marxists but also from some idealistic liberals.[27] With varying degrees of hostility and rationality, polemicists denied him the honorific title of reformer and labeled him a conservative or reactionary defender of the old order.

169

Marxists simply asserted that he had displayed his "bourgeois in-
stincts," while liberal critics attacked him on three grounds: (1) that
identification with the Christian church was incompatible with the
struggle for freedom, (2) that his position remained meaningless until
he demonstrated that it could garner a large popular following, and
(3) that his belief that Christian commitment was the key to a freer
and more just life on earth reflected his personal, deeply rooted,
dogmatic temper. The first, of course, was probably the deepest
rooted of all liberal convictions, but there was no logical necessity
that it should be so in the twentieth century. The last two could not be
held by early-twentieth-century Russian liberals without threatening
their own position.

No inherent reason existed why Bulgakov's church had to be
incommensurable with a reform-oriented social position simply because churches in the past had been associated largely with conservative political forces. The church upon which he placed his hopes
would be an enlightened church, which had recognized the Christian
value of social reform and whose leaders and priests understood the
interrelations of modern social, political, and economic structures
and how to work within them for human good. Moreover, a very wide
range of diversity in these areas of life was possible within the fabric
of a general Christian world view. There was no reason why the slate
of liberal political reforms and partly socialist social and economic
measures advocated by Russian liberals could not have been im-
plemented in a society impregnated with the principles enunciated by
Bulgakov in his turn to the church. It would seem that Russian liberals
stood on firmer ground when they challenged Bulgakov to prove his
ideas in practice by attracting mass support.

Russian liberals endangered their own position in asserting that
Bulgakov's ideas should be ignored because they could not be popular. This had been the very argument directed at philosophical
idealism by Leonid Slonimsky writing in the long-time liberal journal
Vestnik Evropy (European Courier).[28] He had argued that, however
intelligent and admirable its approach to philosophical questions,
idealistic liberalism had no political importance, for the people would
never see any connection between their needs and the complex
abstract arguments of the idealists. In response to the attitude expressed by Slonimsky, the idealists had repeated many times their
conviction that utilitarian standards should not be applied to ques-

tions of truth. To apply the test of democratic success to Bulgakov's thought was to invite its application to their own.

Bulgakov *did* impress some intellectuals as an inherently dogmatic man, who felt it necessary to embody philosophical belief and social action in an institutionalized framework, a party, or a church. Nonetheless, he showed great willingness to work with others of different points of view, which he treated as serious, honest attempts to deal with human problems. Perhaps not much more can be asked of a social thinker than that he honestly study opposing views and find ways to adjust his thought to embody insights which it is permitted to him to see in them, while remaining largely intractable on certain ultimate positions. Bulgakov did this at least as well as any of his critics. In any case, the *ad hominem* argument of "natural dogmatism" was not the issue so much as whether liberal opponents could afford to dismiss his religious ideas as resting ultimately on authority attractive to a dogmatic man.

Bulgakov believed that if men would truly join the Christian church, a richer, happier life and eventual eternal salvation would result. Leaving aside the Christian view of salvation, the idealistic liberals promised a similar great improvement in the conditions of human life if men would enter the embrace of culture. Was culture as Novgorodtsev, Frank, and Struve understood it any less an "objective" repository of truth than the church to which Bulgakov asked men to turn? It would seem not. Like the church, it transcended humanity, so that men could be ignorant of it, could reject it, or could actively pursue it. The latter choice was ultimately transformative, leading to the internalization of the good, the true, and the beautiful and to personhood. Was the belief by urban, highly educated intellectuals that the Russian masses would adopt culture's transformative value system any less dogmatic than Bulgakov's assurance of the transfiguring power of the church?

Did the liberals have any empirically or logically persuasive reason to believe that education of the type they offered would lead the millions of Russian peasants to desire the kind of freedom they found satisfying? It would be a vast oversimplification to point to Western European experience as evidence for that belief. Leaving aside the question of the importance of varying historical traditions, the fact remained that the idealistic liberals themselves found the ultimate basis of Western humanistic values in religious teaching and experience, while they prescribed for Russia the exposure of the masses to secular individualistic humanism. What the effect of this on the peasants might be they could not know. The results of its confrontation with the much older cultural tradition of the Russian people was unpredictable. In the end, the idealistic liberal belief in the transformative power of culture was no less a dogmatic faith than that of Bulgakov in the church. Indeed, when a few hundred prescribe a future for one hundred million, the effort always partakes of dogmatism.

THE REVOLUTION OF SENSIBILITY
AND THE GNOSIS OF MODERNITY

The limitations of classes, institutions, and states as agents of liberating change lead back to the heart of the alternatives to Marxism—the *person*. Idealistic liberalism and Christian socialism claimed to deal with the realities of modern life and at the same time to preserve the autonomy of the person. The needs and demands of poverty-stricken multitudes and of possessing classes competing in complex ways were to be met, while the individual's freedoms were to be respected and, to a degree, satisfied. Novgorodtsev and Bulgakov rejected positivism and Marxism because these deterministic philosophies would in the long run lead to the destruction of liberty. And if socialism's belief in the ''laws of history'' did not lead it into repression, its utopian promises would. It dangled before men a chiliastic reconciliation on this earth of all contradictions of life, which it could not deliver. And the reaction of politicians when men would begin to deny their authority because of their false promises could be predicted. As a disciple of Boehme and Schelling, Bulgakov had to face the suspicion that, though he had forsaken Marxism for religious thought, he still purveyed a chiliastic doctrine.

As a philosophy of liberation, Bulgakov's Christian socialism verged toward what Eric Voegelin calls the ''gnosis of modernity.''[29] Bulgakov has been accused of leaning toward a ''gnostic'' position. The question revolves around Saint Augustine's distinction between sacred and profane history. Gnostic modes of thought are those which insist that profane history not only contains development toward divinization, but also that at some point in history man and nature would be fully realized as God. In other words, gnostic ways of thought hold that man can fully understand and describe the end of sacred history. Bulgakov never claimed the latter. But in his sophiological doctrine he did put development to Godmanhood at the center of the historical process. In so doing he brought all men under the sway of a deterministic principle, Sophia, the divine in the world, and he tended to situate aspects of man not acting under that influence under the sign of evil. He did not enter, but moved toward the ranks of those who believed that their knowledge of the course and end of history gave them the insight needed to separate the saved from the damned.

By 1917, Bulgakov had begun to reach the sophiological doctrine which became an essential part of his theological writings. As this was expressed in *Philosophy of Economics* and *Svet Nevechernyi* (*The Unfading Light*), it proved partially incompatible with the freedom of the person.[30] Sophia became the leading principle of the world. Partaking of both God and the world, she directed the world toward the fulfillment of God's purpose, the return of mankind to His bosom. Sophia presented to mankind the ideas which it needed to play its role in world salvation. The process could not be consummated without man's free choices, but Sophia directed history above and through man and, in so doing, made his freedom, at the least, problematic. For Bulgakov, the role of Sophia in the world made freedom "perceived necessity," the recognition that Divine Providence moves men in accordance with law. As for mankind, in its experience and consciousness, it provided a picture of the world in terms of which Sophia determined the earthly course. Man was the creative "eye" of Sophia.

Bulgakov assigned mankind, not individual men, the power to act creatively in history. Each individual man partook of mankind's freedom through his "holy personality," which was beyond time and space. As a "holy personality" each man entered a collectivity in which all the experiences, triumphant joys, and sufferings of the cosmos were simultaneously present. It was the concentration point of all truth, goodness, and beauty and knew no development, no change, no past, or future. Man's task was to return fully to it through immersion in the church, the Body of Christ, its rituals and its prayers, and through his actions, including those aimed at social and economic reform.

The other part of man, the individual, wallowed in selfhood for eons. It was ruled by passions and deeply involved in the world, which was a "stranger to freedom." Shrouded in the darkness of egoism, it resisted Sophia's profferred consciousness of the evil of a life dedicated to arbitrary actions. Bulgakov viewed as destructive behavior much human activity which even the idealist Novgorodtsev would consider legitimate for free persons. Despite the force with which he supported social, economic, and political reforms aimed at greatly improving the living standards of the Russian people, he deeply distrusted too much wealth, consumption, and luxury. To the degree that populations in developing societies came to manifest the psychology of rising expectations, a point would surely arise at which the Christian ascetic perspective in Bulgakov's thought would conflict with the economic, socialist drive toward greater production and consumption of material goods.[31] Perhaps, then, like Luther, he would pronounce a radical judgment on the evil world and cast aside those who believed that he would approve of their secular struggles. Here stood a firm objective limit to Bulgakov's influence as a reformer. The person whose autonomy he desired to protect would become increasingly scarce with the modernization of Russia. A fervent proponent of modernization, Novgorodtsev nonetheless also projected an attitude to the world unlikely to attract substantial support in his Russia.

Novgorodtsev's personalism suffered from a multiplicity of subjects. He defended the claims to autonomy of the Orthodox Christian person, the rational-possessive person, and the romantic person. The Christian person sought to relate to the world through love, the eighteenth-century individual by cognition and individualistic rational activity, and the nineteenth-century romanticist by fulfillment of his own integrated cognitive and feeling needs.[32] Novgorodtsev believed that love provided a base for sociability; reason, a means of establishing rules for everyday political and economic relationships; and feeling, a way of tempering the latter with the former. But, in fact, they represent aspects of human intercourse which are often incompatible with one another—Christ, Socrates, and Goethe. And, with regard to romantic vistas, he placed a foot in the world of his future and moved well beyond the possibilities of his day in Western Europe and, *a fortiori*, in Russia.

The romantic man sought to go beyond positivities not only as a rationally understood possessor of an autonomous will, but also as a feeling person whose emotional needs placed legitimate demands before society. This demand has formed the core of the revolution of sensibility which has emerged so sharply in affluent late-twentieth-century societies. Important members of "advanced" societies have found that neither political freedom nor economic well-being have brought them happiness and a sense of self-worth, but rather the omnipresent uneasiness stemming from a nagging, hard-to-define feeling of needs and potentialities unfulfilled. They have asked society to provide more than the political democracy, nourishment, and education for economic success sufficient for reasonable security.

The vision of a therapeutic society has captivated many in the liberal band of the political spectrum. Its center would be not the political arena, not the market, but the hospital, taking that to mean a widespread network of social relations in which each is at the same time patient and therapist concerned above all with his own and the other's range of emotional satisfactions and self-esteem as well as material, rational, and spiritual needs.[33] Novgorodtsev made no such explicit claim in his theory, but it is implicit in the Schleiermacherian-Schillerian-Goethean romantic person, so much wider and deeper in content than the rational man of Kant or the economic man of Bentham, whose needs modern political orders had to satisfy. It is safe to say that this conception of the rights of persons would be imcomprehensible to the large majority of early-twentieth-century Russian liberals outside academic and artistic circles.

Novgorodtsev could make the plea for the romantic person because of the tentativeness of his secular commitments. He did not want to eradicate the incompatibilities in his concepts of the person and related social thought. He reveled in tension, sought no release, mistrusted all resolutions; more, he found them dangerous. An independent man, he felt safer navigating through the reefs and hidden islands of uncharted waters than in the calm and peace of a snug harbor. His refuge was Russian Orthodoxy, but that was more of an ultimate sanctuary, another world, than a place of retreat in the midst of the tumult of daily life in society. In pitting himself against the obstacles, the rebuffs, the destruction which life visited upon his ideals and goals, he felt himself a man, and feared that in a secular phalanstery he would be unmanned. He was admirable, but would find few followers and little leverage in the world.

Novgorodtsev asked the suffering millions to postpone gratification, cautioned that reversals of progressive gains were always probable, and expressed doubts about the capacity of human beings to live together in harmony. As progenitor of progressive change he offered the great *culture* which led from classical civilization and Christianity to the embodiment of respect for human dignity and the striving toward higher ideals of truth, beauty, and goodness. Over time humanism could bring the illiterate Russian millions to a point where their personhood would be activated and a lasting free state possible. But even that was problematical, for it always posed the threat of an elitist domination of the minds of the many. What men could find a satisfactory base for work in the world within the suspended multiple options of Novgorodtsev's personalism?

Only the disabused, the disenchanted, the wise in the ways of Ecclesiastes would answer Novgorodtsev's call—the sober, the manly, the hopeful, but pessimistic, the toiler in the vineyards not overwhelmed by enthusiasm. In Russia, with 80 percent of its population nearly illiterate peasants, its two or three greatest cities packed with several million workers leading almost bestial lives, there were precious few of these. They were to be found among the very thin stratum of business men, progressive landlords, enlightened bureaucrats, doctors, lawyers, and professors. But few of them were active politically and those that were found it exceedingly difficult to move the weight of liberal and socialist parties, much less the stubbornly anarchistic mass.

The Bolsheviks drove Novgorodtsev in 1920 and Bulgakov in 1923 from Russia. Bulgakov had become a priest in 1918, beginning a career which made him before his death in 1944 a beloved man to Orthodox Christians and a theologian of world-wide reputation. In 1924 he joined the Russian Faculty of Law which Novgorodtsev had established at Prague University. Directly after the Bolshevik seizure of power, Novgorodtsev's strong religious convictions rose to the surface and dominated his thought. While offering the religious faith and relation toward the world of the Russian peasant as a standard for the Christian person, he sharply attacked the Western thought and culture which played such an important part in his prerevolutionary life. He seemed at last to have made his choice, but as time went by, seemed to move back toward his former complexity of thought and feeling. He died of heart disease in 1924.[34] Speaking over his grave, Bulgakov addressed him as "My father, my brother, my son."

NOTES

NOTES FOR CHAPTER I

1. For a representative selection from his writings, see James M. Edie, James P. Scanlan, Mary-Barbara Zeldin, and George L. Kline, eds., *Russian Philosophy* (Chicago: Quadrangle, 1965), vol. 3, pp. 352–89. See also Samuel H. Baron, *Plekhanov, The Father of Russian Marxism* (Stanford, Calif.: Stanford Univ. Press, 1966), pp. 145–46, 289–95.

2. The term is Mach's. See A.V. Lunacharskii, "Osnovnye idei empirio-krititsizma," *Obrazovanie*, 12, No. 2(1903), pp. 113–50; and V.A. Bazarov, "Avtoritarnaia metafizika i avtonomaia lichnost'," in *Ocherki realisticheskago mirovozzreniia, sbornik statei* (St. Petersburg: Motvid, 1904), pp. 186–261.

3. *Materializm i Empiriokrititsizm* (1908; reprint ed., Moscow: Izd. politicheskoi literatury, 1967).

4. *Problemy Idealizma*, ed. P.I. Novgorodtsev (Moscow: Izd. Moskovskago Psikhologicheskago Obshchestva, 1902).

5. See Struve's "Predislovie" to N. Berdiaev's *Subektivizm i individualizm v obshchestvennoi filosofii* (St. Petersburg: O.N. Popov, 1901), pp. I-LXXXIV. See also, Struve, "K kharakteristike nashego filosofskago razvitiia," *Problemy Idealizma*, pp. 315–38.

6. Actually, William von Humboldt had undertaken as early as 1791 Novgorodtsev's effort to "combine Kantian ethics and Idealist epistemology with political liberalism." See Humboldt, *The Limits of State Action*, trans., ed., and with introd. by J.W. Burrow, (1854; reprint ed., Cambridge: The Univ. Press, 1969).

7. Lamennais published in 1834 the very much read *Paroles d'un croyant*, which stimulated consideration of the connections between religion and socialism. Buchez, who founded Roman Catholic Christian socialism, based much of his thought on Saint Simon's *Nouveau Christianisme* (1825). See

177

F.M.H. Markham, ed. and trans., *Henri Comte de Saint-Simon, Selected Writings* (Oxford: Basil Blackwell, 1952), pp. 81–116. Kingsley's novel, *Alton Locke* (London, 1850), had the greatest impact. On the great influence of Morris and Ruskin, on the Continent as well as in England, see Donald Drew Egbert, *Social Radicalism and the Arts/Western Europe* (New York: Knopf, 1970), throughout.

8. On Ketteler, see Walter Schütze, "Die Idee der sozialen Gerechtigheit im neu-Kantischen und Christlich-sozialen Schrifttum in der zweiten Hälfte des 19 Jahrhunderts," Ph. D. diss, Univ. of Leipzig, 1938. Naumann's ideas are outlined in Hans Kohn's *The Mind of Modern Germany* (New York: Harper, 1960), pp. 277–89.

9. See Wolfgang Deresch, *Der Glaube der religiösen Sozialisten, ausgewählte text* (Hamburg: Furche-Verlag, 1972).

10. G.V. Florovskii, *Puti russkago bogosloviia* (Paris: YMCA Press, 1937); G.P. Fedotov, "The Church and Social Justice," *Cross Currents*, 14, No. 4(1964), pp. 424–27; G.V. Florovskii, "Empire and Desert: Antinomies of Christian History," *Cross Currents*, 9, No. 3(1959), pp. 233–53.

11. V.V. Zenkovskii, *Russian Thinkers and Europe*, trans. Galia S. Bodde (Ann Arbor: American Council of Learned Societies, 1953).

12. The slogan originated by Count S. S. Uvarov in 1832. Czar Nicholas I and the court believed that Russian education should show the interconnections and truly Russian nature of these three principles.

13. A group of friends led by M.V. Butashevich-Petrashevsky, who engaged in literary receptions at which the ideas of Fourier and other socialists were discussed. Dostoevsky attended and spoke at some meetings and was arrested along with others on April 22, 1849. He was sentenced to four years at hard labor to be followed by six years of army service in Siberia. See K. Mochulsky, *Dostoevsky: His Life and Work*, trans. Michael A. Minihan (Princeton: Princeton Univ. Press, 1971), pp. 114–54.

14. See below, p. 51–53.

15. See his *A Journey from St. Petersburg to Moscow*, trans. L. Wiener, ed. R.P. Thaler (Cambridge, Mass: Harvard Univ. Press, 1958).

16. See his *From the Other Shore*, trans. Moura Budberg (London: Weidenfeld and Nicholson, 1956).

17. P.I. Novgorodtsev, *Boris Nik. Chicherin* (Moscow: Moscow Univ., 1905); on Chicherin's philosophy, see N. O. Lossky, *History of Russian Philosophy* (New York: International Universities Press, 1951), pp. 134–43. On his liberalism, see L.B. Schapiro, *Rationalism and Nationalism in Russian Nineteenth Century Political Thought* (New Haven: Yale Univ. Press, 1967), pp. 89–101.

18. V.E. Evgrafov et al., *Istoriia filosofii v SSSR* (Moscow: "Nauka," 1971), vol. 4, chs. 2–5.

19. Peter L. Berger and Thomas Luckmann, *The Social Construction of Reality* (Garden City, N.Y.: Doubleday, 1966), pp. 5–7.

20. See V. Evgen'ev-Maksimov and D. Maksimov, *Iz proshlogo russkoi zhurnalistiki* (Leningrad: Izd. pisatelei v Leningrade, 1930), pp. 141–48. See also *Rech'*, 16 Jan. 1909, p. 5, for a report attacking speakers at the

Religious-Philosophical Society for being the "spokesmen of the trading-manufacturing class." For similar comments by Potresov, see pp. 46–47.

21. The weakness of Mannheim's claim has been demonstrated by many writers. See A.H. Child, "The Problem of Truth in the Sociology of Knowledge," *Ethics*, 58(1947), pp. 18–34. Child published several articles in *Ethics* and elsewhere which examine Mannheim's position exhaustively and leave little of it standing. In his customary calm and incisive manner, John Plamenatz subjects the position of Mannheim and others to critical analysis in *Ideology* (London: Macmillan, 1971). James E. Curtis and John W. Petras have edited a good collection of essays in *The Sociology of Knowledge* (New York: Praeger, 1970).

22. John Ruskin is an outstanding example of this. See John D. Rosenberg, ed., *The Genius of John Ruskin* (New York: G. Braziller, 1963), pp. 139–217, "The Stones of Venice" and pp. 229–72, "Unto This Last." Cf. S.N. Bulgakov, "Sotsial'noe mirovozzrenie Dzh. Reskina," *VFP*, 20, No. 5/100(1909), pp. 395–436.

23. See K. Mannheim, *Ideology and Utopia* (New York: Harcourt, 1936), pp. 153–64, and *Essays on the Sociology of Culture* (London: Routledge and Kegan Paul, 1956), pp. 91–170.

24. J. Piaget, *Six Psychological Studies*, trans. A. Tenzer, ed. D. Elkind (New York: Vintage Books/Random House, 1968), contains a bibliography of Piaget's major works; B. Bernstein, *Class, Codes and Control*, 2d rev. ed. (London: Routledge and Kegan Paul, 1974); M. Douglas, *Natural Symbols* (London: Barrie and Rockliff, 1970); M. Mathiot, *An Approach to the Cognitive Study of Language* (Bloomington: Indiana Univ. Press, 1968); P. Friedrich, "Semantic Structure and Social Structure," in *Explorations in Cultural Anthropology*, ed. Ward H. Goodenough (New York: McGraw-Hill, 1964), pp. 131–65; also, "Structural Implications of Russian Pronomial Usage," in *Sociolinguistics*, ed. W. Bright (The Hague: Mouton, 1966), pp. 214–59; E. Gellner, *Thought and Change* (Chicago: Univ. of Chicago Press, 1965).

25. A good effort to be "fair" about this is in John Lewis's "Idealism and Ideologies," in *Marxism and the Open Mind* (London: Routledge and Kegan Paul, 1957), pp. 1–23; L. Kolakowski demonstrates well the close similarity between ancient and enduring religious and philosophical questions and positions and those much alive in contemporary Marxist circles in "The Priest and the Jester," in *Toward a Marxist Humanism* (New York: Grove Press, 1969), ch. 1, pp. 9–37.

26. *From the Other Shore*, p. 120. No one expressed this point of view better than Blaise Pascal in his *Pensées*, trans. W.F. Trotter (London: J.M. Dent, 1954), pp. 14–70.

27. See Arnold Brecht, *Political Theory*, 2d paperback ed. (Princeton: Princeton Univ. Press, 1969), pp. 466–79.

28. H. Heine, *Religion and Philosophy in Germany* (1882; reprint ed., Boston: Beacon Press, 1959); G. Santayana, *The German Mind* (New York: Crowell, 1968); M. Malia, *Alexander Herzen and the Birth of Russian Socialism, 1812–1855* (Cambridge, Mass.: Harvard Univ. Press, 1961), pp. 69–98.

29. See S. Pepper, *World Hypotheses* (Berkeley: Univ. of California Press, 1966).

30. See M. Scheler, *Die Wissensformen und die Gesellschaft. Gesammelte Werke*, ed. Maria Scheler (Bern: Francke, 1960), vol. 8, p. 81, for a view that links theology and positivism as coming together in their opposition to metaphysics (idealism).

NOTES FOR CHAPTER II

1. There are several reliable works on the rise of Russian Social Democracy. Especially good is J.L.H. Keep, *The Rise of Social Democracy in Russia* (London: Oxford Univ. Press, 1963). Useful on the relation of the party to the workers in the period are A. Wildman, *The Making of a Workers' Revolution* (Chicago: Univ. of Chicago Press, 1967); and R. Pipes, *Social Democracy and the St. Petersburg Labor Movement* (Cambridge, Mass.: Harvard Univ. Press, 1963). The origins and program of the Social Revolutionary party are described in D. Treadgold, *Lenin and His Rivals* (London: Methuen, 1955) pp. 60–82, 138–53.

2. The organization and the development of the Liberation Movement is detailed in S. Galai, *The Liberation Movement in Russia* (Cambridge: The Univ. Press, 1973). It is also well treated in G. Fischer, *Russian Liberalism* (Cambridge, Mass.: Harvard Univ. Press, 1958).

3. Contributors to the collection of essays were S.N. Bulgakov, Kniaz' E.N. Trubetskoi, P.G. (Peter Struve), N.A. Berdiaev, S.K. Frank, S.A. Askol'dov, Kniaz' S.N. Trubetskoi, P.I. Novgorodtsev, B.A. Kistiakovskii, A.S. Lappo-Danilevskii, S.O. Oldenburg, and D.E. Zhukovskii. The main division was between S. Bulgakov, N. Berdiaev, S. Askol'dov, and E. and S. Trubetskoi, rather strongly oriented toward Christian religious solutions of philosophical and social-political problems, and such contributors as P. Struve, S. Frank, B.A. Kistiakovsky, and P. Novgorodtsev.

4. "Predislovie," *Problemy idealizma*, p. I; "Nravstvennyi idealizm v filosofii prava," in *PI*, pp. 236–37; "O filosofskom dvizhenii nashikh dnei," *NP*, No. 10(1904), pp. 59–67.

5. M.N. Ershov, *Puti razvitiia filosofii v Rossii* (Vladivostok: Izd. Gos. Dal'nevostochnago universiteta, 1922), p. 25. On Sept. 15, 1905, Novgorodtsev was hissed while lecturing at Moscow Univ. See V.O. Kliuchevskii, *Pis'ma, dnevniki, aforizmy i mysli ob istorii*, ed. M.V. Nechkina (Moscow: "Nauka," 1968), p. 293. A further indication of the negative attitude of radical youth to Novgorodtsev can be found in K.V. Ostrovitianov, *Dumy o proshlom* (Moscow: "Nauka," 1967), pp. 78, 93, 94, 185.

6. Kniaz' E.N. Trubetskoi, *Vospominaniia* (Sofia: Rossisko-bulgarskoe knigoizdatel'stvo, 1921), pp. 72–91. For a point of view which sees the positivism of the 1870–1880s as a form of idealism, see V.F. Asmus, "Bor'ba filosofskikh techenii v Moskovskikh universitetakh v 70-x godakh XIX veka," in *Izbrannye filosofskie trudy* (Moscow: Moscow Univ., 1969), vol. 1, pp. 238–66.

7. E.N. Trubetskoi, *Vospominaniia*; M. Ershov, *Puti*.

8. V.V. Zenkovskii, *A History of Russian Philosophy*, trans. George L. Kline (New York: Columbia Univ. Press, 1953), vol. 1, pp. 406–10, 453–65; vol. 2, pp. 606–20.

9. N.D. Vinogradov, "Kratkii istoricheskii ocherk deiatel'nosti Mosk. Psikh. Obshchestva za 25 let," *VFP*, 21, No. 3/103(1910), pp. 249–62.

10. "O filosofskom dvizhenii nashikh dnei," *NP*, No. 10(1904), p. 65.

11. Examples of this could be multiplied indefinitely. See Novgorodtsev, "Kant, kak moralist'," *VFP*, 16, No. 1/76(1905), pp. 21–23; S. L. Frank, "O kriticheskom idealizme," *Mir Bozhii*, 13, No. 12(1904), p. 257.

12. Novgorodtsev, "Nravstvennaia problema v filosofii Kanta," *VFP*, 15, No. 2/72(1904), pp. 283–85; Frank, "O kriticheskom idealizme," pp. 226–27.

13. Frank, "O kriticheskom idealizme," pp. 261–63. Of course, anyone following Kant in ethics must place this principle at the base of his thought. Novgorodtsev emphasized, however, that the pursuit of happiness was a powerful force for good in the world.

14. *Pervaia Gosudarstvennaia Duma, alfavitnyi spisok i podrobniia biografii* (Moscow, 1906), p. 126.

15. N. Alekseev, "V burnye gody," *Novyi Zhurnal*, No. 52(1958), pp. 176–77; No. 54(1958), pp. 149–50. See also A.A. Kizevetter, *Na rubezhe dvukh stoletii* (Prague: "Orbis," 1929), pp. 305–307.

16. Mark Vishniak, *Dan proshlomu* (New York: Chekhov, 1954), p. 50.

17. V.R. Leikina-sbirskaia, *Intelligentsiia v rossii vo vtoroi polovine XIX veka* (Moscow: "Mysl'," 1971), pp. 261–62; Kizevetter, *Na rubezhe*, pp. 305–307.

18. Kniazhna Ol'ga Trubetskaia, *Kniaz' S.N. Trubetskoi* (New York: Chekhov, 1953), pp. 213–14. The Student Historical-Philosophical Society discussed in these pages was the forerunner of the "Moscow Religious-Philosophical Society in honor of Vl. Soloviev." See pp. 69–71; T. Riha, *A Russian European* (Notre Dame: Univ. of Notre Dame Press, 1969), p. 73.

19. N. Alekseev, "V burnye gody."

20. *Ibid*.

21. *The Logic of Liberty* (Chicago: Univ. of Chicago Press, 1951), especially ch. 7.

22. M. Mauss, "Une categorie de l'esprit humain, la notion de personne, celle de 'Moi'," in *Sociologie et Anthropologie* (Paris: Presses universitaires de France, 1960), p. 358.

23. Vladimir Solov'ev, *Opravdanie dobra. Polnoe Sobranie Sochinenii*, 2d ed., ed. and with notes by S.M. Solov'ev and E.L. Radlov (St. Petersburg: Prosveshchenie, 1911), vol. 8, pp. 273–79. See also Vladimir Lossky, *The Mystical Theology of the Eastern Church* (London: James Clark, 1968), pp. 53, 114–34.

24. "Moral i poznanie," *VFP*, 13, No. 4/64(1902), p. 837.

25. I. Kant (1793). A translation appears in Carl J. Friedrich, ed., *The Philosophy of Kant* (New York: Modern Library, 1949), pp. 356–411.

26. "Sushchestvo russkago pravoslavnago soznaniia," in *Pravoslavie i Kul'tura*, ed. V.V. Zenkovskii (Berlin: "Russkaia Kniga," 1923), p. 7.

27. Novgorodtsev, *Kant i Hegel v ikh ucheniiakh o prave i gosudarstve* (Moscow: Moscow Univ., 1901), p. 80.
28. Michael Polanyi, *The Tacit Dimension* (London: Routledge and Kegan Paul, 1967), pp. 3–25.
29. "Sushchestvo russkago pravoslavnago soznaniia," pp. 14–23.
30. *Kant i Hegel*, pp. 82–90, 110–11; "Moral i poznanie," pp. 826–28.
31. "Nravstvennaia problema v filosofii Kanta," pp. 305–10; "Moral i poznanie," p. 833; *Kant i Hegel*, pp. 161–63, 167, and throughout pt. 3. For an excellent discussion of this question, see W. Kaufmann, *Hegel, Reinterpretation, Texts and Commentary* (Garden City, N.Y.: Doubleday, 1965), pp. 44–58. On Schleiermacher, see below, pp. 138–39.
32. Kaufmann, *Hegel*, pp. 102–103.
33. *Kant i Hegel*, p. 212. As so often in his thought, Novgorodtsev cites Georg Simmel; in this case, *Einleitung in die Moralwissenschaft* (Berlin: Hertz [Besser], 1893), vol. 1, p. 183.
34. *Kant i Hegel*, pp. 149–50; R. Stammler, *Wirtschaft und Recht nach der materialistischen Geschichtsauffassung* (Leipzig: Veit, 1896), p. 185.
35. For a systematic presentation of the many meanings attributed to "natural law" see Erik Wolf, *Das Problem der Naturrechtslehre* (Karlsruhe: C.F. Müller, 1955). Arnold Brecht's review in *Natural Law Forum*, 3, No. 1(1958), pp. 192–98, reproduces Wolf's categories. See also Carl J. Friedrich, *The Philosophy of Law in Historical Perspective* (Chicago: Univ. of Chicago Press, 1969), throughout.
36. "Pravo i nravstvennost'," in *Sbornik po obshchestvenno-iuridicheskim naukam*, ed. Iu. S. Gambarov, No. 1, (St. Petersburg: O.N. Popov, 1899), p. 129.
37. *Kant i Hegel*, p. 147; "Uchenie Kanta o prave i gosudarstve," *VFP*, 12, No. 3/58(1901), pp. 353–54.
38. Novgorodtsev also discusses natural law in the following: "Pravo estestvennoe," *Entsiklopedicheskii Slovar'* (St. Petersburg: Brokgaus i Efron, 1898), vol. 48, pp. 885–90; "Moral i poznanie"; "Nravstvennyi idealizm v filosofii prava," in *Problemy idealizma*, pp. 236–96; see I. Kant, *The Metaphysical Elements of Justice*, trans. and ed. John Ladd (New York: Bobbs-Merrill, 1965). See also R. Stammler, *The Theory of Justice*, trans. I. Husik from the 1902 ed. (New York: Macmillan, 1925), ch. 3, "Just Law and Law of Nature," pp. 72–93; W. Windelband, "O printsipe morali," in *Preliudii*, trans. S. Frank from 2d German ed. (St. Petersburg: Zhukovskii, 1904), pp. 252–77; P. Natorp, *Sozialpädegogik* (Stuttgart: F. Frommann [E. Hauff], 1899). For a useful treatment of Natorp's social ideas, see Walter Schütze, "Die Idee der sozialen Gerechtigheit."
39. *Kant i Hegel*, p. 148; "Pravo i nravstvennost'," p. 118; See also, "Dva pravovykh ideala," *Nauchnoe Slovo*, 2, No. 10(1904), pp. 112–27. This is a very free translation of section 7, "Grundgesetz der reinen praktischen Vernunft." Kant, *Werke in Sechs Banden*, ed. Wilhelm Weischedel (Wiesbaden: Insel-Verlag, 1956), vol. 4, pp. 143–44.
40. On "rationalization," see R. Aron, *German Sociology* (Glencoe, Ill.: Free Press, 1957), pp. 105–106.

41. See below, pp. 143–50, 174–76.

42. R. Kindersley analyzes this well in his *The First Russian Revisionists* (Oxford: Clarendon, 1962). See also A. Mendel, *Dilemmas of Progress in Tsarist Russia* (Cambridge, Mass.: Harvard Univ. Press, 1961), pp. 213–26. The best single source for Bulgakov's critique of positivism is his "O realisticheskom mirovozzrenii (Neskol 'ko slov po pov. vykhoda v svete sbornika "Och. realis. mirov.")," *VFP*, 15, No. 3/73(1904), pp. 380–403.

43. S. Bulgakov, *Avtobiograficheskiia zametki* (Paris: YMCA Press, 1946), p. 16.

44. *Kapitalizm i zemledelie*, 2 vols. (St. Petersburg: V.A. Tikhanov, 1900). See also his *O rynkakh pri kapitalisticheskom proizvodstve* (Moscow: M. I. Vodovozov, 1897).

45. See the introduction to his *Ot marksizma k idealizmu* (1904; reprint ed., Ann Arbor: University Microfilms, 1965).

46. "Voprosy filosofii i psikhologii v 1904 godu," *VZh*, No. 2(1905), p. 304.

47. L.Z. Slonimskii, "Noveishie idealisty," *Vestnik Evropy*, 38, No. 5(1903), pp. 313–24; N.A. Rozhkov, "Znachenie i sud'by noveishago idealizma v rossii," *VFP*, 14, No. 2/67 (1903), pp. 326–27. See also V.A. Bazarov, "Mistitsizm i realizm nashego vremeni," in *Ocherki po filosofii marksizma* (St. Petersburg: V. Bezobrazov, 1908), pp. 3–71, and "Sud'by russkago 'idealizma' za poslednee desiatiletie," in *Iz istorii noveishei russkoi literatury* (Moscow: "Zerno," 1910), pp. 151–95.

48. "Ortodoks," (Akselrod, Liubov'), "O 'Problemakh idealizma'," in *Protiv idealizma* (Moscow, 1922), pp. 13–31; *ibid.*, p. 27.

49. Aleksandr N. Potresov, "Evoliutsiia obshch.-politicheskoi mysli v predrevoliutsionniiu epokhu," in *Obshchestvennoe dvizhenie v Rossii v nachale XX-go veka*, ed. L. Martov *et al.* (St. Petersburg: "Obshchestvennaia pol'za," 1909), pp. 594–97.

50. "Bez plana," *VZh*, No. 3(1905), pp. 388–93; Bulgakov, "Chto daet sovremennomu soznaniiu filosofiia Vladimira Solov'eva?" *VFP*, 14, No. 1/66(1903), pp. 52–96; 2/67(1903), pp. 125–26, in *Ot marksizma*, pp. 198–241.

51. "Osnovnyia problemy teorii progressa," in *Problemy idealizma* (1902), pp. 1–47, in *Ot marksizma*, pp. 114–17, 121, 128–29.

52. *Ibid.*, p. 131.

53. P.A. Florenskii, "O simvolakh beskonechnosti, ocherki idei G. Kantora," *NP*, No. 9(1904), pp. 173–235. See also, Florenskii, "O tipakh vozrastaniia," *Bogoslovskii Vestnik*, 15, No. 7(1906), pp. 530–68. For a brief explanation of the ideas of Cantor which Florensky tried to use for religious ends, see E.T. Bell, *Men of Mathematics* (Harmondsworth, England: Penguin, 1965), vol. 2, pp. 612–40.

54. Florenskii, "O simvolakh," p. 175.

55. *Ibid.*, p. 178.

56. *Ibid.*, p. 179.

57. Bulgakov, "Osnovnyia problemy," pp. 132–36.

58. F. Nietzsche, *Von Nutzen und Nachteil der Historie für das Leben* (Basel: Verlag Birkhause, n.d.), pp. 8–11.

59. Bulgakov, "Osnovnyia problemy," p. 136.
60. Quoted in Philip Merlan, *Monopsychism, Mysticism, Metaconsciousness* (The Hague: Martinus Nijhoff, 1963), p. 116, n. 4.
61. *Ibid.*
62. Other ex-Marxists and Novgorodtsev feared the theocratic tendencies in Soloviev's thought. See P. Struve, "Pamiati Vladimira Solov'eva," in *Na raznyia temy* (St. Petersburg: A.E. Kolpinski, 1902), pp. 197–202; S.L. Frank, "O kriticheskom idealizme," p. 245; N.A. Berdiaev, "O novom russkom idealizme," *VFP*, 15, No. 5/75(1904), pp. 683–724, in *Sub specie aeternitatis* (St. Petersburg: M.V. Pirozhkov, 1907), p. 171; P.I. Novgorodtsev, "Ideia prava v filosofii V.S. Solov'eva," *VFP*, 12, No. 1/56(1901), pp. 112–19.
63. Bulgakov expressed the following basic principles of Soloviev's philosophy in his "Chto daet sovremennomu soznaniiu filosofiia Vladimira Solov'eva?"
64. "Bez plana," *VZh*, No. 3(1905), p. 401.
65. N.V. Valentinov, *Vstrechi s Leninym* (New York: Chekhov, 1953), pp. 216–35.
66. "Any attempt to speak without speaking any particular language is not more hopeless than the attempt to have a religion that shall be no religion in particular. . . ." George Santayana, quoted in Clifford Geertz, "Religion As a Cultural System," in *Anthropological Approaches to the Study of Religion*, ed. M. Banton (London: Tavistock, 1969), p. 1.
67. See below, pp. 61–62.
68. See below, pp. 70, 78–79.

NOTES FOR CHAPTER III

1. See S. Harcave, *The Russian Revolution of 1905* (London: Collier, 1970); L. Haimson, "The Problem of Social Stability in Urban Russia, 1905–1917(Part Two)," *Slavic Review*, 24, No. 1(1965), pp. 1–21.
2. *Vekhi*, 4th ed. with appended biblio. on "Vekhi" (Moscow: N. Kushnerev, 1909).
3. P.P. Pertsov, *Literaturnye vospominaniia, 1890–1902gg.* (Moscow–St. Petersburg: "Akademiia," 1933), pp. 272–308; T. Pachmuss, *Zinaida Hippius, An Intellectual Profile* (Carbondale and Edwardsville: Southern Illinois Univ. Press, 1971), pp. 7–9; and the same writer's "Zinaida Hippius, Epokha Mira Iskusstva," *Vozrozhdenie*, No. 203(1968), pp. 66–73. This and other articles published by Pachmuss in the past five years in *Vozrozhdenie* are excellent guides to the Merezhkovsky-Hippius world of the early twentieth century.
4. Mark Etkind, *A.N. Benua, 1870–1960* (Leningrad-Moscow: "Iskusstvo," 1965), p. 55; I.E. Grabar', *Moia zhizn'* (Moscow-Leningrad, 1937), p. 280.
5. *Literaturnyi dnevnik: 1899–1907* (St. Petersburg: M.V. Pirozhkov, 1908), pp. 36–38.
6. V.A. Maevskii, *Vnutreniaia missiia i ee osnovopolozhnik* (Buenos

Aires: 1954), pp. 104–18. See also Hippius, *Dmitrii Merezhkovskii* (Paris: YMCA Press, 1951), pp. 86–90; and Sergei Makovskii, *Na parnase "Serebriannogo veka"* (Munich: Izd. Tsentral'nogo Obedineniia Politicheskikh Emigrantov iz SSSR, 1962), pp. 25–33.

7. *Valerii Briusov v avtobiograficheskikh zapisiakh, pis'makh, vospominaniiakh sovremennikov i otzyvakh kritiki*, comp. N. Ashukin (Moscow: "Federatsiia," 1929), pp. 157–61.

8. For the details of the founding and operation of *Novyi Put'*, see V. Evgen'ev-Maksimov and D. Maksimov, *Iz proshlogo russkoi zhurnalistiki* (Leningrad: Izd. pisatelei v Leningrade, 1930), pp. 131–254.

9. See George F. Putnam, "Vasilii V. Rozanov: Sex, Marriage and Christianity," *Canadian Slavic Studies*, 5, No. 3(1971), pp. 301–26.

10. See Karl Löwith, *Meaning in History* (Chicago: Univ. of Chicago Press, 1949), pp. 145–59. F. Schelling (1775–1854) expressed the idea in a form close to that of Merezhkovsky. See F. Copleston, S.J., *A History of Philosophy* (Garden City, N.Y.: Doubleday, 1965), vol. 7, pt. 1, p. 175. For a more detailed discussion, see Xavier Tilliette, *Schelling, Une Philosophie en Devenir* (Paris: Libraire Philosophique J. Vrin, 1970), vol. 2, pp. 435–88, especially pp. 459–69. Merezhkovsky developed this scheme before 1905 in the following: "Predislovie," *L. Tolstoi i Dostoevskii* in *Polnoe sobranie sochinenii* (Moscow: Sytin, 1914), vol. 11; *The Death of the Gods*, trans. B.G. Guerney (New York: Modern Library, 1929); *The Romance of Leonardo da Vinci*, trans. H. Trent (New York: Washington Square Press, 1963); "Zapiski religiozno-filosofskago sobraniia," Meeting 3, p. 175, *NP*, No. 2(1903); 10, pp. 226–27, *NP*, No. 5(1903); 17, pp. 426–27, *NP*, No. 11 (1903); 18, pp. 470–72, *Ibid*. See also his "Novyi Vavilon," *NP*, No. 3(1904), p. 174.

The convenient outline presented here comes from Merezhkovsky's "O Tserkvi griadushchago," in *Zapiski S-Petersburgskago religiozno-filosofskago obshchestva*, vol. 2 (St. Petersburg: Herol'd, 1908), pp. 1–4.

11. "Otzyv o. Ioann Kronshtadskago o 'Novom Puti'," *NP*, No. 3(1903), p. 253.

12. *Russkii Vestnik, Khristianskoe Chtenie* and, most fully, *Missionerskoe Obozrenie*, carried excerpts from the religious-philosophical meetings and *Novyi Put'*, and much critical comment, 1903–1904. A good summary of the "official" church's position on several issues discussed at the meetings in St. Petersburg is in *Voprosy Zhizni* (St. Petersburg: Sv. Synod, 1904). Statements on major issues by important churchmen, such as Archimandrite Serge, Bishop Serge, Bishop Anthony, and the Synodal official V.M. Skvortsov may be consulted in the notes of the religious-philosophical meetings published as supplements to *Novyi Put'* in 1903–1904; Meeting 1, pp. 1–5, 26–27, 31–33, *NP*, No. 1(1903); 2, p. 43, *ibid*.; 3, pp. 77–78; 7, pp. 137–39, 146–48, *NP*, No. 3(1903); 8, pp. 159–64, 169, *NP*, No. 4(1903); 9, pp. 178–85, 194–95, *ibid*.; 10, p. 238; 15, p. 362, *NP*, No. 9(1903); 17, p. 427; 19, pp. 526–27, *NP*, No. 12(1903). See also P.P. Kudriavtsev, "K voprosu ob otnoshenii khristianstva k iazychestvu," *Trudy Kievskoi Dukhovnoi Akademii*, 44, No. 5(1903), pp. 30–78.

13. Romanskii (A.V.Kartashev), "Religiozno-filosofskaia khronika," *NP*, No. 7(1903), p. 266.

14. Romanskii (A.V. Kartashev), "Otklikaiutsia," *NP*, No. 1 (1904), p. 268. See also "Religiozno-filosofskaia khronika," *NP*, No. 5(1903), pp. 202–10.

15. Kudriavtsev, "K voprosu": "ZRFS(11)," p. 237, *NP*, No. 6(1903); F.S. Ornatskii, "Po povodu novago zhurnala, 'Novyi Put'," " *Trudy Kievskoi Dukhovnoi Akademii*, 44, No. 3(1903), pp. 450–52.

16. S. Bulgakov, "O. Aleksandr El'chaninov, stat'ia iz zhurnala 'Put'," " in *Pamiati ottsa Aleksandra El'chaninova* (Paris: YMCA Press, 1935), p. 62.

17. N. Berdiaev, "Religiozno-filosofskoe obshchestvo pamiati V. Solov'eva," *Vek*, No. 22(1907), pp. 342–43.

18. E. (A. El'chaninov), "Religiozno-filosofskoe obshchestvo pamiati Vl. S. Solov'eva v Moskve," *Vek*, No. 9(1907), pp. 107–108; quotations in the section are from this source. See also "Religiozno-obshchestvennaia zhizn'," *Vek*, No. 13(1907), p. 163.

19. "Religiozno-filosofskoe obshchestvo."

20. N.S. Arseniev, "O moskovskikh religiozno-filosofskikh i literaturnikh kruzhkakh i sobraniakh nachala XX veka," *Sovremennik*, No. 6(1962), pp. 30–42; "Iz iunosti (kartiny moskovskoi zhizni)," *Vozrozhdenie*, No. 18(1951), pp. 71–86; "Gody iunosti v Moskve," *Mosty*, vol. 7(1959), pp. 369–71.

21. See Father S. Chetverikov, "Khristianskoe Bratstvo Bor'by i ego programma pri svete Pravoslaviia," *Moskovskii Golos*, 22 Mar. 1907, pp. 5–8. For details of the cases of other priests silenced or arrested by the church for "revolutionary activity," see V.F. Ern, "Staroobriadtsy i sovremennye religioznie zaprosy," *Zhivaia Zhizn'*, No. 1 (1908), pp. 9–16; and *Pastyr novago tipa* (Moscow: Efimov, 1907). The latter discusses the actions and fate of Father Ion Brikhnichev of Tiflis.

22. El'chaninov, "Religiozno-filosofskoe obshchestvo."

23. V. Sventsitskii, *Religioznaia smysl' 'Branda' Ibsena*, (St. Petersburg: Otto Unfug, 1907), p. 6. V.F. Ern, *Sem' Svobod* (Moscow: Efimov, 1906).

24. M. Karpovich, "Iunosheskie gody ottsa Aleksandra (vospominaniia druga)," in *Pamiati ottsa Aleksandra El'chaninova* (Paris: YMCA Press, 1935), pp. 25–31.

25. During these years Florensky wrote his major work, *Stolp i utverzhdenie istiny*, 1 (Moscow: Vil'de, 1908); 2(Moscow: A.A. Chervrevoi, 1908); *Stolp i utverzhdenie istiny* (Moscow: "Put'," 1914).

26. *Pis'ma ko vsem* (Moscow: Poplavskii, 1907), p. 37.

27. See V. Murvar, "Messianism in Russia: Religious and Revolutionary," *Journal for the Scientific Study of Religion*, 10, No. 4(1971), pp. 277–338; Yonina Talmon, "Pursuit of the Millennium: The relation between religious and social change," *European Journal of Sociology*, 3, No. 2(1962), pp. 125–48; Anthony F. C. Wallace, "Revitalization movements," *American Anthropologist*, 58, No. 2(1956), pp. 264–81.

28. A complete description of the activities of the Brotherhood of Christian Struggle is in V. Sventsitskii, "Khristianskoe bratstvo bor'by" i ego

programma (Moscow: Poplavskii, 1906). The Brotherhood existed for four months, Feb.–May, 1906.

29. When Sventsitsky published "Otkrytoe pis'mo veruiushchago k Pravoslavnoi Tserkvi," in *Poliarnaia Zvezda*, 3 Feb. 1906, pp. 561–64, both he and the journal's editor, Peter Struve, were fined 100 rubles for "agitation against the state."

30. In addition to those written by the Brotherhood, this series included booklets on industrial workers' problems and on the activities of the "revolutionary priest," Father John Brikhnichev.

31. A large proportion of the writings of Ern and Sventsitsky refer negatively to private property. The following offer the fullest treatments: V. F. Ern, *Khristianskoe otnoshenie k sobstvennosti* (Moscow: Efimov, 1906), "Tserkovnoe vozrozhdenie," *Voprosy Religii*, No. 1(1906), pp. 127–32; V. Sventsitskii, *Chto nuzhno krest'ianinu?* (Moscow: Efimov, 1906), pp. 9–11; *Pis'ma ko vsem*, pp. 37–45.

32. Ern, "Tserkovnoe vozrozhdenie."

33. *Pis'ma ko vsem*, p. 40.

34. See above, pp. 36–37; Polanyi, *The Logic of Liberty*, ch. 7.

35. *Pis'ma ko vsem*, pp. 40–41.

36. *Ibid.*, pp. 43–44.

37. V. Ern, "O zhiznennoi pravde," *Voprosy Religii*, No. 2(1908), pp. 38–45, 48; *Kak nuzhno zhit' khristianinu?* (Moscow: Efimov, 1906): "Nasha vina," *Vek*, No. 3(1907), pp. 34–35.

38. V. Ern, "Tserkovnoe vozrozhdenie," p. 126; "O zhiznennoi pravde," pp. 60–61; "Khristos v revoliutsii," *Vek*, No. 7(1907), pp. 83–85; Sventsitskii, "Smert' i bessmertie," in *Svobodnaia Sovest'*, vol. 1 (Moscow: Sytin, 1906), pp. 34–67.

39. V. Ern, "O zhiznennoi pravde," p. 61; "Katakomby i sovremennost'," in F. Buass'e, *Katakomby* (Moscow: Efimov, 1907), p. 4; V. Sventsitskii and V.F. Ern, *Vzyskuiushchim Grada* (Moscow: Efimov, 1906), pp. 54–69; V. Sventsitskii, *Lev Tolstoi i Vladimir Solov'ev* (St. Petersburg: Otto Unfug, 1907), p. 5. Of course the Brotherhood devoted substantial effort to "exposing" the illogicalities and possible evil consequences of secular socialist thought. Ern, "Sotsializm i problema svobody," *Zhivaia Zhizn'*, No. 2(1907), pp. 40–87; "Sotsialism i obshchee mirovozzrenie," *Bogoslovskii Vestnik*, 16, No. 9(1907), pp. 35–60. "Plekhanov ob Ibsene," *Vek*, No. 11 (1907), pp. 133–35; V. Sventsitskii, *Pis'ma ko vsem*, pp. 49–66.

40. Sventsitskii and Ern, *Vzyskuiushchim Grada*, pp. 57–61; Sventsitskii, *Religioznaia smysl' 'Branda' Ibsena*, pp. 23–24; V. Ern, "O zhiznennoi pravde," p. 61; "Katakomby," p. 11.

41. See above ch. 3, n. 27. See also Mary Douglas, *Natural Symbols*, and Bryan Wilson, *Religious Sects* (London: Weidenfeld and Nicolson, 1970), pp. 48–65.

42. A. Kartashev, "Moi ranniia vstrechi s o. Sergiem," *Pravoslavnaia Mysl'*, No. 3(1951), pp. 47–55.

43. See also the violent attack on "liberals" by Metropolitan Antony (Khrapovitsky), "O strashnom sude i o sovremennykh sobytiiakh," 20 Feb.

1905; in Episkop Nikon (Rklitskii), *Zhizneopisanie Blazhenneishago Antoniia, Mitropolita Kievskago i Galitskago* (New York: Izd. Severo-Amerikanskoi i kanadskoi eparkhii, 1956), vol. 2, pp. 155–65.

44. "Religiozno-obshchestvennaia khronika," *Vek*, No. 8 (1907), p. 208; B. Kremnev, "Religiozno-filosofskoe sobranie v Peterburge," *Pereval*, Nos. 8–9(1907), pp. 93–94.

45. *Rech'*, No. 214, 11 Sept. 1907, p. 4.

46. *Rech'*, No. 235, 5 Oct. 1907, p. 4.

47. *Zapiski S. Peterburgskago religiozno-filosofskago obshchestva*, No. 1, pp. 1–3. (St. Petersburg, "Herol'd," 1908.)

48. *Ibid.*, p. 2.

49. The main source for this listing of meetings is *Rech'*, which carried reports on most meetings above the signature N. O. (perhaps N. Ognev, since Lossky, whose name was used in the founding of the society and whose initials were N. O., claimed that he played no active role in the society). See his *Vospominaniia* (Munich: Wilhelm Fink, 1968), p. 148.

50. See above, pp. 63–66.

51. "Khristianstvo i mir (otvet D.S. Merezhkovskomu)," *Zhivaia Zhizn'*, No. 1(1907), pp. 15–46. Ern and Sventsitsky expressed deep contempt for the ideas and attitudes of many of the literary figures and hangers-on involved in the religious-philosophical meetings in Moscow and St. Petersburg, but they respected Merezhkovsky.

52. "Khristianstvo i mir," p. 22.

53. *Ibid.*, pp. 32–38.

54. *Istoriia religii, Pravoslavie*, with appendix by Prof. S.N. Bulgakov (Moscow: "Pol'za," 1909); El'chaninov, ch. 1–4, 7; El'chaninov and Ern, ch. 5; El'chaninov and Florensky, ch. 6.

55. *Pravoslavie*, pp. 164–70.

56. See also, G.P. Fedotov, *The Russian Religious Mind* (New York: Harper, 1960), vol. 1, pp. 3–60.

57. V. O. Kliuchevskii, *Kurs russkoi istorii*, in *Sochineniia*, 2d ed. (1906; reprint ed., Moscow: Gosizdat. politicheskoi literatury, 1956), vol. 1, pt. 1, Lecture 4, pp. 61–73.

58. *Pravoslavie*, pp. 171–85.

59. Quoted in N.A. Berdiaev, "Religiozno-obshchestvennaia khronika," *VZh*, No. 2(1905), pp. 381–82.

60. "Tragicheskii zverinets," *Zhivaia Zhizn'*, No. 1(1908), pp. 17–24; *Pravoslavie*; *O samoupravlenie* (Moscow: Sytin, 1906); *Zhitie sv. Frantsiska Assizskago* (Moscow: Efimov, 1906).

61. *Pravoslavie*, pp. 187–88.

62. See Mary Douglas, *Natural Symbols*, pp. 1–18 and throughout; Clifford Geertz, "Religion As a Cultural System."

63. Sviashch. S. Shchukin, "Deistvitel'nost' i deistvennost'," *ME*, No. 8(1907), p. 18.

64. I have in mind here insights provided by Erik Erikson in *Identity and the Life Cycle* (New York: International Universities Press, 1959), pp. 55–65.

NOTES FOR CHAPTER IV

1. From the beginning, the Godseeking poets viewed with alarm the introduction of the "pedantic" professor into their midst. See D. V. Filosofov, "Propoved' idealizma, (Sbornik 'Problemy idealizma,' Moscow, 1903)," *NP*, No. 10(1903), p. 182; Letter of Briusov to Pertsov, Jan. 4, 1903, published in "V. Briusov i Novyi Put'," *Literaturnoe nasledstvo* (Moscow, 1937), vols. 27–28, p. 291; A. Belyi, "Idealisty i 'Novyi Put','" *Vesy*, No. 11(1904), pp. 66–67; Georgii Chulkov, *Gody stranstvii* (Moscow: "Federatsiia," 1930), p. 59.

2. "Bez plana," *VZh*, No. 2(1905), pp. 347–48. See also, "Filosofiia kn. S.N. Trubetskago i dukhovnaia bor'ba sovremennosti," *Kriticheskoe Obozrenie*, No. 1(1909), pp. 8–12; also published in *Dva grada*, 2 vols. (Moscow: "Put'," 1911), vol. 2, pp. 255–59.

3. "Bez plana," *VZh*, No. 2(1905), pp. 348–51; No. 3(1905), pp. 400–401; "Venets ternovyi," *Svoboda i Kul'tura*, 1 Apr. 1906, pp. 32–33, in *Dva grada*, vol. 2, pp. 223–43.

4. "Tserkov' i kul'tura," *Dva grada*, vol. 2, pp. 311–12, originally published in *Voprosy Religii*, No. 1(1906), pp. 38–52; "Chekhov, kak myslitel'," *NP*, No. 10(1904), pp. 35–38; "Bez plana," *VZh*, No. 6(1905), p. 293.

5. "Bez plana," *VZh*, No. 6(1905), p. 317; "Kn. S. N. Trubetskoi, kak religioznyi myslitel'," *ME*, No. 14 (1908), pp. 11–13.

6. See above, pp. 76–78.

7. "Paskhal'nye dumy," *Narod*, No. 1(1906), p. 1.

8. "Pis'mo intelligenta," No. 7(1906), p. 2.

9. Thinking that they might be arrested for revolutionary activity, Merezhkovsky and his associates had fled to the West during the Revolution of 1905.

10. *Rech'*, 17 July 1908, p. 3. See Merezhkovskii, Hippius, Filosofov, *Le Tsar et la Révolution* (Paris: Mercure de France, 1907), especially pp. 129–30. Articles exhibiting the ideas of the "revolutionary" Merezhkovsky in the period 1905–1907 are published in vols. 13 and 14 of his *Polnoe sobranie sochinenii* (Moscow: Sytin, 1914). I should like to acknowledge the kindness of B.A. Pyman (then married and living in the USSR) for allowing me to microfilm and use her Ph.D. diss., "The Russian Decadents, 1890–1905, with special reference to D.S. Merezhkovsky," Cambridge Univ. 3516, 1959.

11. "Intelligentsiia i religiia," *Rech'*, 29 Oct. 1908, p. 2.

12. *Rech'*, 3 Feb. 1909, p. 5.

13. *Ibid.*

14. *Rech'*, 18 Apr. 1909; 2 Feb. 1910, p. 4.

15. This list has been compiled largely from reports in *Rech'*. However, in some cases where reports did not appear in *Rech'*, they were found elsewhere, i.e.: *Novaia Rus'*, 3 Jan. 1909, p. 4 for the Dec. 30 meeting; *Nasha Gazeta*, 1 Jan. 1909, pp. 4–5. For Chukovsky's report, see *Nasha Gazeta*, 3 Jan. 1909, p. 4; On Ivanovich's report, see *Nasha Gazeta*, 16 Jan. 1909, p. 4; on Filosofov's report, see *Nasha Gazeta*, 22 Jan. 1909, p. 4.

16. *Rech'*, 31 Apr. 1908, p. 7, and other reports in 1909.

17. On Blok's participation, see George F. Putnam's "Aleksandr Blok and the Russian Intelligentsia," *Slavic and East European Journal*, 9, No. 1 (1965), pp. 29-46.

18. See A.V. Lunacharskii, *Religiia i sotsializm*, 2 vols. (St. Petersburg: Shipovnik, 1908, 1911), especially vol. 1, pp. 36-49, and vol. 2, pp. 244-59, 321-47. Bazarov's views were published in "Bogoiskatel'stvo i bogostroitel'stvo," in *Vershiny* (St. Petersburg: "Obshchestvennaia pol'za," 1909), pp. 332-65; see also *Rech'*, 11 Jan. 1909, p. 6. I. K. "Nebesnyi revizionizm," *ME*, No. 27(1908), pp. 23-29. See also M. Gorkii, "Ispoved'," in *Sbornik "Znanie" za 1908 god* (St. Petersburg: "Znanie," 1908), pp. 1-206, especially pp. 154-57, 171-74, 200-206.

19. "Pis'mo v redaktsiiu," *Rech'*, 24 Jan. 1907, p. 4. See also "Neobkhodimoe raziasnenie," *Vek*, No. 5(1907), pp. 58-59. Bulgakov served on the Kadet committee on church reform, along with P. I. Novgorodtsev, Kn. P. Dolgorukov, and several priests. See *Nov'*, 29 Dec. 1906, p. 2. In 1905, Bulgakov supported the program of the left wing of the Kadet party, but also demanded the elimination of capitalism in industry and agriculture. See "Bez plana," *NP*, No. 11(1904), pp. 348-60, and "Neotlozhnaia zadacha (O soiuze khristianskoi politiki)," *VZh*, No. 9 (1905), pp. 340-49.

20. "Religiia i politika," *Poliarnaia Zvezda*, 12 Mar. 1906, p. 121.

21. "Srednevekovyi ideal i noveishaia kul'tura," in *Dva grada*, vol. 1, pp. 150-77; originally *RM*, 28, No. 1(1907), pp. 61-83.

22. "Tserkov' i kul'tura," in *Dva grada*, vol. 2, pp. 303-307; "Dushevnaia drama Gertsena," *VFP*, 13, No. 4/64(1902), pp. 1248-75; 13, No. 5/65(1902), pp. 1363-78; in *Ot marksizma*, pp. 191-92.

23. Neotlozhnaia zadacha," pp. 352-54; " 'Tragediia chelovechestva,' Emerikha Madacha," *VZh*, No. 2(1905), pp. 213-20.

24. N. Ezerskii, "Religiia i politika," *RM*, 28, No. 1(1907), pp. 106-26; Sviashch. S. Shchukin, "Deistvitel'nost' i deistvennost'," *ME*, No. 8(1907), pp. 15-29; N. Ezerskii, "Otkrytoe pis'mo k ottsu S. Shchukinu," *ME*, No. 13(1907), pp. 30-35; Shchukin, "Po povodu 'pis'ma s drugago berega' (otkrytoe pis'mo k N. Ezerskomu)," *ME*, No. 14(1907), pp. 25-30; N. Ezerskii, "Vtoroe pis'mo ottsu S. Shchukinu," *ME*, Nos. 24-25 (1907), pp. 28-35.

See also S. Lur'e, "Sektantstvo i partiinost'," *ME*, No. 30(1906), pp. 28-36; Lur'e, "Religioznaia mistika i filosofiia," *RM*, 29, No. 4(1908), pp. 41-56; Lur'e, "Religioznye iskaniia v sovremennoi literature," *RM*, 29, No. 10(1908), pp. 44-67; E. Trubetskoi, "Dva slova po povodu polemiki S. Lur'e i S.N. Bulgakova," *ME*, No. 30(1906), pp. 37-39; E. Trubetskoi, "Tserkov' i sovremennoe obshchestvennoe dvizhenie," *Pravo*, No. 15(1905), pp. 1169-75.

25. "Religiia i politika."

26. *Ibid.*

27. *Poliarnaia Zvezda*, 3 Feb. 1906, p. 561.

28. "Neskol'ko slov po povodu stat'i S.N. Bulgakova," *Poliarnaia Zvezda*, 12 Mar. 1906, pp. 128-30.

29. *Ibid.*

30. *Rech'*, Mar. 1909, p. 6; P. Struve, "Religiia i sotsializm," *RM*, 30, No. 8(1909), pp. 148–56; see also Struve, "Na raznyia temy," *RM*, 29, No. 2(1908), pp. 177–79; Struve, "Otryvki o gosudarstve i natsii," *RM*, 29, No. 5(1908), pp. 192–93; Struve, "Lev Tolstoi," *RM*, 29, No. 8(1908), pp. 218–30; Struve, "Na raznyia temy," *RM*, 30, No. 1(1909), pp. 208–10; Struve, "Na raznyia temy," *RM*, 31, No. 2(1910), pp. 182–83; Struve, "Pochemu zastoialas' nasha dukhovnaia zhizn'?" *RM*, 35, No. 3(1914), p. 118; and Struve, "Religiia i obshchestvennost', otvet Z.N. Hippius," *RM*, 35, No. 5(1914), pp. 134–40.

31. Bulgakov, "Religiozno-obshchestvennaia khronika, politicheskoe osvobozhdenie i tserkovnaia reforma," *VZh*, Nos. 4–5(1905), pp. 517–21; Bulgakov, "Religiia chelovekobozhiia v russkoi revoliutsii," in *Dva grada*, vol. 2, pp. 129–31, 135, 156–57, originally published in *RM*, 29, No. 3(1908), pp. 72–103. J.T. Merz, in *A History of European Thought in the Nineteenth Century* (New York: Dover, 1965), vol. 3, p. 561, calls Büchner's *Force and Matter* the "gospel of materialism."

32. See ch. 4, n. 23.

33. Bulgakov, "Tserkov' i kul'tura," in *Dva grada*, vol. 2, p. 305; Bulgakov "Religiia chelovekobozhiia u L. Feierbakha," *VZh*, Nos. 10–11(1905), pp. 236–73, and No. 12(1905), pp. 74–102; Bulgakov, "Religiia i politika," p. 122; Bulgakov, "Karl Marks, kak religioznyi tip," *ME*, No. 22(1906), pp. 34–43; No. 23(1906), pp. 24–33; No. 24(1906), pp. 42–50; No. 25(1906), pp. 46–54; in *Dva grada*, vol. 1, pp. 69–105.

34. Bulgakov's *Narod* lasted but ten days, and its "official" editor, Lashniukov, was jailed. In it appeared what was perhaps Vasilii Zenkovsky's first published article, "Predchuvstviia marksizma," No. 1(1906), pp. 2–3, praising Marx's "scientific" discoveries and concern for the poor. It was enough to end the life of the newspaper.

Bulgakov was also a founder of the Kiev Religious-Philosophical Society. Information on this is contained in V. V. Zenkovsky's "Memoirs, 1900–1920," which are held at the Russian and East European Archive, Columbia Univ. Library, New York. Important members were P.P. Kudriavtsev, V.I. Ekzempliarskii, I.P. Chetvernikov, and V.Z. Zavitnevich.

35. "Bez plana," *VZh*, No. 3(1905), pp. 393, 401–13; Nos. 4–5(1905), pp. 492–94, 496, 508. *Tovarishch*, 6 Dec. 1906, pp. 1–2; Bulgakov, "Tserkovnyi vopros v Gosudarstvennoi Dume," *Vek*, No. 10(1907), pp. 119–20.

36. "Na vyborakh (iz dnevnika)," *RM*, 33, No. 11(1912), pp. 185–92; the quotation, p. 187.

37. "Na vyborakh"; Bulgakov, "Chemu uchit delo episkopa Germogena?" *RM*, 33, No. 2, pt. 2(1912), pp. 50–53.

38. "Individualizm ili sobornost'," *Narod*, No. 6 (1906), pp. 3–4. V. Ern, "O zhiznennoi pravde," pp. 58–61.

39. See below, pp. 111, 116, 120, 170.

40. Bulgakov, "O neobkhodimosti vvedeniia obshchestvennykh nauk v programmu dukhovnoi shkoly," *Bogoslovskii Vestnik*, 15, No. 2(1906), pp. 345–56. E. Trubetskoi considered this to be an incorrect approach. He argued that to complete Soloviev's work the religious thinkers should ap-

proach the lay intellectuals rather than the church, "Pamiati V.S. Solov'eva, otkrytoe pis'mo S.N. Bulgakovu," *VZh*, No. 2(1905), pp. 386–90. See also Bulgakov's "Neotlozhnaia zadacha" and "Sotsial'nye obiazannosti tserkvi," *Narod*, No. 5(1906), pp. 1–2; and "Vremennoe i vechnoe," *Vek*, No. 7(1906), pp. 78–79.

41. "Bez plana," *VZh*, No. 6(1905), pp. 301–302, 312–14.

42. *Kratkii ocherk politicheskoi ekonomii* (Moscow: Efimov, 1907), pp. 15, 24–25; "Osnovnyia problemy teorii progressa," in *Ot marksizma*, pp. 122–25; Consult Bulgakov's article "Zadachi politicheskoi ekonomii," in *Ot marksizma*, pp. 317–47, for many of the points raised in this section. See also, "Khristianstvo i sotsial'nyi vopros," in *Dva grada*, vol. 1, pp. 212–13, originally published in *Voprosy Religii*, No. 1(1906), pp. 298–334.

43. "Pod znamenem universiteta," *VFP*, 17, No. 5/85(1906), p. 461.

44. "Pod znamenem universiteta," pp. 463–68. See also, Evgenii Ivanov, "Universitet," *VZh*, Nos. 4–5(1905), pp. 264–67.

45. On this, see F. Nietzsche, *Von Nutzen und Nachteil der Historie für das Leben*, Sections VIII–X, pp. 71–112.

46. Bulgakov, *Kratkii ocherk*, pp. 5–6. *Filosofiia khoziaistva, chast' pervaia* (Moscow: "Put'," 1912), pp. 89–126, 135. See also "Priroda v filosofii Vl. Solov'eva," in *O Solov'eve* (Moscow: "Put'," 1911), pp. 1–31. In this article, Bulgakov emphasizes Schelling's primary emphasis on the "spiritualization of nature," as this was presented by Solov'ev. See also his "Khristianstvo i mifologiia," *RM*, 32, No. 8(1911), pp. 121, 125–26; "Filosofiia khoziaistva," *RM*, 34, No. 5(1913), pp. 70–79.

47. "Khristianstvo i sotsial'nyi vopros," *Dva grada*, vol. 1, p. 228; *Kratkii ocherk*, p. 6.

48. *Kratkii ocherk*, pp. 7, 17; See also, "Ob ekonomicheskom ideale," *Nauchnoe Slovo*, No. 5(1903), in *Ot marksizma*, pp. 263–70; "Khristianstvo i sotsial'nyi vopros," pp. 227–33.

49. "Narodnoe khoziaistvo i religioznaia lichnost'," *ME*, No. 24(1909), p. 30, in *Dva grada*, vol. 1, pp. 178–205.

50. "Khristianstvo i sotsial'nyi vopros," *Dva grada*, vol. 1, pp. 212, 231–32. *Kratkii ocherk*, pp. 11–13.

51. "Khristianstvo i sotsial'nyi vopros," *Dva grada*, vol. 1, pp. 223–24; "Karleil i Tolstoi," *NP*, No. 12(1904), pp. 227–60 and *VZh*, No. 1(1905), pp. 16–38. See also, "Po povodu raziasneniia Sv. Sinoda otnositel'no chestvovaniia L.N. Tolstogo," *ME*, No. 36(1908), pp. 26–28.

52. "Narodnoe khoziaistvo i religioznaia lichnost'," pp. 28–30.

53. *Ibid.*, p. 32. See also, "Ekonomicheskii materializm kak filosofiia khoziaistva," *RM*, 33, No. 1(1912), pp. 44–64.

54. *Bedenken und Ergebung*, in *Werke*, 40 vols. (Stuttgart and Tübingen: J. G. Cotta, 1840), vol. 40, pp. 425; quoted in Karl Löwith, *From Hegel to Nietzsche*, trans. David E. Green (New York: Holt, 1964), p. 7.

55. Löwith, *Hegel to Nietzsche*, p. 9.

56. A.M. Pankratova, L.M. Ivanov, and V. D. Mochalov, eds., *Istoriia Moskvy* (Moscow: Izd. Akad. Nauk SSSR, 1955), vol. 5, pp. 454–58.

NOTES FOR CHAPTER V

1. "Sovremennye otzvuki slavianofil'stva," *VZh*, No. 6(1905), p. 372.

2. "Dva etiuda," *Poliarnaia Zvezda*, 30 Dec. 1905, pp. 210–11.

3. "Prof. B. I. Ger'e o pervoi Gosudarstvennoi Dume," *RM*, 28, No. 1(1907), pp. 19–25.

4. I. L. Goremykin, chairman of the council of ministers, in a speech to the Duma, May 13, 1905; see Michael Florinsky, *Russia: A History and an Interpretation* (New York: Macmillan, 1965), vol. 2, pp. 1188–92.

5. Statement by Professor George Katkov, of the University of London. Professor Isaiah Berlin communicated it to me.

6. See R. Cumming, *Human Nature and History* (Chicago: Univ. of Chicago Press, 1969), vol. 1, pp. 1–16.

7. *Ibid.*, 2, pp. 275–398.

8. "Dva etiuda," pp. 214–15.

9. *Ibid.*, p. 217.

10. Trans. G.D.H. Cole (New York: Dutton, 1950), pp. 13–14.

11. Novgorodtsev, "Uchenie Kanta o prave i gosudarstve," pp. 355–56.

12. *Ibid.*, pp. 349–50; "Moral i poznanie," p. 833; *Kant i Hegel*, pp. 190, 194–95.

13. *Kant i Hegel*, p. 235.

14. "Krizis sovremennago pravosoznaniia," *VFP*, 17, No. 4/84(1906), pp. 415–20.

15. "Krizis," *VFP*, 19, No. 4/94(1908), pp. 434–35; "Sovremennye otzvuki slavianofil'stva," p. 375.

16. "Krizis," *VFP*, 18, No. 5/90(1907), pp. 441–51.

17. "Krizis," *VFP*, 17, No. 4/84(1906), pp. 440–50; No. 18, 5/90(1907), pp. 438, 455, 462–65, 474, 481, 487; 19, No. 1/91(1908), pp. 80–108; *Ob obshchestvennom ideale*, 3d ed. (Berlin: "Slovo," 1921), pp. 11, 25, appeared first as a series of articles in *VFP*, 1911–16.

18. "Gosudarstvo i pravo," 1, *VFP*, 15, No. 4/74(1904), p. 405; "Krizis," *VFP*, 18, No. 5/90(1907), pp. 437, 487.

19. "Gosudarstvo i pravo," 1, pp. 403, 416–19.

20. *Ibid.*, pp. 440–44.

21. "Uchenie Kanta o prave i gosudarstve," p. 316; "Gosudarstvo i pravo," 1, p. 411.

22. See Alfred Levin, *The Second Duma*, 2d. ed. (Hamden, Conn.: Archon Books, 1966).

23. "Krizis," *VFP*, 18, No. 4/89(1907), pp. 377–79; 19, No. 1/91(1908), pp. 116–17.

24. "Krizis," *VFP*, 18, No. 5/90(1907), p. 438.

25. On "Wholes and Parts," see *Parts and Wholes*, ed. Daniel Lerner (New York: Free Press, 1963), especially C. Kluckhohn, "Parts and Wholes in Cultural Analysis," p. 111–33, and E. Nagel, "Wholes, Sums and Organic Unities," pp. 135–55. Jean Piaget offers a provocative statement based on his genetic psychology in *Études Sociologiques* (Geneva: Libraire Droz, 1965), pp. 26–38 and throughout.

26. "Gosudarstvo i pravo," 2, *VFP*, 15, No. 5/75(1904), pp. 508, 529–30.

27. *Kant i Hegel*, pp. 146–56.

28. "Sovremennoe polozhenie problemy estestvennago prava," *Iuridicheskii Vestnik*, No. 1(1913), p. 19.

29. *Ibid.*, p. 22; see also "Psikhologicheskaia teoriia prava i filosofiia estestvennago prava," *Iuridicheskii Vestnik*, No. 3(1913), pp. 5–34.

30. "Krizis," *VFP*, 19, No. 4/94(1908), pp. 391–95, 405–407; 412; See G. Simmel, *Kant*, 2d ed. (Leipzig: Duncker und Humblot, 1905), pp. 170–81.

31. "Krizis," *VFP*, 19, No. 4/94(1908), pp. 404, 413–26, 432; *Ob obshchestvennom ideale*, p. 18.

32. The following summary of Goethean positions comes from S. Frank, "K kharakteristike Gete," in *Filosofiia i zhizn'* (St. Petersburg: Zhukovskii, 1910), pp. 355–66. Both Frank and Novgorodtsev were strongly influenced by Simmel. See G. Simmel, "Kant i Gete," trans. S. Frank, *RM*, 29, No. 6(1908), pp. 39–69. Of course, Hegel believed that individuality based solely on the "law of the heart" would lead to utter subjectivity and a war of all against all. *The Phenomenology of the Mind*, 2d ed., rev. and cor., trans. J.B. Baillie (New York: Macmillan, 1955), p. 399.

33. See S. Frank, "Lichnost' i mirovozzrenie Fr. Shleiermakhera," *RM*, 32, No. 9(1911), pp. 1–28, on "feeling," pp. 15–20. Friedrich Schleiermacher, *Reden über die Religion* (1821), 3d ed., trans. by J. Oman (1893); abridged with intro. by E. Graham Waring as *On Religion, Speeches to Its Cultural Despisers* (New York: Ungar, 1955), pp. 33–38.

34. Frank, "Lichnost' i mirovozzrenie Fr. Shleiermakhera," p. 26. Schleiermacher, *Monologen* (1800), trans. by H. L. Friess as *Schleiermacher's Soliloquies* (Chicago: Open Court, 1957), pp. 27–29, 74–77.

35. *Ob obshchestvennom ideale*, pp. 1, 102–109.

36. "Krizis," *VFP*, 17, No. 4/84(1906), pp. 408–10. *Ob obshchestvennom ideale*, pp. 58–59, 62, 125–27, 132, 135. For Bulgakov's similar views, see "Karleil i Tolstoi," pp. 239–40.

37. "Krizis," *VFP*, 19, No. 4/94(1908), pp. 432–37. See Simmel, *Einleitung in die Moralwissenschaft* (Berlin: Hertz [Besser], 1893), vol. 2, pp. 380–426.

38. "Krizis," *VFP*, 19, No. 4/94(1908), pp. 427–31, 439.

39. *Ob obshchestvennom ideale*, p. 112.

40. "Krizis," *VFP*, 19, No. 4/94(1908), pp. 437–38; Simmel, "Die Grossstadt und das geistesleben," in *Die Grossstadt* (Dresden: Zahn und Jaensch, 1903), pp. 185–206, see *The Sociology of George Simmel*, trans. and ed. Kurt H. Wolff (New York: Free Press, 1964), pp. 409–24.

41. "Krizis," *VFP*, 19, No. 5/95(1908), pp. 513–18. As works exemplifying German "new liberalism," Novgorodtsev pointed to I. Jastrow, *Die Aufgaben des Liberalismus in Preussen*, 2d ed. (Berlin: Rosenbaum und Hart, 1894), and H. Dietzel, *Das Neünzehnte Jahrhundert und das Programm des Liberalismus* (Bonn: Röhrscheide und Ebbecke, 1900).

42. "Krizis," *VFP*, 19, No. 5/95(1908), pp. 524, 541, 545–52; See also "Pravo na dostoinoe chelovecheskoe sushchestvovanie," in *Sotsial'nofilosofskie etiudy* (St. Petersburg–Moscow: M.O. Volf, 1911), pp. 3–13.

43. "Krizis," *VFP*, 19, No. 5/95(1908), pp. 575–78, 583–87.
44. *Ibid.*, p. 537.
45. *Ibid.*, pp. 559–65, 594.
46. Particularly in *Smoke* (1866); see *The Borzoi Turgenev*, trans. Harry Stevens (New York: Knopf, 1955), pp. 3–164, especially pp. 77–93. See also, *Turgenev's Letters*, ed. Edgar H. Lehrman (New York: Knopf, 1961), pp. 140–44.
47. "Sushchestvo russkago pravoslavnago soznaniia," in *Pravoslavie i Kul'tura*, ed. V.V. Zenkovskii (Berlin: "Russkaia Kniga," 1923), pp. 7–23.
48. "Krizis," *VFP*, 19, No. 5/95(1908), p. 587; See also, S.A. Kotliarevskii, "Predposylka demokratii," *VFP*, 16, No. 2/77(1905), pp. 122–23.
49. "Krizis," *VFP*, 19, No. 5/95(1908), pp. 569–72. Novgorodtsev took as an excellent statement of the "culture and personality" theme the articles of P. Struve and S. Frank, "Ocherki filosofii kul'tury," pt. 1, *Poliarnaia Zvezda*, 22 Dec. 1905, pp. 104–17; pt. 2, 30 Dec. 1905, pp. 170–84.
50. "Krizis," *VFP*, No. 5/95(1908), pp. 571, 595. Novgorodtsev criticizes not only Struve and Frank, but also Windelband, who believed that higher ideals, expressed in the articulation of culture by creative individuals, became determinative for the life of the populace. This Neo-Kantian idea also reflected Fichtean elitism. See George A. Kelly, *Idealism, Politics and History* (London: Cambridge Univ. Press, 1969), pt. 4, "J.G. Fichte," especially pp. 269–85.
51. *Ob obshchestvennom ideale*, pp. 37, 74–78.
52. *Ob obshchestvennom ideale*, pp. 80–85; see also, "Dva pravovykh ideala," pp. 112–27.
53. *Ob obshchestvennom ideale*, pp. 3, 9, 17, 29–31. Novgorodtsev interpreted in this way Marx's view that "Only when man does not separate social forces from himself in the form of political forces will human emancipation be complete." See "The Jewish Question," in *The Marx-Engels Reader*, ed. R.G. Tucker (New York: Norton, 1972), pp. 44–45.
54. *Ob obshchestvennom ideale*, pp. 42–48, 51–54. Again, Novgorodtsev relies on Simmel, *Soziologie* (Leipzig: Duncker und Humblot, 1908), pp. 600–13, "Die Selbsterhaltung der Gruppe."
55. *Ob obshchestvennom ideale*, pp. 19–21, 79–87. See Simmel, *Die Probleme der Geschichtephilosophie*, 3d ed. (Leipzig: Duncker und Humblot, 1907), pp. 160–62.
56. *Ob obshchestvennom ideale*, pp. 71–74, 89–91; R. Stammler, *Wirtschaft und Recht nach der materialistischen Geschichtsauffassung*, 2d ed., enlarged (Leipzig: Veit, 1896), pp. 577–602.
57. *Ob obshchestvennom ideale*, pp. 95–96; again, Simmel, *Die Religion* (Frankfort on the Main: Rütten und Loening, 1906), pp. 22, 28–29.
58. *Ob obshchestvennom ideale*, pp. 132–37.
59. P.B. Struve, "Intelligentsiia i revoliutsiia," in *Vekhi* (Moscow: N. Kushnerev, 1909) pp. 156–74.
60. In *Intelligentsiia v Rossii* (St. Petersburg: Knigoizdat. "Zemlia," 1910), pp. 89–191.
61. *Ob obshchestvennom ideale*, p. 113.

NOTES FOR CHAPTER VI

1. A.N. Whitehead, *Science and the Modern World* (New York: New American Library, 1948), pp. 41-55.

2. See C. Renouvier, *Le personnalisme* (Paris: F. Alcan, 1903) and John A. Scott, *Republican Ideas and the Liberal Tradition in France, 1870-1914* (New York: Columbia Univ. Press, 1951), pp. 50-88. Hobhouse's ideas may be studied in his *Liberalism* (1911; reprint ed., introd. Allen P. Grimes, London: Oxford Univ. Press, 1969), p. 8 and throughout. See also, the "new liberalism" in *English Liberalism and the State*, ed. Harold J. Schultz (Lexington, Mass.: Heath, 1972), pp. 75-122.

3. See above, pp. 10-11.

4. On personalism, see F. Copleston, S.J., *A History of Philosophy* (Garden City, N.Y.: Doubleday, 1967), vol. 8, pt. 1, pp. 267-83; pt. 2, pp. 45-55.

5. See R. Dahrendorf, *Essays in the Theory of Society* (Stanford, Calif.: Stanford Univ. Press, 1968), pp. 19-87; R. Musil, *The Man Without Qualities*, trans. Eithne Wilkins and E. Kaiser (London: Secker and Warburg, 1953), vol. 1, p. 34. In its entirety, Musil's novel is filled with provocative ideas about the intellectual climate of early twentieth-century Central Europe. So, also, is Herman Bloch's *The Sleepwalkers*, trans. Willa and Edwin Muir (New York: Grosset, 1947). See the chapters on the "Disintegration of Values," interspersed with the narrative.

6. I would consider that much of the "Godbuilding" and empiriomonist social thought of Lunacharsky was an "alternative to" rather than a form of Marxism. For a sharp critique of present-day Western "imaginary and unintelligible Marxism," which I consider applicable to Lunacharsky's "Godbuilding," see Ernest Gellner's "The Soviet and the Savage," *Times Literary Supplement*, 16 Oct. 1974, p. 1166.

7. The terms "mystical-dogmatic" and "rational-critical" are used by Eugene Dais in "Law, Authority and Social Change," *Archiv für Rechts- und Sozial-Philosophie,* 57, No. 2(1971), pp. 161-85. Of course, these concepts stem from the work of Max Weber. See "The Types of Authority," in *Theories of Society*, ed. Talcott Parsons *et al.*, trans. A.M. Henderson and Talcott Parsons (Glencoe, Ill.: Free Press, 1961). vol. 1, pp. 626-32.

8. See Cyril E. Black, ed., *The Transformation of Russian Society* (Cambridge, Mass.: Harvard Univ. Press, 1960). From the substantial literature on "modernization," the following are excellent: C.E. Black, *The Dynamics of Modernization* (New York: Harper, 1967); S.N. Eisenstadt, *Tradition, Change and Modernity* (New York: Wiley, 1973); Marion J. Levy, Jr., *Modernization and the Structure of Societies* (Princeton: Princeton Univ. Press, 1970). Particularly thought-provoking is Ernest Gellner's *Thought and Change* (Chicago: Univ. of Chicago Press, 1965), especially pp. 126-221.

9. On "rationalization," see *From Max Weber: Essays in Sociology*, trans. and eds. H.H. Gerth and C. Wright Mills (London: Routledge and Kegan Paul, 1952), pp. 196-264 (bureaucracy), and pp. 267-301 (religion).

10. Novgorodtsev, *Ob obshchestvennom ideale*, p. 41. Foucault, *The Order of Things*, translation of *Les Mots et les choses* (London: Tavistock. 1970), p. 320.

11. See above, pp. 108–10.

12. John Shelton Curtis, *Church and State in Russia* (1940; reprint ed., New York: Octagon Books, 1972), pp. 71–72, and throughout. A.V. Kartashev, "The Russian Church During the Synodal Period of Her History," *The Christian East*, July–Dec. 1936, p. 119. Gerhard Simon, *Die Kirchen in Russland* (Munich: Manz, 1970), pp. 9–36.

13. "Deistvitel'nost' i deistvennost'," pp. 24–27; and "Po povodu 'pis'ma s drugago berega,' (otkrytoe pis'mo k N. Ezerskomu)," *ME*, No. 14(1907), pp. 25–30.

14. P.I. Novgorodtsev, "Pravoslavnaia tserkov' v eia otnoshenii k dukhovnoi zhizni novoi Rossii," *Russkaia Mysl'* (Prague), Nos. 1–2(1922), pp. 193–221. A.V. Kartashev, "The Russian Church," pp. 112–25. Gerhard Simon, *Die Kirchen*, pp. 43–61 and "Church, State and Society," in *Russia Enters the Twentieth Century*, eds. G. Katkov *et al.* (London: Temple Smith, 1971), pp. 199–235.

15. Curtis, *Church and State* and Simon, *Die Kirchen*. See also, A.A. Bogolepov, "Church Reform in Russia," trans. A.E. Moorhouse, *St. Vladimir Seminary Quarterly,* Nos. 1–2(1966), pp. 12–66. I. Smolich, "Predsobornoe prisutstvie," *Put'*, 38 (1933), pp. 65–75. On the reform movement among the St. Petersburg clergy, see A.V. Kartashev, *Russkaia tserkov' v 1905* (St. Petersburg: Merushev, 1906). See also *Tserkovnoe Obnovlenie*, No. 1(1906), pp. 13–16, and *Vek*, No. 1(1906), pp. 1–4.

16. Alexander Vucinich, "Politics, Universities and Science," in *Russia Under the Last Tsar*, ed. T.V. Stavrou (Minneapolis: Univ. of Minnesota Press, 1969), p. 159.

17. *Ibid.*, pp. 156–58.

18. *Ibid.*

19. See a provocative study of the "theoretic attitude" and the "religious attitude" in E. Spranger, *Types of Men, the Psychology and Ethics of Personality*, trans. Paul J.W. Pigors (1928; reprint ed., New York: Johnson, 1966), pp. 109–30, 210–46.

20. "O putiakh i zadachakh russkoi intelligentsii," in *Iz Glubiny*, 2d ed. (1918; reprinted, Paris: YMCA Press, 1967), pp. 263–65.

21. *Ibid.*

22. "Pravo i nravstvennost'," pp. 130–32.

23. "Na vyborakh (iz dnevnika)," *RM*, 33, No. 11(1912), pp. 186–88.

24. *Avtobiograficheskiia zametki*, pp. 73–93.

25. He said that he did not support a police state and did not move to the "right." *Ibid.*, p. 82. See also his "Na vyborakh," pp. 185–92.

26. *Dva grada*, vol. 2, pp. 121–22.

27. See above, pp. 46–47. See also A.S. Izgoev, "Bessilie religioznykh intelligentov," *Rech'*, 5 Apr. 1908, p. 5.

28. L. Z. Slonimskii, "Noveishie idealisty," pp. 313–24.

29. E. Voegelin, *The New Science of Politics* (Chicago: Univ. of Chicago Press, 1952), pp. 107–35. See J. Danzas, "Les réminiscences gnostiques dans la philosophie russe moderne," *Revue des Sciences Philosophiques et Théologiques*, 25(1936), pp. 658–85. It should be noted that tendencies in this

direction lead some to question Bulgakov's credentials as a spokesman for Russian Orthodoxy. See P. Evdokimov, *Le Christ dans la Pensée Russe* (Paris: Les Éditions du Cerf, 1970), pp. 179–94, especially, 192–94. Yves-Noël Lelouvier, *Perspectives Russes Sur L'église* (Paris: Éditions du Centurion, 1968), p. 37.

30. In *Svet nevechernyi* (Moscow: "Put'," 1917), Bulgakov presents his religious philosophy as it had developed up until 1917. In the interpretation of Bulgakov's sophiology in that work, I have followed the guidance of V.V. Zenkovsky, *A History of Russian Philosophy*, trans. George L. Kline (New York: Columbia Univ. Press, 1953), vol. 2, pp. 897–904, and Nicholas O. Lossky, *History of Russian Philosophy* (New York: International Universities Press, 1951), pp. 206–14.

31. See above, p. 112.

32. On the "possessive individual," see C.B. Macpherson, *The Political Theory of Possessive Individualism* (London: Oxford Univ. Press, 1970), pp. 263–77.

33. In a different context and with different emphases than that of the "revolution of sensibility" Philip Rieff considers the idea of the "therapeutic society" in *The Triumph of the Therapeutic* (New York: Harper, 1966) summarizing his views in ch. 8, pp. 232–61. See also the chapter "The Emergence of Psychological Man" in his *Freud, The Mind of a Moralist* (New York: Viking, 1959), pp. 329–57. A related range of ideas is discussed in Fred Weinstein and Gerald Platt's *The Wish to Be Free* (Berkeley: Univ. of California Press, 1969). My primary debt in this and much else is to Carl Schorske. See his article, "Politics and the Psyche in *fin-de-siècle* Vienna: Schnitzler and Hofmannsthal," *American Historical Review*, No. 4(1961), pp. 930–46.

34. Novgorodtsev's critique of the West is in his "Sushchestvo russkago pravoslavnago soznaniia," The details on the end of his life come from a witness, Professor George Katkov. They were transmitted to me by Professor Isaiah Berlin.

BIBLIOGRAPHY

RUSSIAN PERIODICALS AND NEWSPAPERS (1890–1914) furnished one of the major sources for this work. Equally important are books published in the late nineteenth and early twentieth century by the writers who pursued idealistic and religious themes. Also valuable are the memoirs of Russians active in intellectual circles in the last two decades before 1914. The Chekhov publishing house directed by Michael Karpovich carried out important work in this area, while other books and articles containing memoirs were published by emigré presses in New York, London, Paris, Berlin, Munich, Prague, Belgrade, and Sofia.

Because of the topic of my research, I could not gain access to known archival materials while in the Soviet Union. However, research in the Saltykov-Shchedrin Library in Leningrad uncovered many titles not available and, in some cases, not known in any Western library. The newspaper holdings on Fontanka were also very useful, since they contained important materials not available in the West. Some valuable memoirs and letters were consulted in the Archive of Russian and East European Culture at Columbia University. For anyone wishing to do further research in this area, there are rich periodical holdings, particularly at Harvard, Columbia, and Stanford universities, New York Public Library, and the library of St. Vladimir's Seminary. Most of the essential books can be found in one or another of the scholarly libraries in the United States, England, West Germany, and Helsinki, Finland.

Little scholarly literature exists on idealistic liberalism, the religious-philosophical societies, and Christian socialism in twentieth-century Russia. In "The Main Currents of Contemporary Russian Thought" Pierre Pascal offers a useful survey for the late nineteenth and early twentieth century. Other recent surveys appear in James Billington's *The Icon and the Axe* and Donald Treadgold's *The West in Russia and China, Religious and Secular Thought in Modern Times*, Vol. I: *Russia 1472–1917*. The works by Edie, Scanlan, and Zeldin, Bubnoff, Frank, Schmeman, Schultze, and Shein listed in the bibliography contain substantial translated readings from the work of religious and idealistic thinkers.

Several scholars have produced works on the thought of non-Marxist early-twentieth-century Russian thinkers. Arthur Mendel, in his book *Dilemmas of Progress in Tsarist Russia* examines the ideas of P. Struve, N. Berdiaev, and S. Bulgakov in the context of the "Marxist-Populist debate" of the 1890s. He expends the bulk of his effort on a description and evaluation of the economic and political views of these rivals. Richard Kindersley presents the ideas of the same thinkers, along with S. Frank and M. Tugan-Baranovsky in *The First Russian Revisionists*, a work which offers useful personal backgrounds of the Legal Marxists and delves into the philosophical basis of their critique of Marxism. The most recent work, R. Pipes' *Struve: Liberal on the Left*, offers not only an excellent study of its protagonist, but also a good treatment of the political and general intellectual currents of his time. Also valuable is Klaus von Beyme's monograph, *Political Sociology in Tsarist Russia*, which, though it is faithful to its title, deals with the relation of liberalism to philosophical idealism and to the crisis situation in Russia at the beginning of the twentieth century.

Until very recently, except for the Reverend George Florovsky's *Paths of Russian Theology*, no substantial scholarly work had been devoted to the religious-philosophical currents of thought of the early twentieth century. Interest has quickened in the past decade, and the religious-philosophical thought treated herein has attracted notice from scholars. In 1963 Nicholas Zernov produced a rather encyclopedic survey in *The Russian Religious Renaissance of the Twentieth Century*. Peter Scheibert published a substantial article "The Petersburg Religious-Philosophical Meetings of 1902 and 1903." Along with presenting for the first time in print an organized discussion of the points of view articulated at the meetings, this article provides in a short space a good summary and evaluation of related developments within the church and among the intelligentsia of the early twentieth century. An excellent description of the activities of the religious-philosophical societies has been provided by J. Scherrer in *The Petersburg Religious-Philosophical Associations: The Religious Self-Comprehension of their Intelligentsia-Members* (1973). Like Zernov's book, it does not probe sufficiently into the varieties of religious thought and commitment manifested by the many intellectuals involved. James Scanlan provided a philosophical treatment of "The New Religious Consciousness: Merezhkovsky and Berdiaev," while George L. Kline's *Religious and Anti-Religious Thought in Russia* offered useful chapters on "Religious Neo-Conservatives: Leontyev and Rozanov" and "The 'God-Builders': Gorky and Lunacharski." Temira Pachmuss provided new information and insight into the activities and ideas of the Merezhkovsky group in the religious-philosophical meetings and societies in *Zinaida Hippius, An Intellectual Portrait* and several articles and documents.

In the past decade, Soviet scholars have devoted increasing attention to the religious and non-Marxist currents of thought at the turn of the century. Important is Volume Four (1971) of their *History of Philosophy in the USSR*, produced by many scholars. It offers four chapters on "Noble landlord, liberal bourgeois and bourgeois democratic tendencies in philosophy and sociology in Russia," and one on "Philosophical revisionism in the Russian Social Democratic movement (Machists)." In *Essays on the History of Modern and Contemporary Bourgeois Thought* (1960), K. S. Bakradze tried to show the "subjective idealist" character of the Machist, Neo-Kantian, and Shuppeian ideas employed by non-Marxist thinkers in early-twentieth-century Russia. G. S. Vasetskii and others outlined Lenin's ideological struggle with revisionists, "legal Marxists," liberals, and Neo-Kantians in *Essays on the History of Philosophy in Russia (Second Half of the Nineteenth and Beginning of the Twentieth Centuries)*, pt. 2 (1960). In *A Critique of Intuitionism in Russia* (1963) I.P. Chueva sharply criticized the work of N. Lossky and S. Frank. M.I. Shakhnovich, in *Lenin and the Problem of Atheism* (1965), devoted sections to the idealists and the "God-builders"; E.I. Vodzinskii's book *Russian Neo-Kantianism at the End of the Nineteenth and Beginning of the Twentieth Centuries* concentrates on the professional philosophers A.I. Vvedenskii and I.

Lapshin, and the philosopher-psychologist G. Chelpanov. These men were teachers and colleagues of the philosophers treated in this volume.

Lenin as a Philosopher (1969) presented essays on "Struvism," "God-seeking," "God-building," and Machism. Another Leninist critique of Machism appears in A.I. Korneeva's *Lenin's Critique of Machism and the Struggle against Contemporary Idealism* (1971). V.N. Sherdakov and others edited a volume on *Atheism, Religion and Modern Times* (1973), which contains an essay by E.S. Lukashevich on "The Basic Directions in Russian God-seeking in the Beginning of the Twentieth Century." The ideas of Bulgakov and, to a lesser degree, Novgorodtsev are discussed by N.I. Bochkarev in *V.I. Lenin and Bourgeois Sociology in Russia* (1973). In *K. Marx's "Das Kapital" and Philosophical Thought in Russia* (1974), V.F. Pustarnakov criticized the economic ideas of Bulgakov and Struve. All of these works assert, rather than demonstrate, their conclusions and suffer from rigid use of unproven and restrictive Marxist notions about the relationship of complex thought to social categories. But they also deal directly with the texts and raise important questions about the adoption of idealistic, religious, and Machian positivist philosophies in the twentieth century.

The bibliography which follows includes works cited in the notes and a selection of other useful books and articles. Where more than one work is included for a given author, the items are listed in chronological order. The following abbreviations are used for often-cited periodicals: *Moskovskii Ezhenedel'nik–ME*, *Novyi Put'–NP*, *Russkaia Mysl'–RM*, *Voprosy Filosofii i Psikhologii–VFP*, and *Voprosy Zhizni–VZh*.

Aggeev, Konstantin Sviashch. " 'Vozrozhdaiushchiisia idealizm v miroso-zertsaniia russkago obrazovannago obshchestva," *Vera i Razum*, 2, No. 5(1904), otdel filosofskii, pp. 171–90; No. 6, 235–42; No. 7, 361–80.
_____. "Religiia i politika," *Vek*, No. 10(1907), pp. 120–22; No. 12, 142–43.
Aivazov, Ivan G. *Religioznoe obnovlenie nashikh dnei ("Novoputeistsy," "Vekhi")*. 3d ed. Moscow: "Russkaia Pechatnaia," 1910.
Alekseev, N. "V burnye gody," *Novyi Zhurnal*, No. 52(1958), pp. 172–88.
_____. "V burnye gody," *Novyi Zhurnal*, No. 54(1958), pp. 148–63.
Alekseev, Sergei. "Razlozhenie marksizma." *NP*, No. 12(1904), pp. 86–115.
Aron, Raymond. *German Sociology*. Glencoe, Ill.: Free Press, 1957.
Arseniev, Nicholas S. "Iz iunosti (kartiny moskovskoi zhizni)," *Vozrozhdenie*, No. 18(1951), pp. 71–86.

_____. "Gody iunosti v Moskve," *Mosty*, vol. 7(1959), pp. 363–73.

_____. "O moskovskikh religiozno-filosofskikh i literaturnikh kruzhkakh i sobraniakh nachala XX veka," *Sovremennik*, No. 6(1962), pp. 30–42.

_____. "A.S. Khomiakov i V.A. Kozhevnikov," *Vozrozhdenie*, No. 216(1970), pp. 35–55.

Asmus, Valentin F. "Bor'ba filosofskikh techenii̯ v Moskovskikh universitetakh v 70-x godakh XIX veka." In *Izbrannye filosofskie trudy*, vol. 1, pp. 238–66. Moscow: Moscow Univ., 1969.

Avenarius, Richard. *Kritika chistago opyta*. Ed. A.V. Lunacharskii. Moscow: S. Dorovatsky and A. Charushnikov, 1905.

Bakradze, Konstantin S. *Ocherki po istorii noveishei i sovremennoi burzhuaznoi filosofii*. Tbilisi: "Sabchota Sakartvelo," 1960.

Baron, Samuel H. *Plekhanov, The Father of Russian Marxism*. Stanford, Calif.: Stanford Univ. Press, 1966.

Bazarov, Vladimir A. "Avtoritarnaia metafizika i avtonomaia lichnost'." In *Ocherki realisticheskago mirovozzreniia, sbornik statei*, pp. 186–261. St. Petersburg: Motvid, 1904.

_____. "Mistitsizm i realizm nashego vremeni." In *Ocherki po filosofii marksizma, sbornik statei*, pp. 3–71. St. Petersburg: V. Bezobrazov, 1908.

_____. "Bogoiskatel'stvo i bogostroitel'stvo." In *Vershiny, sbornik statei*, No. 1, pp. 332–65. St. Petersburg: "Obshchestvennaia pol'za," 1909.

_____. "Sud'by russkago 'idealizma' za poslednee desiatiletie." In *Iz istorii noveishei russkoi literatury, sbornik statei*, pp. 151–95. Moscow: "Zerno," 1910.

Bell, E.T. *Men of Mathematics*. 2 vols. Harmondsworth, England: Penguin, 1965.

Belyi, Andrei. "Idealisty i 'Novyi Put'," " *Vesy*, No. 11(1904), pp. 66–67.

Berdiaev, Nikolai A. *Subektivizm i individualizm v obshchestvennoi filosofii: kriticheskii etiud o N. K. Mikhailovskom*. St. Petersburg: O.N. Popov, 1901.

_____. "O novom russkom idealizme," *VFP*, 15, No. 5/75 (1904), pp. 683–724. In *Sub specie aeternitatis, sbornik statei*, pp. 152–90. St. Petersburg: M.V. Pirozhkov, 1907.

_____. "Religiozno-obshchestvennaia khronika," *VZh*, No. 2(1905), pp. 380–85.

_____. *Novoe religioznoe soznanie, sbornik statei*. St. Petersburg: M.V. Pirozhkov, 1907.

_____. "Religiozno-filosofskoe obshchestvo pamiati V. Solov'eva," *Vek*, No. 22(1907), pp. 342–43.

_____. *Dukhovnyi krizis intelligentsii, sbornik statei*. St. Petersburg: "Obshchestvennaia pol'za," 1910.

Berger, Peter L., and Thomas Luckmann. *The Social Construction of Reality, A Treatise in the Sociology of Knowledge*. Garden City, N.Y.: Doubleday, 1966.

Bernstein, Basil. *Class, Codes and Control, I: Theoretical Studies Towards a Sociology of Language*. 2d rev. ed. London: Routledge and Kegan Paul, 1974.

Beyme, Klaus von. *Politische Soziologie im zaristischen Russland*. Wiesbaden: O. Harrassowitz, 1965.

Billington, James. *The Icon and the Axe, An Interpretive History of Russian Culture*. New York: Knopf, 1966.

Black, Cyril E., ed. *The Transformation of Russian Society*. Cambridge, Mass.: Harvard Univ. Press, 1960.

_____. *The Dynamics of Modernization*. New York: Harper, 1967.

Bloch, Herman. *The Sleepwalkers*. Trans. Willa and Edwin Muir. New York: Grosset, 1947.

Bochkarev, N.I. *V.I. Lenin i burzhuaznaia sotsiologiia v rossii*. Moscow: Moscow Univ., 1973.

Bogolepov, Alexander A. "Church Reform in Russia," trans. A.E. Moorhouse, *St. Vladimir Seminary Quarterly*, Nos. 1–2(1966), pp. 12–66.

Bogoslovskii Vestnik, a Moscow monthly theological journal, 1892–1918.

"Bogostroitel'stvo i bogoiskatel'stvo," *Nasha Gazeta*, 13 Jan. 1909, p. 2.

The Borzoi Turgenev. Trans. Harry Stevens. New York: Knopf, 1955.

Brecht, Arnold. Rev. of E. Wolf. *Das Problem der Naturrechtslehre, Natural Law Forum*, 3, No. 1(1958), pp. 192–98.

_____. *Political Theory: The Foundations of Twentieth Century Political Thought*. 2d paperback ed. Princeton: Princeton Univ. Press, 1969.

Buass'e, F. *Katakomby*. Moscow: Efimov, 1907.

Bubnov, Nikolai, and H. Ehrenberg, eds. *Ostliches Christentum, Dokumente*. Munich: C.H. Becksche, 1925.

Bubnoff, Nikolai, ed. *Russische Religionsphilosophen, Dokumente*. Heidelberg: Lambert Schreider, 1956.

Büchner, Ludwig. *Force and Matter, or Principles of the Natural Order of the Universe*. Trans. from 15th German ed. New York: Eckler, 1891.

Bulgakov, Sergei N. "O zakonomernosti sotsial'nykh iavlenii." *VFP*, 7, No. 5/35(1896), pp. 575–611.

_____. *O rynkakh pri kapitalisticheskom proizvodstve*. Moscow: M.I. Vodovozov, 1897.

_____. *Kapitalizm i zemledelie*. 2 vols. St. Petersburg: V.A. Tikhanov, 1900.

_____. "Vasnetsov, Dostoevskii, Vl. Soloviev, i L. Tolstoi." in *Literaturnoe delo, sbornik statei*, pp. 119–39. St. Petersburg: A. E. Kolpinskii, 1902.

_____. "Dushevnaia drama Gertsena." *VFP*, 13, No. 4/64(1902), pp. 1248–75; 13, No. 5/65(1902), pp. 1363–78. In *Ot marksizma*, pp. 161–94.

_____. "Osnovnyia problemy teorii progressa." In *Problemy idealizma* (1902), pp. 1–47, and *Ot marksizma*, pp. 113–60.

_____. "Chto daet sovremennomu soznaniiu filosofiia Vladimira Solov'eva?" *VFP*, 14, No. 1/66(1903), pp. 52–96; 2/67(1903), pp. 125–66. In *Ot marksizma*, pp. 195–262.

_____. "Ob ekonomicheskom ideale," *Nauchnoe Slovo*, No. 5(1903). In *Ot marksizma*, pp. 263–87.

_____. "Zadachi politicheskoi ekonomii." In *Ot marksizma*, pp. 317–47.

_____. *Ot marksizma k idealizmu, sbornik statei (1896–1903)*. 1904. Reprint. Ann Arbor: University Microfilms, 1965.

_____. "O realisticheskom mirovozzrenii (Neskol'ko slov po pov. vykhoda v svete sbornika "Och. realis. mirov."")," *VFP*, 15, No. 3/73(1904), pp. 380–403.

_____. "Chekhov, kak myslitel'," *NP*, No. 10(1904), pp. 32–54; No. 11, pp. 138–52.

_____. "Bez Plana. Idealizm i obshchestvennaia programma," *NP*, No. 11(1904), pp. 348–60.

_____. "Karleil i Tolstoi," *NP*, No. 12(1904), pp. 227–60; *VZh*, No. 1(1905), pp. 16–38.

_____. " 'Tragediia chelovechestva,' Emerikha Madacha," *VZh*, No. 2(1905), pp. 205–22.

_____. "Voprosy filosofii i psikhologii v 1904 godu," *VZh*, No. 2(1905), pp. 299–304.

_____. "Bez plana. 'Voprosy Zhizni' i voprosy zhizni," *VZh*, No. 2(1905), pp. 347–68.

_____. "Bez plana. O puti Solov'eva-otvet kn. E.N. Trubetskomu," *VZh*, No. 3(1905), pp. 388–414.

_____. "Religiozno-obshchestvennaia khronika, politicheskoe osvobozhdenie i tserkovnaia reforma," *VZh*, Nos. 4–5 (1905), pp. 491–522.

_____. "Bez plana. Neskol'ko zamechanii po povodu stat'i G.I. Chulkova o poezii Vl. Solov'eva," *VZh*, No. 6(1905), pp. 293–317.

_____. "Neotlozhnaia zadacha (O soiuze khristianskoi politiki)," *VZh*, No. 9(1905), pp. 332–60.

_____. "Religiia chelovekobozhiia u L. Feierbakha," *VZh*, Nos. 10–11(1905), pp. 236–73; No. 12(1905), pp. 74–102.

_____. *Neotlozhnaia zadacha*. Moscow: Sytin, 1906.

_____. "O neobkhodimosti vvedeniia obshchestvennykh nauk v programmu dukhovnoi shkoly," *Bogoslovskii Vestnik*, 15, No. 2(1906), pp. 345–56.

_____. "Tserkov' i kul'tura," *Voprosy Religii*, No. 1(1906), pp. 38–52. In *Dva grada*, vol. 2, pp. 303–13.

_____. "Tserkov' i gosudarstvo," *Voprosy Religii,* No. 1(1906), pp. 53–101.

_____. "Khristianstvo i sotsial'nyi vopros," *Voprosy Religii*, No. 1(1906), pp. 298–334. In *Dva grada*, vol. 1, pp. 206–33.

_____. "Religiia i politika," *Poliarnaia Zvezda*, 12 Mar. 1906, pp. 118–27.

_____. "Venets ternovyi. Pamiati F.M. Dostoevskago," *Svoboda i Kul'tura*, 1 Apr. 1906, pp. 17–36. In *Dva grada*, vol. 2, pp. 223–43.

_____. "Karl Marks, kak religioznyi tip," *ME*, No. 22(1906), pp. 34–43; No. 23(1906), pp. 24–33; No. 24(1906), pp. 42–50; No. 25(1906), pp. 46–54. In *Dva grada*, vol. 1, pp. 69–105.

_____. "Paskhal'nye dumy," *Narod*, No. 1(1906), p. 1.

_____. "Sotsial'nye obiazannosti tserkvi," *Narod*, No. 5(1906), pp. 1–2.

_____. "Individualizm ili sobornost'," *Narod*, No. 6(1906), pp. 3–4.

_____. "Pis'mo intelligenta," *Narod*, No. 7(1906), p. 2.

_____. "Vremennoe i vechnoe," *Vek*, No. 7(1906), pp. 78–79.

_____. "Dukhovenstvo i politika," *Tovarishch*, 6 Dec. 1906, pp. 1–2.

_____. "Pod znamenem universiteta," *VFP*, 17, No. 5/85(1906), pp. 453–68.

_____. *Kratkii ocherk politicheskoi ekonomii*. Moscow: Efimov, 1907.

_____. "Srednevekovyi ideal i noveishaia kul'tura." *RM*, 28, No. 1(1907), pp. 61–83. In *Dva grada*, vol. 1, pp. 150–77.

_____. "Pis'mo v redaktsiiu," *Rech'*, 24 Jan. 1907, p. 4.

_____. "Neobkhodimoe raziasnenie," *Vek*, No. 5(1907), pp. 58–59.

_____. "Tserkovnyi vopros v Gosudarstvennoi Dume," *Vek*, No. 10(1907), pp. 119–20.

_____. "Voskresenie Khristovo i sovremennoe soznanie," *Vek*, No. 16(1907), pp. 215–19. In *Dva grada*, vol. 2, pp. 166–76.

_____. "Svoboda sovesti i prinuditel'naia religioznost'," *Rech'*, 10 May 1907, p. 1.

_____. "Religiia chelovekobozhiia v russkoi revoliutsii," *RM*, 29, No. 3(1908), pp. 72–103. In *Dva grada*, vol. 2, pp. 128–66.

_____. "Kn. S.N. Trubetskoi, kak religioznyi myslitel'," *ME*, No. 14(1908), pp. 11–22.

_____. "Po povodu raziasneniia Sv. Sinoda otnositel'no chestvovaniia L.N. Tolstogo," *ME*, No. 36(1908), pp. 24–30.

_____. "Filosofiia kn. S.N. Trubetskago i dukhovnaia bor'ba sovremennosti," *Kriticheskoe Obozrenie*, No. 1(1909), pp. 8–12. In *Dva grada*, vol. 2, pp. 243–54.

_____. "Pervokhristianstvo i noveishii sotsializm," *VFP*, 20, No. 3/98(1909), pp. 215–68. In *Dva grada*, vol. 2, pp. 1–50.

_____. "Narodnoe khoziaistvo i religioznaia lichnost'," *ME*, No. 23(1909), pp. 25–28; No. 24(1909), pp. 17–34. In *Dva grada*, vol. 1, pp. 178–205.

_____. "Sotsial'noe mirovozzrenie Dzh. Reskina," *VFP*, 20, No. 5/100(1909), pp. 395–436.

_____. "Vechnyi gorod," *ME*, No. 5(1910), pp. 43–52.

_____. "Revoliutsiia i reaktsiia," *ME*, No. 8(1910), pp. 23–36.

_____. "Problemy filosofii khoziaistva," *VFP*, 21, No. 4/104(1910), pp. 504–27.

_____. *Dva grada, izsledovaniia o prirode obshchestvennykh idealov*. 2 vols. Moscow: "Put'," 1911.

_____. "Priroda v filosofii Vl. Solov'eva." In *O Solov'eve, sbornik statei*, pp. 1–31. Moscow: "Put'," 1911.

_____. "Khristianstvo i mifologiia." *RM*, 32, No. 8(1911), pp. 112–33.

_____. *Filosofiia khoziaistva, chast' pervaia*. Moscow: "Put'," 1912.

_____. "Ekonomicheskii materializm kak filosofiia khoziaistva," *RM*, 33, No. 1(1912), pp. 44–64.

_____. "Chemu uchit delo episkopa Germogena?" *RM*, 33, No. 2, pt. 2(1912), pp. 50–53.

_____. "Na vyborakh (iz dnevnika)," *RM*, 33, No. 11(1912), pp. 185–92.

_____. *Istoriia sotsial'nykh uchenii v XIX veka*. 2d ed. Moscow, 1913.

_____. "Filosofiia khoziaistva," *RM*, 34, No. 5(1913), pp. 70–79.

_____. "Transtsendental'naia problema religii (vstupitel'naia glava k podgotovliaemomu issledovaniiu po filosofii religii)," *VFP*, 25, No. 4/124(1914), pp. 580–652; No. 5/125, pp. 728–80.

_____. "Sofiinost' tvari (kosmoditseia)," *VFP*, 27, 2–3/132–33 (1916), pp. 79–194.

_____. *Svet nevechernyi*. Moscow: "Put'," 1917.

_____. *Tikhie dumy, iz statei 1911–15*. Moscow: Leman i Sakharov, 1918.
_____. "O. Aleksandr El'chaninov, stat'ia iz zhurnala 'Put'." In *Pamiati ottsa Aleksandra El'chaninova*, pp. 60–64. Paris: YMCA Press, 1935.
_____. *Avtobiograficheskiia zametki*. Paris: YMCA Press, 1946.
Chetverikov, I.T. "Kriticheskii individualizm v russkoi filosofii," *Trudy Kievskoi Dukhovnoi Akademii*, No. 9(1905), pp. 120–32.
Chetverikov, Father S. "Khristianskoe Bratstvo Bor'by i ego programma pri svete Pravoslaviia," *Moskovskii Golos*, 22 Mar. 1907, pp. 5–8.
Child, Arthur H. "The Problem of Truth in the Sociology of Knowledge," *Ethics*, 58(1947), pp. 18–34.
Chueva, Izida. *Kritika idei intuitivizma v. rossii*. Moscow-Leningrad: Akad. Nauk SSSR, 1963.
Chulkov, Georgii, "Poeziia Vladimira Solov'eva," *VZh*, Nos. 4–5(1905), pp. 101–17.
_____. *Gody stranstvii*. Moscow: "Federatsiia," 1930.
Copleston, Frederick, S.J. *A History of Philosophy*. Vols. 7 and 8. Garden City, N.Y.: Doubleday, 1965, 1967.
Cumming, Robert D. *Human Nature and History, A Study of the Development of Liberal Political Thought*. 2 vols. Chicago: Univ. of Chicago Press, 1969.
Curtis, James E., and John W. Petras, eds. *The Sociology of Knowledge, a Reader*. New York: Praeger, 1970.
Curtis, John Shelton. *Church and State in Russia, The Last Years of the Empire*. 1940. Reprint. New York: Octagon Books, 1972.
Dahrendorf, Rolf. *Essays in the Theory of Society*. Stanford, Calif.: Stanford Univ. Press, 1968.
Dais, Eugene. "Law, Authority and Social Change." *Archiv für Rechts-und Sozial-Philosophie*, 57, No. 2(1971), pp. 161–85.
Danzas, J. "Les réminiscences gnostiques dans la philosophie russe moderne," *Revue des Sciences Philosophiques et Théologiques*, 25(1936), pp. 658–85.
David, Zdenek. "The Influence of Jacob Boehme on Russian Religious Thought," *The Slavic Review*, 22, No. 1(1962), pp. 43–64.
Deresch, Wolfgang. *Der Glaube der religiösen Sozialisten, ausgewählte text*. Hamburg: Furche-Verlag, 1972.
Dietzel, H. *Das Neünzehnte Jahrhundert und das Programm des Liberalismus*. Bonn: Röhrscheide und Ebbecke, 1900.
Douglas, Mary. *Natural Symbols, Explorations in Cosmology*. London: Barrie and Rockliff, 1970.
Edie, James M., James P. Scanlan, Mary-Barbara Zeldin, and George L. Kline, eds. *Russian Philosophy*. Chicago: Quadrangle, 1965, vol. 3.
Egbert, Donald Drew. *Social Radicalism and the Arts/Western Europe, a Cultural History from the French Revolution to 1968*. New York: Knopf, 1970.
Eisenstadt, Shmuel N. *Tradition, Change and Modernity*. New York: Wiley, 1973.
El'chaninov, Aleksandr. *Zhitie sv. Frantsiska Assizskago*. Moscow: Efimov, 1906.

————. *O samoupravlenie*. Moscow: Sytin, 1906.

————. "Kanony i tserkovnaia organizatsiia." *Zhivaia Zhizn'*, No. 1(1907), pp. 9–14.

————. "Religiozno-filosofskoe obshchestvo pamiati Vl. S. Solov'eva v Moskve," *Vek*, No. 9(1907), pp. 107–108.

————. "Religiozno-obshchestvennaia zhizn'," *Vek*, No. 13(1907), p. 163.

————. "Tragicheskii zverinets," *Zhivaia Zhizn'*, No. 1(1908), pp. 17–24.

————, and G. Vekilov. "Bibliografiia," *Voprosy Religii*, No. 2(1908), pp. 385–416.

El'chaninov, A., V.F. Ern, and P.A. Florenskii. *Istoriia religii, Pravoslavie*. With app. by Prof. S.N. Bulgakov. Moscow: "Pol'za," 1909.

English Liberalism and the State. Ed. Harold J. Schultz. Lexington, Mass.: Heath, 1972.

Erikson, Erik. *Identity and the Life Cycle, Selected Papers*. New York: International Universities Press, 1959.

Ern, Vladimir F. *Kak nuzhno zhit' khristianinu?* Moscow: Efimov, 1906.

————. *Khristianskoe otnoshenie k sobstvennosti*. Moscow: Efimov, 1906.

————. *Sem' Svobod*. Moscow: Efimov, 1906.

————. "Tserkovnoe vozrozhdenie," *Voprosy Religii*, No. 1(1906), pp. 102–42.

————. "Sotsializm i obshchee mirovozzrenie," *Bogoslovskii Vestnik*, 16, No. 9(1907), pp. 35–60.

————. "Katakomby i sovremennost'." In F. Buass'e. *Katakomby*. Moscow: Efimov, 1907, pp. 3–11.

————. "Khristianstvo i mir (otvet D.S. Merezhkovskomu)," *Zhivaia Zhizn'*, No. 1(1907), pp. 15–46.

————. "Sotsializm i problema svobody," *Zhivaia Zhizn'*, No. 2(1907), pp. 40–87.

————. "Nasha vina," *Vek*, No. 3(1907), pp. 34–35.

————. "Khristos v revoliutsii," *Vek*, No. 7(1907), pp. 83–85.

————. "Tainstva i vozrozhdenie Tserkvi," *Tserkovnoe Obnovlenie*, No. 9(1907), pp. 65–66.

————. "Istoricheskaia Tserkov'," *Tserkovnoe Obnovlenie*, No. 11(1907), pp. 81–83.

————. "Plekhanov ob Ibsene," *Vek*, No. 11(1907), pp. 133–35.

————. *Pastyr novago tipa*. Moscow: Efimov, 1907.

————. "Staroobriadtsy i sovremennye religioznie zaprosy," *Zhivaia Zhizn'*, No. 1(1908), pp. 9–16.

————. "O zhiznennoi pravde," *Voprosy Religii*, No. 2(1908), pp. 29–61.

————. "Chto delat'?" *Voprosy Religii*, No. 2(1908), pp. 62–91.

————. "Ideia katastroficheskago progressa," *RM*, 30, No. 10, pt. 2(1909), pp. 142–59.

————. *Bor'ba za logos, opyty filosofskie i kriticheskie*. Moscow: "Put'," 1911.

Ershov, M.N. *Puti razvitiia filosofii v Rossii*. Vladivostok: Izd. Gos. Dal'nevostochnago universiteta, 1922.

Etkind, Mark. *A.N. Benua, 1870–1960*. Leningrad-Moscow: "Iskusstvo," 1965.

Evdokimov, Paul. *Le Christ dans la Pensée Russe*. Paris: Les Éditions du Cerf, 1970.

Evgen'ev-Maksimov, V., and D. Maksimov. *Iz proshlogo russkoi zhurnalistiki*. Leningrad: Izd. pisatelei v Leningrade, 1930.

Evgrafov, V.E., *et al. Istoriia filosofii v SSSR*. Vol. 4. Moscow: "Nauka," 1971.

Ezerskii, N. "Religiia i politika," *RM*, 28, No. 1(1907), pp. 106–26.

──────. "Otkrytoe pis'mo k ottsu S. Shchukinu," *ME*, No. 13(1907), pp. 30–35.

──────. "Vtoroe pis'mo ottsu S. Shchukinu," *ME*, Nos. 24–25(1907), pp. 28–35.

Fedotov, George P. "Le renouveau spirituel en Russie," *Cahiers de la Quinzaine*, Series 28, Book 1(1931), pp. 53–77.

──────. *The Russian Religious Mind, Kievan Christianity, the Tenth to the Thirteenth Centuries*. New York: Harper, 1960.

──────. "The Church and Social Justice," *Cross Currents*, 14, No. 4(1964), pp. 424–27.

Fichte, Johann. *The Vocation of Man*. Trans. R. Chisholm. Indianapolis–New York: Bobbs-Merrill, 1956.

Filosofskaia Entsiklopediia, 5 vols. Moscow: "Sovetskaia Entsiklopediia," 1960–1970.

Filosofov, Dmitrii V. "Propoved' idealizma (Sbornik 'Problemy idealizma,' Moscow, 1903)," *NP*, No. 10(1903), pp. 177–84.

──────. "Religiozno-filosofskiia sobraniia," *Slovo*, 20 Oct. 1908, p. 2.

──────. "Druziia ili vraga (bogostroitel'stvo i bogoiskatel'stvo v rossii)," *RM*, 30, No. 8(1909), pp. 120–47.

Fischer, George. *Russian Liberalism: From Gentry to Intelligentsia*. Cambridge, Mass.: Harvard Univ. Press, 1958.

Florenskii, Pavel A. "O simvolakh beskonechnosti, ocherki idei G. Kantora," *NP*, No. 9(1904), pp. 173–235.

──────. "O tipakh vozrastaniia," *Bogoslovskii Vestnik*, 15, No. 7(1906), pp. 530–68.

──────. *Stolp i utverzhdenie istiny, 1(pis'ma k drugu, 1–7)*. Moscow: Vil'de, 1908.

──────. *Stolp i utverzhdenie istiny, 2, pis'mo 8*. Moscow: A.A. Chervrevoi, 1908.

────── *Stolp i utverzhdenie istiny, opyt pravoslavnoi feoditsei v dvenadtsati pis'makh*. Moscow: "Put'," 1914.

Florinsky, Michael. *Russia: A History and an Interpretation*. 2 vols. New York: Macmillan, 1965.

Florovsky, George V. *Puti russkago bogosloviia*. Paris: YMCA Press, 1937.

──────. "Empire and Desert: Antinomies of Christian History," *Cross Currents*, 9, No. 3(1959), pp. 233–53.

Foucault, Michael. *The Order of Things (Les mots et les choses [1966])*. Trans. not identified. London: Tavistock, 1970.

Frank, Semen L. "Gosudarstvo i lichnost'," *NP*, No. 11(1904), pp. 308–17.

_____. "O kriticheskom idealizme," *Mir Bozhii*, 13, No. 12(1904), pp. 224–64.

_____. "O zadachii religiozno-filosofskago obshchestva," *Slovo*, 21 Oct. 1908, p. 3.

_____. *Filosofiia i zhizn', sbornik statei*. St. Petersburg: Zhukovskii, 1910.

_____. "K kharakteristike Gete." In *Filosofiia i zhizn'*, pp. 355–66. St. Petersburg: Zhukovskii, 1910.

_____. "Lichnost' i mirovozzrenie Fr. Shleiermakhera," *RM*, 32, No. 9(1911), pp. 1–28.

_____, ed. *Iz istorii russkoi filosofskoi mysli kontsa XIX-go i nachala XX-go Veka, Antologiia*. New York: Inter Language Literary Associates, 1965.

Friedrich, Carl J., ed. *The Philosophy of Kant*. New York: Modern Library, 1949.

_____. *The Philosophy of Law in Historical Perspective*. Chicago: Univ. of Chicago Press, 1969.

Friedrich, Paul. "Semantic Structure and Social Structure." In *Explorations in Cultural Anthropology*, ed. Ward H. Goodenough, pp. 131–65. New York: McGraw-Hill, 1964.

_____. "Structural Implications of Russian Pronomial Usage." In *Sociolinguistics*, ed. W. Bright, pp. 214–59. The Hague: Mouton, 1966.

From Max Weber: Essays in Sociology. Trans. and eds. H. H. Gerth and C. Wright Mills, pp. 196–301. London: Routledge and Kegan Paul, 1952.

Galai, Shmuel. *The Liberation Movement in Russia (1900–1905)*. Cambridge: The Univ. Press, 1973.

Geertz, Clifford. "Religion As a Cultural System." In *Anthropological Approaches to the Study of Religion*, ed. M. Banton, pp. 1–46. London: Tavistock, 1969.

Gellner, Ernest. "The Soviet and the Savage," *Times Literary Supplement*, 16 Oct. 1974, p. 1166.

_____. *Thought and Change*. Chicago: Univ. of Chicago Press, 1965.

Goethe, Johann W. von. *Bedenken und Ergebung*. In *Werke*, 40 vols. Stuttgart and Tübingen: J. G. Cotta, vol. 40, 1840.

Gorkii, Maksim. "Ispoved'." In *Sbornik "Znanie" za 1908 god*. pp. 1–206. St. Petersburg: "Znanie," 1908.

Grabar', Igor' E. *Moia zhizn'*. Moscow-Leningrad, 1937.

Haase, Felix. *Russische Kirche und Sozializmus*. Leipzig and Berlin: Heubner, 1922.

Haimson, Leopold. "The Problem of Social Stability in Urban Russia, 1905–1917 (Part Two)," *Slavic Review*, 24, No. 1 (1965), pp. 1–21.

Harcave, Sydney. *The Russian Revolution of 1905*. London: Collier, 1970.

Hecker, Julius. *Religion and Communism, a study of religion and atheism in Soviet Russia*. New York: Wiley, 1934.

Hegel, Georg. *Reason in History, a General Introduction to the Philosophy of History*. Trans. R. Hartman. Indianapolis–New York: Bobbs-Merrill, 1953.

_____. *The Philosophy of Right*. Trans. and ed. T. Knox. Oxford: Clarendon Press, 1952.

_____. *The Phenomenology of Mind*. 2d ed., rev. and cor. Trans. J.B. Baillie. New York: Macmillan, 1955.

Heine, Heinrich. *Religion and Philosophy in Germany*. 1882. Reprint. Boston: Beacon Press, 1959.

Herzen, Alexander I. *From the Other Shore*. Trans. Moura Budberg. London: Weidenfeld and Nicholson, 1956.

Hippius, Zinaida. *Literaturnyi dnevnik:* 1897–1907. St. Petersburg: M.V. Pirozhkov, 1908.

_____. *Dmitrii Merezhkovskii*. Paris: YMCA Press, 1951.

Hobhouse, Leonard. *Liberalism*. 1911. Reprint. London: Oxford Univ. Press, 1969.

Humboldt, Wilhelm von. *The Limits of State Action*. 1854. Reprint. Trans., ed. and introd. J. W. Burrow. Cambridge: The Univ. Press, 1969.

I.K. "Nebesnyi revizionizm," *ME*, No. 27(1908), pp. 23–29.

Intelligentsiia v Rossii, sbornik statei. St. Petersburg: Knigoizdat. "Zemlia," 1910.

Iuridicheskii Vestnik, a Moscow monthly journal, 1913–1916.

Ivanov, Evgenii. "Universitet," *VZh*, Nos. 4–5(1905), pp. 264–67.

Iz Glubiny, sbornik statei o russkoi revoliutsii. 2d ed. 1918. Reprint. Paris: YMCA Press, 1967.

Izgoev, Aleksandr S. "Bessilie religioznykh intelligentov," *Rech'*, 5 Apr. 1908, p. 5.

Iz istorii noveishei russkoi literatury. Moscow: "Zerno," 1910.

Jastrow, I. *Die Aufgaben des Liberalismus in Preussen*. 2d ed. Berlin: Rosenbaum und Hart, 1894.

"The Jewish Question." In *The Marx-Engels Reader*, ed. Robert G. Tucker. New York: Norton, 1972.

Kant, Immanuel. *The Metaphysical Elements of Justice*. Trans. and ed. John Ladd. New York: Bobbs-Merrill, 1965.

_____. *Prolegomena to Any Future Metaphysics*. Trans. P. Lucas. Manchester, England: Manchester Univ. Press, 1950.

_____. "Grundgesetz der reinen praktischen Vernunft." *Werke in Sechs Banden*. Ed. Wilhelm Weischedel. Vol. 4, pp. 143–44. Wiesbaden: Insel-Verlag, 1956.

Kareev, A. "Po povodu zapiski revniteli tserkovnago obnovleniia," *Tovarishch*, 13 Mar. 1906, p. 2.

Karpovich, Michael. "Iunosheskie gody ottsa Aleksandra (vospominaniia druga)," In *Pamiati ottsa Aleksandra El'chaninova*. pp. 25–31. Paris: YMCA Press, 1935.

Kartashev, Anton V. *Russkaia tserkov' v 1905*. St. Petersburg: Merushev, 1906.

_____. *Reforma, reformatsiia i ispolnenie tserkvi*. Petrograd: "Korabl," 1916.

_____. "The Russian Church During the Synodal Period of Her History," *The Christian East*, Vol. XVI, Nos. 3–4 (July–Dec. 1936), pp. 112–24.

_____. "Moi ranniia vstrechi s o. Sergiem," *Pravoslavnaia Mysl'*, No. 8(1951), pp. 47–55.

Kaufmann, Walter. *Hegel, Reinterpretation, Texts and Commentary*. Garden City, N.Y.: Doubleday, 1965.

Keep, John L. H. *The Rise of Social Democracy in Russia, 1898–1907*. London: Oxford Univ. Press, 1963.

Kelly, George A. *Idealism, Politics and History, Sources of Hegelian Thought*. London: Cambridge Univ. Press, 1969.

Khristianskoe Chtenie. A St. Petersburg monthly theological journal, 1821–1916.

Kindersley, Richard. *The First Russian Revisionists, A Study of Legal Marxism in Russia*. Oxford: Clarendon, 1962.

Kingsley, Charles. *Alton Locke, tailor and poet*. London: Chapman and Hall, 1850.

Kistiakovskii, Bogdan. "Kategorii neobkhodimosti i spravedlivosti pri izsledovanii sotsial'nykh iavlenii," *Zhizn'*, No. 5(1900), pp. 284–306; No. 6(1900), pp. 127–48.

Kizevetter, Aleksandr A. *Na rubezhe dvukh stoletii*, *(Vospominaniia* 1881–1914). Prague: "Orbis," 1929.

Klarr, Herman. *Die Utopie vom Erdenparadiese bei Nowgorodzeff*. Leipzig: R. Noske, 1936.

Kline, George. "Theoretische Ethik im Russischen Frühmarxismus," *Forschungen zur Osteuropaischen Geschichte*, 9(1963), pp. 269–79.

―――. *Religious and Anti-Religious Thought in Russia, The Weil Lectures*. Chicago: Univ. of Chicago Press, 1968.

Kliuchevskii, Vasilii O. *Kurs russkoi istorii*. In *Sochineniia*, 2d ed. 1906, Reprint. Vol. 1, pt. 1, Lecture 4, pp. 61–73. Moscow: Gosizdat. politicheskoi literatury, 1956.

―――. *Pis'ma, dnevniki, aforizmy i mysli ob istorii*, Ed. M.V. Nechkina. Moscow: "Nauka," 1968.

Kogan, Petr S. *Ocherki po istorii noveishei russkoi literatury*. Vol. 3. No. 3. *Mystiki i bogoiskateli*. Moscow: "Zaria," 1911.

Kohn, Hans. *The Mind of Modern Germany*. New York: Harper, 1960.

Kolakowski, Leszek. "The Priest and the Jester." In *Toward a Marxist Humanism, Essays on the Left Today*. Ch. 1. New York: Grove Press, 1969.

Korneeva, A.I. *Leninskaia kritika makhizma i bor'ba protiv sovremennogo idealizma*. Moscow: "Mysl," 1971.

Kotliarevskii, Serge A. "Ob istinnom i mnimon realizme (po pov. "Ocherki realistich. mirovoz.")," *VFP*, 15, No. 5/75(1904), pp. 624–44.

―――. "Predposylka demokratii," *VFP*, 16, No. 2/77(1905), pp. 104–27.

Kovalevsky, Pierre. "Messianisme et millenarisme," *Archives de sociologie des religions*, 5(1958), pp. 47–70.

Kozhevnikov, Vladimir. *Otnoshenie sotsializma k religii*. Moscow, 1908.

Kremnev, B. "Religiozno-filosofskoe sobranie v Peterburge," *Pereval*, Nos. 8–9(1907), pp. 93–94.

Kudriavtsev, Petr P. "Slovo o znachenii i sile very," *Trudy Kievskoi Dukhovnoi Akademii*, 43 No. 4(1902), pp. 609–23.

―――. "K voprosu ob otnoshenii khristianstva k iazychestvu," *Trudy Kievskoi Dukhovnoi Akademii*, 44, No. 5(1903), pp. 30–78.

_____. *Absoliutizm ili reliativizm, Opyt istoriko-kriticheskago izucheniia chistago empirizma noveishago vremeni v ego otnoshenii k nravstvennosti i religii*. Kiev: N.I. Chokalov, 1908.

Lamennais, Félicité R. de. *Paroles d'un croyant*. 1834. Reprint. Paris: Flammarion, 1973.

Leikina-sbirskaia, V.R. *Intelligentsiia v rossii vo vtoroi polovine XIX veka*. Moscow: "Mysl'," 1971.

Lelouvier, Yves-Noël. *Perspectives Russes Sur L'église, un théologien contemporaine: Georges Florovsky*. Paris: Éditions du Centurion, 1968.

Lenin, Vladimir I. *Materializm i Empiriokrititsizm: Kriticheskie zametki ob odnoi reaktsionnoi filosofii*. 1908. Reprint. Moscow: Izd. politicheskoi literatury, 1967.

_____. *Filosofskie tetradi*. Moscow: Izd. politicheskoi literatury, 1965.

_____. *O religii i tserkvi*. Ed. E.G. Filimonov, and I.A. Galitskaia, Moscow: Izd. politicheskoi literatury, 1966.

Levin, Alfred. *The Second Duma, A Study of the Social Democratic Party and the Russian Constitutional Experiment*. 2d ed. Hamden, Conn.: Archon Books, 1966.

Levitskii, Sergei. *Ocherki po istorii russkoi filosofii i obshchestvennoi mysli*. Frankfort on the Main: Posev Verlag, 1968.

_____. "On Some Characteristic Traits of Russian Philosophic Thought," *St. Vladimir's Theological Quarterly*, 13, No. 3(1969), pp. 149–61.

Levy, Marion J., Jr. *Modernization and the Structure of Societies, A Setting for International Affairs*. Princeton: Princeton Univ. Press, 1970.

Lewis, John. "Idealism and Ideologies." In *Marxism and the Open Mind*, pp. 1–23. London: Routledge and Kegan Paul, 1957.

Literaturnyi raspad, kriticheskii sbornik, No. 1. St. Petersburg: "Zerno," 1908.

Literaturnyi raspad, No. 2. St. Petersburg: Knigoizdatel'stvo "EOS," 1909.

Lossky, Nicholas O. *History of Russian Philosophy*. New York: International Universities Press, 1951.

_____. *Vospominaniia*. Munich: Wilhelm Fink, 1968.

Lossky, Vladimir. *The Mystical Theology of the Eastern Church*. London: James Clark, 1968.

Löwith, Karl. *From Hegel to Nietzsche, the Revolution in Nineteenth Century Thought*. Trans. David E. Green. New York: Holt, 1964.

_____. *Meaning in History, the Theological Implications of the Philosophy of History*. Chicago: Univ. of Chicago Press, 1949.

Lunacharskii, Anatolii V. "Osnovnye idei empiriokrititsizma," *Obrazovanie*, 12, No. 2(1903), pp. 113–50.

_____. *Religiia i sotsializm*. 2 vols. St. Petersburg: Shipovnik, 1908, 1911.

Lur'e, S. "Sektantstvo i partiinost'," *ME*, No. 30(1906), pp. 28–36.

_____. "Religioznaia mistika i filosofiia," *RM*, 29, No. 4(1908), pp. 41–56.

_____. "Religioznye iskaniia v sovremennoi literature," *RM*, 29, No. 10(1908), pp. 44–67.

Macpherson, C.B. *The Political Theory of Possessive Individualism*. London: Oxford Univ. Press, 1970.

Maevskii, Vladimir A. *Vnutreniaia missiia i ee osnovopolozhnik*. Buenos Aires: 1954.

Makovskii, Sergei. *Na Parnase "Serebriannogo veka."* Munich: Izd. Tsentral'nogo Obedineniia Politicheskikh Emigrantov iz Sssr, 1962.

Malia, Martin. *Alexander Herzen and the Birth of Russian Socialism, 1812–1855*. Cambridge, Mass.: Harvard Univ. Press, 1961.

Mannheim, Karl. *Ideology and Utopia, An Introduction to the Sociology of Knowledge*. New York: Harcourt, 1936.

———. *Essays on the Sociology of Culture*. London: Routledge and Kegan Paul, 1956.

Markham, F.M.H., ed. and trans. *Henri Comte de Saint-Simon, Selected Writings*. Oxford: Basil Blackwell, 1952.

Martynov, Aleksandr S. *Khristianstvo i sotsial-demokratiia*. St. Petersburg: "Berezhlivost'," 1906.

The Marx-Engels Reader. Ed. Robert G. Tucker, New York: Norton, 1972.

Mathiot, Madeleine. *An Approach to the Cognitive Study of Language*. Bloomington: Indiana Univ. Press, 1968.

Mauss, Marcel. "Une categorie de l'esprit humain, la notion de personne, celle de 'Moi'." In *Sociologie et Anthropologie*. pp. 333–63. Paris: Presses universitaires de France, 1960.

Meier, Aleksandr A. "Intelligentsiia i religiia," *Rech'* 29 Oct. 1908, p. 2.

———. *Religiia i kul'tura, po pov. sovrem. religiozn. iskanii*. St. Petersburg: "Gramotnost'," 1909.

Mendel, Arthur. *Dilemmas of Progress in Tsarist Russia, Legal Marxism and Legal Populism*. Cambridge, Mass.: Harvard Univ. Press, 1961.

Merezhkovskii, Dmitrii S. "Zapiski religiozno-filosofskago sobraniia," Meeting 3, p. 175, *NP*, No. 2(1903); 10, pp. 226–27, *NP*, No. 5(1903); 17, pp. 426–27, *NP*, No. 11(1903); 18, pp. 470–72, *ibid*.

———. "Novyi Vavilon." *NP*, No. 3(1904), pp. 171–77.

———, Zinaida Hippius, and D.V. Filosofov. *Le Tsar et la Révolution*. Paris: Mercure de France, 1907.

———. "O Tserkvi griadushchago." In *Zapiski S-Peterburgskago religiozno-filosofskago obshchestva*. St. Petersburg: Herol'd, 1908, vol. 2, pp. 1–4.

———. *Polnoe sobranie sochinenii*, 24 vols. Moscow: Sytin, 1914, Vols. 11, 13, 14.

———. "Predislovie." *L. Tolstoi i Dostoevskii*. In *Polnoe sobranie sochinenii*. Vol. 11, Moscow: Sytin, 1914.

———. *The Death of the Gods*. Trans. B.G. Guerney. New York: Modern Library, 1929.

———. *The Romance of Leonardo da Vinci*. Trans. H. Trent. New York: Washington Square Press, 1963.

Merlan, Phillip. *Monopsychism, Mysticism, Metaconsciousness, Problems of the Soul in the Neo-Aristotelian and Neo-Platonic Tradition*. The Hague: Martinus Nijhoff, 1963.

Merz, John T. *A History of European Thought in the Nineteenth Century*. 4 vols. New York: Dover, 1965.

Minskii, Nikolai. "Absoliutnaia reakstiia," I. *Slovo*, 29 June 1908, p. 3; II, 1 July, p. 2; III, 3 July, p. 3.
———. "O novom religioznom soznanii," *Nasha Gazeta*, 22 Jan. 1909, pp. 2–3; 25 Feb., pp. 3–4.
Mir Bozhii. A St. Petersburg monthly journal, 1892–1906.
Mir Iskusstva. A St. Petersburg monthly journal, 1899–1904.
Missionerskoe Obozrenie. A St. Petersburg monthly missionary journal, 1896–1916.
Mochulsky, Konstantin. "The Idea of Social Christianity in Russian Philosophy." *St. Vladimir's Seminary Quarterly*, 12, Nos. 3–4(1968), pp. 157–69.
———. *Dostoevsky: His Life and Work*. Trans. Michael A. Minihan. Princeton: Princeton Univ. Press, 1971.
Moskovskii Ezhenedel'nik. A Moscow weekly journal, 1906–1910.
Moskovskii Golos. A Moscow weekly newspaper, 1906–1907.
Murvar, Vatro. "Russian Religious Structures: A Study in Persistent Church Subservience." *Journal for the Scientific Study of Religion*, 7, No. 1(1968), pp. 1–22.
———. "Messianism in Russia: Religious and Revolutionary," *Journal for the Scientific Study of Religion*, 10, No. 4(1971), pp. 277–338.
Musil, Robert. *The Man Without Qualities*. 3 vols. Trans. Eithne Wilkins and E. Kaiser. London: Secker and Warburg, 1953.
Myshchtsyn, V. "Iz periodicheskoi pechati-politicheskaia rol' dukhovenstva-soiuz khristianskoi politiki," *Bogoslovskii Vestnik*, 15, No. 2(1906), pp. 380–91; No. 3, pp. 597–603; No. 4, pp. 768–83; No. 5, pp. 155–74.
Narod. A Kiev daily, 1906.
Nasha Gazeta. A St. Petersburg daily newspaper, 1904–1908.
Natorp, P. *Sozialpädegogik*. Stuttgart: F. Frommann (E. Hauff), 1899.
Nietzsche, Friedrich. *Von Nutzen und Nachteil der Historie für das Leben*. Basel: Verlag Birkhause, n.d.
Nov'. A Moscow daily newspaper, 1906–1907.
Novaia Rus'. A St. Petersburg daily newspaper, 1908–1910.
Novgorodtsev, Pavel I. *Istoricheskaia shkola iuristov, ee proiskhozhdenie i sud'ba*. Moscow: Moscow Univ., 1896.
———. "Pravo estestvennoe." *Entsiklopedicheskii Slovar'*. Vol. 48, pp. 885–90. St. Petersburg: Brokgaus i Efron, 1898.
———. "Pravo i nravstvennost'." In *Sbornik po obshchestvenno-iuridicheskim naukam*, ed. Iu. S. Gambarov, No. 1, pp. 113–36. St. Petersburg: O.N. Popov, 1899.
———. "K voprosu o sushchnosti teokratii," *VFP*, 10, No. 5/50(1899), pp. 303–11.
———. *Istoriia novoi filosofii prava, kurs lektsii*, 3d expanded ed., Vol. 1. Moscow: Literaturnoe obshchestvo raspredelenii politicheskikh knig, 1900.
———. *Kant i Hegel v ikh ucheniiakh o prave i gosudarstve*. Moscow: Moscow Univ., 1901.

_____. "Ideia prava v filosofii V.S. Solov'eva," *VFP*, 12, No. 1/56(1901), pp. 112–29.

_____. "Uchenie Kanta o prave i gosudarstve," *VFP*, 12, No. 3/58(1901), pp. 315–61.

_____. *O zadachakh sovremennoi filosofii prava*. St. Petersburg: "Slova," 1902.

_____. "Moral i poznanie," *VFP*, 13, No. 4/64(1902), pp. 824–38.

_____. "Nravstvennyi idealizm v filosofii prava." In *Problemy Idealizma*, pp. 236–96.

_____. "Znachenie filosofii," *Nauchnoe Slovo*, No. 4(1903), pp. 108–15.

_____. *Iz lektsii po obshchei teorii prava, chast' metodologicheskaia*. Moscow: Izd. studentov, 1904.

_____. "Nravstvennaia problema v filosofii Kanta," *VFP*, 15, No. 2/72(1904), pp. 279–314.

_____. "Gosudarstvo i pravo," 1. *VFP*, 15, No. 4/74(1904), pp. 397–446; 2, No. 5/75, pp. 508–38.

_____. "O filosofskom dvizhenii nashikh dnei," *NP*, No. 10 (1904), pp. 59–67.

_____. "Dva pravovykh ideala," *Nauchnoe Slovo*, 2, No. 10(1904), pp. 112–27.

_____. *Boris Nik. Chicherin*. Moscow: Moscow Univ., 1905.

_____. "Kant, kak moralist'," *VFP*, 16, No. 1/76(1905), pp. 19–36.

_____. "Sovremennye otzvuki slavianofil'stva," *VZh*, No. 6 (1905), pp. 354–82.

_____. "Dva etiuda," *Poliarnaia Zvezda*, 30 Dec. 1905, pp. 210–22.

_____. "Speech on the means of communication between the Duma, the Council of Ministers and the Emperor," *Stenograficheskii otchet, Gosudarstvennaia Duma*, 1906, pp. 245–46, 248.

_____. "Speech on the inviolability of the person," *S.O.*, pp. 295–98, 316–17, 371–72.

_____. "Speech on the verification of the rights of members of the Duma from Perm gub." *S.O.*, pp. 1082–85.

_____. "Krizis sovremennago pravosoznaniia," *VFP*, 17, No. 4/84(1906), pp. 390–451; 18, No. 4/89(1907), pp. 367–432; No. 5/90(1907), pp. 433–91. Vol. 19, No. 1/91(1908), pp. 80–117; No. 3/93(1908), pp. 251–86; No. 4/94(1908), pp. 337–440; No. 5/95(1908), pp. 513–97.

_____. "Prof. B. I. Ger'e o pervoi Gosudarstvennoi Dume," *RM*, 28, No. 1(1907), pp. 19–25.

_____. "Russkii posledovatel' G. Kogena," *VFP*, 20, No. 4/99(1909), pp. 636–61.

_____. "Ucheniye sofistov o estestvennom prave," *VFP*, 21, No. 1/101(1910), pp. 109–23.

_____. "Pravo na dostoinoe chelovecheskoe sushchestvovanie." In *Sotsial'no-filosofskie etiudy*, pp. 1–13. St. Petersburg–Moscow: M.O. Volf, 1911.

_____. "Ob obshchestvennom ideale," *VFP*, 22, No. 4/109(1911), pp. 395–439; No. 5/110(1911), pp. 491–530; 23, No. 5/115(1912), pp. 361–98; 24, No.

4/119(1913), pp. 279–312; 25, No. 1/121(1914), pp. 1–146; 27, No. 2–3/132–33 (1916), pp. 356–409; 27, No. 4/134(1916), pp. 400–511.

———. *Politicheskie ideali drevnago i novago mira*. Vols. 1 and 2. Moscow: Moscow Univ., 1910, 1913.

———. "Sovremennoe polozhenie problemy estestvennago prava," *Iuridicheskii Vestnik*, No. 1(1913), pp. 18–24.

———. "Psikhologicheskaia teoriia prava i filosofiia estestvennago prava," *Iuridicheskii Vestnik*, No. 3 (1913), pp. 5–34.

———. "O putiakh i zadachakh russkoi intelligentsii," In *Iz Glubiny, sobornik statei o russkoi revoliutsii*, 2d ed. 1918. Reprint. Paris: YMCA Press, 1967, pp. 247–68.

———. *Ob obshchestvennom ideale*. 3d ed. Berlin: "Slovo," 1921.

———. "Pravoslavnaia tserkov' v eia otnoshenii k dukhovnoi zhizni novoi Rossii," *Russkaia Mysl'* (Prague), Nos. 1–2(1922), pp. 193–221.

———. "Sushchestvo russkago pravoslavnago soznaniia." In *Pravoslavie i Kul'tura*, ed. V.V. Zenkovskii, pp. 7–23. Berlin: "Russkaia Kniga," 1923.

Novyi Put'. A St. Petersburg monthly journal, 1903–1904.

Novyi Zhurnal. New York journal, 1941–present.

Obrazovanie. A St. Petersburg monthly journal, 1892–1909.

Obshchestvennoe dvizhenie v Rossii v nachale XX-go veka. Eds. L. Martov, P. Maslov, and A. Potresov. St. Petersburg: "Obshchestvennaia pol'za," 1909–1914.

Ocherki filosofii marksizma, sbornik statei, St. Petersburg: V. Bezobrazov, 1908.

Ocherki realisticheskago mirovozzreniia, sbornik statei, St. Petersburg: Motvid, 1904.

Ognev, N. *Tserkovnyi sobor i religioznye zaprosy obshchestva*. St. Petersburg, 1908.

Ornatskii, F.S. "Po povodu novago zhurnala, 'Novyi Put','" *Trudy Kievskoi Dukhovnoi Akademii*, 44, No. 3(1903), pp. 440–54.

"Ortodoks" (Akselrod, Liubov'). "O 'Problemakh idealizma.' " In *Protiv idealizma, sbornik statei*, pp. 13–31. Moscow, 1922.

Ostrovitianov, Konstantin V. *Dumy o proshlom*. Moscow: "Nauka," 1967.

"Ot otnoshenii tserkvi i sviashchenstva k sovremennoi obshchestvenno-politicheskoi zhizni, Zapiski Soiuz Revnit. Tserk. Obnov." *Rech'*, 11 Mar. 1906, p. 2.

"Otzyv o. Ioann Kronshtadskago o 'Novom Puti'," *NP*, No. 3(1903), p. 253.

Pachmuss, Temira. "Zinaida Hippius, Epokha Mira Iskusstva," *Vozrozhdenie*, No. 203(1968), pp. 66–73.

———. *Zinaida Hippius, An Intellectual Profile*. Carbondale and Edwardsville: Southern Illinois Univ. Press, 1971.

Pankratova, A.M., L.M. Ivanov, and V.D. Mochalov, eds. *Istoriia Moskvy*. Moscow: Izd. Akad. Nauk SSSR, 1955, vol. 5.

Parts and Wholes. Ed. Daniel Lerner. New York: Free Press, 1963.

Pascal, Blaise. *Pensées*. Trans. W.F. Trotter. London: J.M. Dent, 1954.

Pascal, Pierre. "La religion du peuple russe." *Revue de Psychologie des Peuples*, 2, No. 5(1947), pp. 138–54; No. 7, pp. 262–84.

_____. "Les Grands Courants de la Pensée Russe Contemporaine." *Cahiers du Monde Russe et Soviétique*, 3, No. 1(1962), pp. 5–58.
_____. "La Culture Russe Au Tournant du Siècle." Conference: *La Philosophie Idéaliste en Russie*. Aix-en-Provence, 25–29 Mar. 1968.
Pepper, Stephen. *World Hypotheses, A Study in Evidence*. Berkeley: Univ. of California Press, 1966.
Pereval. A Moscow monthly journal, 1906–1907.
Pertsov, Petr P. *Literaturnye vospominaniia, 1890–1902gg*. Moscow–St. Petersburg: "Akademiia," 1933.
Pervaia Gosudarstvennaia Duma, alfavitnyi spisok i podrobniia biografii. Moscow, 1906.
Piaget, Jean. *Études Sociologiques*. Geneva: Libraire Droz, 1965.
_____. *Six Psychological Studies*. Trans. A. Tenzer. Ed. D. Elkind. New York: Vintage Books/Random House, 1968.
Pipes, Richard. *Social Democracy and the St. Petersburg Labor Movement, 1885–1897*. Cambridge, Mass.: Harvard Univ. Press, 1963.
_____. *Struve, Liberal on the Left, 1870–1905*. Vol. 1, Cambridge, Mass.: Harvard Univ. Press, 1970.
Plamenatz, John. *Ideology*. London: Macmillan, 1971.
Plekhanov, Georgii. *G. V. Plekhanov o religii i tserkvi, izbrannye proizvedeniia*. Moscow: Izd. Akad. Nauk SSSR, 1957.
Polanyi, Michael. *The Logic of Liberty, Reflections and Rejoinders*. Chicago: Univ. of Chicago Press, 1951.
_____. *The Tacit Dimension*. London: Routledge and Kegan Paul, 1967.
Poliarnaia Zvezda. A St. Petersburg weekly journal, 1905–1906.
Popov, Sergei I. *Kant i Kantianstvo*. Moscow: Moscow Univ., 1961.
Poltoratzkii, Nikolai. "Russian religious philosophy." *St. Vladimir's Seminary Quarterly*, NS1, No. 3(1957), pp. 23–35.
Potresov, Aleksandr N. "Evoliutsiia obshch.-politicheskoi mysli v pred-revoliutsionniiu epokhu." In *Obshchestvennoe dvizhenie v Rossii v nachale XX-go veka*, ed. L. Martov *et al.*, pp. 584–98. St. Petersburg: "Obshchestvennaia pol'za," 1909.
Problemy idealizma, sbornik statei. Ed. P.I. Novgorodtsev. Moscow: Izd. Moskovskago Psikhologicheskago Obshchestva, 1902.
Pustarnakov, V.F. *"Kapital" K. Marksa i filosofskaia mysl' v rossii*. Moscow: "Nauka," 1974.
Putnam, George F. "Aleksandr Blok and the Russian Intelligentsia," *Slavic and East European Journal*, 9, No. 1(1965), pp. 29–46.
_____. "Vasilii V. Rozanov: Sex, Marriage and Christianity," *Canadian Slavic Studies*, 5, No. 3(1971), pp. 301–26.
Put'. A Paris journal, 1925–1939.
Pyman, B.A. "The Russian Decadents, 1890–1905, with special reference to D.S. Merezhkovsky." Ph.D. diss., Cambridge Univ. 3516, 1959.
Radishchev, Alexander N. *A Journey from St. Petersburg to Moscow*. Trans. L. Wiener. Ed. R.P. Thaler. Cambridge, Mass.: Harvard Univ. Press, 1958.
Ratner, M. "Problemy idealizma v russkoi literature." *Russkoe Bogatstvo*,

No. 8(1903), pt. 2, pp. 1–30; No. 9(1903), pt. 2, pp. 1–32; No. 10(1903), pt. 2, pp. 1–29.

Rech'. A St. Petersburg daily newspaper, 1906–1917.

"Religioznaia problema v sovremennom osveshchenii," *Bogoslovskii Vestnik*, 18, No. 1(1909), pp. 58–84, 234–60, 424–49; continued as "Religiia i obshchestvennost'," 18, No. 2(1909), pp. 229–59, 424–61.

"Religiozno-obshchestvennaia khronika," *Vek*, No. 8(1907), p. 208.

"Religiozno-obshchestvennaia zhizn'." *Vek*, No. 13(1907), p. 163.

Renouvier, Charles. *Le personnalisme*. Paris: F. Alcan, 1903.

Rieff, Philip. *The Triumph of the Therapeutic, Uses of Faith After Freud*. New York: Harper, 1966.

———. *Freud, The Mind of a Moralist*. New York: Viking, 1959.

Riha, Thomas. *A Russian European; Paul Miliukov in Russian Politics*. Notre Dame: Univ. of Notre Dame Press, 1969.

(Rklitskii), Episkop Nikon. *Zhizneopisanie Blazhenneishago Antoniia, Mitropolita Kievskago i Galitskago*. 2 vols. New York: Izd. Severo-Amerikanskoi i kanadskoi eparkhii, 1956.

Romanskii. "Religiozno-filosofskaia khronika," *NP*, No. 5 (1903), pp. 201–11.

———. "Religiozno-filosofskaia khronika." *NP*, No. 7(1903), pp. 259–76.

———. "Otklikaiutsia." *NP*, No. 1(1904), pp. 268–76.

Rosenberg, John D., ed. *The Genius of John Ruskin*. New York: G. Braziller, 1963.

Rousseau, Jean Jacques. *The Social Contract and Discourses*. Trans. G.D.H. Cole. New York: Dutton, 1950.

Rozanov, Vasilii. "Russkaia tserkov'," *Poliarnaia Zvezda*. 3 Feb. 1906, pp. 524–40.

———. *O slabnuvskii fetish (Psikhol. osnovy russkoi revoliutsii)*. St. Petersburg: M.V. Pirozhkov, 1906.

———. "K pyatomu izdaniiu 'Vekh,' " *ME*, No. 10(1910), pp. 33–46.

Rozental, Mark M. *et al.*, eds. *Lenin kak filosof*. Moscow: Izd. politicheskoi literatury, 1969.

Rozhkov, Nikolai A. "Znachenie i sud'by noveishago idealizma v rossii," *VFP*, 14, No. 2/67(1903), pp. 314–32.

Rudnev, Vladimir A. "Religiia i sotsializm," *Sovremennyia Zapiski*, 35(1928), pp. 473–92; 37(1928), pp. 409–71.

Russkaia Mysl'. A Moscow monthly journal, 1880–1918.

Russkaia Mysl'. Sofia, 1921; Prague, 1922–23; Paris, 1927.

Russkii Vestnik. A Moscow and St. Petersburg monthly journal, 1856–1906.

Sabaneeff, Leonid. "Religious and Mystical Trends in Russia at the Turn of the Century." *The Russian Review*, 24, No. 4(1965), pp. 354–68.

Saint-Simon, Henri. *Nouveau Christianisme*. Paris: Bossange père, 1825.

Santayana, George. *The German Mind: A Philosophical Diagnosis*. New York: Crowell, 1968.

Scanlan, James P. "The New Religious Consciousness: Merezhkovsky and Berdiaev." *Canadian Slavic Studies*, 4, No. 1(1970), pp. 17–35.

Schachnowitsch, M. I. *Lenin und die Fragen des Atheismus*. Berlin: Dietz, 1966.
Schapiro, Leonard B. *Rationalism and Nationalism in Russian Nineteenth Century Political Thought*. New Haven: Yale Univ. Press, 1967.
Scheibert, Peter. "Die Petersburger religiös-philosophischen Zusammen-kunfte von 1902 und 1903," *Jahrbucher für Geschichte OstEuropas*, NS12(1964), pp. 513–60.
Scheler, Max. *Die Wissensformen und die Gesellschaft. Gesammelte Werke*. Vol. 8. Ed. Maria Scheler. Bern: Francke, 1960.
Scherrer, Jutta. "Die Religioes-Philosophischen Gesellschaften," Conference: *La Philosophie Idealiste en Russie*. Aix-en-Provence, 25–29 Mar. 1968.
_____. *Die Petersburger Religiös-Philosophischen Vereinigungen; Die Entwicklung des religiösen Selbstverständnisses ihrer Intelligentcija-Mitglieder (1901–1917)*. Wiesbaden: Otto Harrasowitz im Kommission, 1973.
Schleiermacher, Friedrich. *Reden über die Religion* (1821). 3d ed. trans. by J. Oman (1893); abridged with an intro. by E. Graham Waring as *On Religion, Speeches to Its Cultural Despisers*. New York: Ungar, 1955.
_____. *Schleiermacher's Soliloquies (Monologen*, 1800). Trans. H. L. Friess. Chicago: Open Court, 1957.
Schmemann, Alexander. *Ultimate Questions, An Anthology of Modern Russian Religious Thought*. New York: Holt, 1965.
Schorske, Carl. "Politics and the Psyche in *fin-de-siècle* Vienna: Schnitzler and Hofmannsthal." *American Historical Review*, No. 4(1961), pp. 930–46.
Schultze, Bernhard, ed. *Russische Denker, Ihre Stellung Zu Christus, Kirche und Papstuum*. Vienna: Herder, 1950.
_____. "Die Sozialeprinzipien in der Russischen Religionsphilosophie." *Zeitschrift für katholische Theologie*, 73, No. 4(1951), pp. 385–423.
Schütze, Walter. "Die Idee der sozialen Gerechtigheit im neu-Kantischen und Christlich-sozialen Schrifttum in der zweiten Hälfte des 19 Jahrhunderts." Ph.D. diss., Univ. of Leipzig, 1938.
Scott, John A. *Republican Ideas and the Liberal Tradition in France, 1870–1914*. New York: Columbia Univ. Press, 1951.
Shchukin, Sviashch. S. "Deistvitel'nost' i deistvennost'," *ME*, No. 8(1907), pp. 15–29.
_____. "Po povodu 'pis'ma s drugago berega' (otkrytoe pis'mo k N. Ezerskomu)," *ME*, No. 14(1907), pp. 25–30.
_____. *Okolo tserkvi, sbornik statei*. Moscow: "Put'," 1913.
Shein, Louis J., trans. and ed. *Readings in Russian Philosophical Thought* (late nineteenth and early twentieth centuries). The Hague: Mouton, 1968.
Sherdakov, V.N. *et al. Ateizm, Religiia, Sovremennost'*. Leningrad: "Nauka," 1973.
Simmel, Georg. *Einleitung in die Moralwissenschaft*. 2 vols. Berlin: Hertz (Besser), 1893.
_____. *Die Grossstadt*. Dresden: Zahn und Jaensch, 1903, pp. 185–206.
_____. *Kant*. 2d ed. Leipzig: Duncker und Humblot, 1905.
_____. *Die Religion*. Frankfort on the Main: Rütten und Loening, 1906.

———. *Die Probleme der Geschichtephilosophie*. 3d ed. Leipzig: Duncker und Humblot, 1907.

———. "Kant i Gete," trans. S. Frank, *RM*, 29, No. 6(1908), pp. 39–69.

———. *Soziologie*. Leipzig: Duncker und Humblot, 1908.

Simon, Gerhard. *Die Kirchen in Russland*. Munich: Manz, 1970.

———. "Church, State and Society." In *Russia Enters the Twentieth Century*, eds. G. Katkov *et al.*, pp. 199–235. London: Temple Smith, 1971.

Skvortsov, Vasilii M. *Tserkovnyi svet i gosudarstvennyi razum. Opyt tserkovno-politicheskoi khrestomatii*. 2 vols. St. Petersburg: 1912–1913.

Slonimskii, Leonid Z. "Noveishie idealisty," *Vestnik Evropy*, 38, No. 5(1903), pp. 313–24.

Slovo. A St. Petersburg daily newspaper, 1904–1909.

Smolich, I., "Predsobornoe prisutstvie," *Put'*, 38(1933), pp. 65–75.

The Sociology of George Simmel. Trans. and ed. Kurt H. Wolff. New York: Free Press, 1964.

Solov'ev, Vladimir. *God, Man and the Church*. (*Religiozniia osnovy zhizni, 1882–1884*). Trans. D. Attwater. London: James Clark, n.d.

———. *Opravdanie dobra. Polnoe Sobranie Sochinenii*, 2d ed. Ed. and with notes by S.M. Solov'ev and E.L. Radlov. Vol. 8. St. Petersburg: Prosveshchenie, 1911.

Sovremennye religioznye i tserkovnoe-obshchestvennye voprosy v reshenii ikh vydaiushchimisia dukhovnymi i svetskimi pravoslavno-russkimi pisatel'iami. St. Petersburg, 1903.

Spranger, Eduard. *Types of Men, the Psychology and Ethics of Personality*. Trans. Paul J.W. Pigors, 1928. Reprint. New York: Johnson, 1966.

Stäglich, Dieter. *Vladimir F. Ern, (1882–1917), Sein Philosophisches und Publizistisches Werk*. Bonn, 1967.

Stammler, Rudolf. *Wirtschaft und Recht nach der materialistischen Geschichtsauffassung*, 2d ed., enlarged. Leipzig: Veit, 1896.

———. *The Theory of Justice*. Trans. I. Husik from the 1902 ed. New York: Macmillan, 1925.

Struve, Petr B. "K kharakteristike nashego filosofskago razvitiia." In *Problemy idealizma*, pp. 315–38.

———. "Predislovie." In N. Berdiaev. *Subektivizm i individualizm v obshchestvennoi filosofii: kriticheskii etiud o N. K. Milhailovskom*, pp. i-lxxxiv. St. Petersburg: O. N. Popov, 1901.

———. *Na razniya temy (1893–1901), sbornik statei*. St. Petersburg: A.E. Kolpinski, 1902.

———. "Pamiati Vladimira Solov'eva." In *Na raznyia temy*, sbornik statei, 1893–1901, pp. 197–202. St. Petersburg: A.E. Kolpinski, 1902.

———, and Semen Frank. "Ocherki filosofii kul'tury," pt. 1, *Poliarnaia Zvezda*, 22 Dec. 1905, pp. 104–17; pt. 2, 30 Dec. 1905, pp. 170–84.

———. "Neskol'ko slov po povodu stat'i S.N. Bulgakova," *Poliarnaia Zvezda*, 12 Mar. 1906, pp. 128–30.

———. "Na raznyia temy," *RM*, 29, No. 2(1908), pp. 174–84.

———. "Otryvki o gosudarstve i natsii," *RM*, 29, No. 5(1908), pp. 187–93.

———. "Lev Tolstoi," *RM*, 29, No. 8(1908), pp. 218–30.

———. "Intelligentsiia i revolutsiia." In *Vekhi*. 4th ed. with appended biblio. on "Vekhi," pp. 156–174.

———. "Na raznyia temy," *RM*, 30, No. 1(1909), pp. 208–10.

———. "Religiia i sotsializm," *RM*, 30, No. 8(1909), pp. 148–56.

———. *Patriotica, sbornik statei, (1905–1909)*. St. Petersburg: Zhukovskii, 1910.

———. "Na raznyia temy," *RM*, 31, No. 2(1910), pp. 181–86.

———. "Pochemu zastoialas' nasha dukhovnaia zhizn'?" *RM*, 35, No. 3(1914), pp. 104–18.

———. "Religiia i obshchestvennost', otvet Z.N. Hippius," *RM*, 35, No. 5(1914), pp. 134–40.

Sventsitskii, Valentin. *Chto nuzhno krest'ianinu?* Moscow: Efimov, 1906.

———, and V.F. Ern. *Vzyskuiushchim grada*. Moscow: Efimov, 1906.

———. *"Khristianskoe bratstvo bor'by" i ego programma*. Moscow: Poplavskii, 1906.

———. "Smert' i bessmertie," In *Svobodnaia Sovest', sbornik statei*, pp. 34–67. Moscow; Sytin, 1906.

———. "Otkrytoe pis'mo veruiushchago k Pravoslavnoi Tserkvi." In *Poliarnaia Zvezda*, 3 Feb. 1906, pp. 561–64.

———. *Religioznaia smysl' 'Branda' Ibsena*. St. Petersburg: Otto Unfug, 1907.

———. *Pis'ma ko vsem*. Moscow: Poplavskii, 1907.

———. *Lev Tolstoi i Vladimir Solov'ev*. St. Petersburg: Otto Unfug, 1907.

———. "O novom religioznom soznanii." *Vek*, No. 18(1907), pp. 253–55.

Svoboda i Kul'tura. Successor to *Poliarnaia Zvezda*, 1906.

Svobodnaia Sovest', literaturno-filosofskii sbornik. 2 vols. Moscow: Sytin, 1906.

Talmon, Yonina. "Pursuit of the Millenium: The relation between religious and social change." *European Journal of Sociology*, 3, No. 2(1962), pp. 125–48.

Tilliette, Xavier. *Schelling, Une Philosophie en Devenir*. Paris: Libraire Philosophique J. Vrin, 1970), vol. 2, pp. 435–88.

Tovarishch. A St. Petersburg daily newspaper, 1906–1917.

Treadgold, Donald. *Lenin and His Rivals, The Struggle for Russia's Future, 1898–1906*. London: Methuen, 1955.

———. *The West in Russia and China, Religious and Secular Thought in Modern Times*. Vol. 1 *Russia 1472–1917*. Cambridge: The Univ. Press, 1973.

Trubetskaia, Olga, Kniazhna. *Kniaz' S.N. Trubetskoi, vospominaniia sestry*. New York: Chekhov, 1953.

Trubetskoi, Evgenii N., Kniaz'. "Novoe izsledovanie o filosofii prava Kanta i Hegel'ia." *VFP*, 13, No. 1/61 (1902), pp. 581–605.

———. "Pamiati V.S. Solov'eva, otkrytoe pis'mo S.N. Bulgakovu," *VZh*, No. 2(1905), pp. 386–90.

———. "Tserkov' i sovremennoe obshchestvennoe dvizhenie," *Pravo*, No. 15(1905), pp. 1169–75.

———. *Partiia 'mirnago obnovleniia'*. Moscow: Sytin, 1906.

———. "Dva slova po povodu polemiki S. Lur'e i S.N. Bulgakova," *ME*, No. 30(1906), pp. 37–39.

———. "C togo zhe berega," *ME*, No. 26–27(1907), pp. 24–28.

———. *Vospominaniia*. Sofia: Rossisko-bulgarskoe knigoizdatel'stvo, 1921.

Trubetskoi, Sergei, Kniaz'. *Sobranie sochinenii*, 6 vols. Moscow, 1907–1912.

———. "Na rubezhe," *ME*, No. 9(1906), pp. 268–74; No. 10(1906), pp. 300–303.

Tserkov' v istorii rossii (IXv.–1917g.), kriticheskie ocherki. Moscow: "Nauka," 1967.

Tserkovnoe Obnovlenie. A supplement to *Vek*.

Tugan-Baranovskii, Mikhail I. *K luchshemu budushchemu*. St. Petersburg: "Energiia," 1912.

Turgenev's Letters. Ed. Edgar H. Lehrman. New York: Knopf, 1961.

Tyszkiewicz, S., S.J. "Platonisme et plotinisme dans l'Ecclésiologie russe orthodoxe," *Nouvelle revue théologique*, 15, No. 3(1954), pp. 288–302.

Tyshkevich, S. Svyashch. *Nastavleniia sv. Tikhona zadonskogo po sotsial'nomu voprosu*. Rome: Izd. seminarii "Russkum," 1955.

Uspenskii, V.V. "Vopros o dogmaticheskom razvitii po Peterburgskikh R.F. sobraniiakh." *Khristianskoe Chtenie*, 84, No. 11(1904), pp. 597–612; No. 12(1904), pp. 757–86.

Ustav Religio-filosofskogo obshchestva v Peterburge. St. Petersburg, 1907.

"V. Briusov i Novyi Put'," *Literaturnoe nasledstvo*, 1937, vols. 27–28, pp. 276–98.

"V soiuze tserkovnago obnovleniia," *Rech'*, 24 Mar. 1906, p. 4.

"V soiuze tserkovnago obnovleniia." *Rech'*, 4 Nov. 1906, p. 5.

Valentinov, Nikolai V. *Vstrechi s Leninym*. New York: Chekhov, 1953.

Valerii Briusov v avtobiograficheskikh zapisiakh, pis'makh, vospominaniiakh sovremennikov i otzyvakh kritiki. Comp. N. Ashukin. Moscow: "Federatsiia," 1929.

Vasetskii, G.S. *et al*., eds. *Ocherki po istorii filosofii v rossii (Vtoraia polovina XIX i nachalo XX veka)*. Moscow: Moscow Univ., 1960.

Vekhi, sbornik statei o russkoi intelligentsii. 4th ed. with appended biblio. on "Vekhi." Moscow: N. Kushnerev, 1909.

Vek. A Moscow weekly newspaper, 1906–1907.

Vekilov, G. "Problema khristianskoi obshchestvennosti," *ME*, No. 43 (1907), pp. 20–38.

Vera i Razum. A Kharkov monthly theological journal, 1884–1917.

Vestnik Evropy. A St. Petersburg monthly journal, 1866–1919.

Vinogradov, Nikolai D. "Kratkii istoricheskii ocherk deiatel'nosti Mosk. Psikh. Obshchestva za 25 let." *VFP*, 21, No. 3/103(1910), pp. 249–62.

Vishniak, Mark. *Dan proshlomu*. New York: Chekhov, 1954.

Vodzinskii, Evgenii I. *Russkoe NeoKantianstvo, kontsa XIX-nachala XX vekov*. Leningrad: Leningrad Univ. 1966.

Voegelin, Eric. *The New Science of Politics, An Introduction*. Chicago: Univ. of Chicago Press, 1952.

Voprosy Filosofii i Psikhologii. A Moscow monthly journal, 1889–1917.

Voprosy Religii. A Moscow journal, 1906, 1908.

Voprosy Zhizni. Successor to *Novyi Put'*.

Voprosy Zhizni. St. Petersburg: Sv. Synod, 1904.

Vostrikov, Andrei V. *Bor'ba Lenina protiv neo-Kantianskoi revizii marksizma v Rossii*. Moscow: Gosizd. politicheskoi literatury, 1948.

Vozrozhdenie. Paris journal, 1949–present.

Vucinich, Alexander. "Politics, Universities and Science." In *Russia Under the Last Tsar*, ed. T.V. Stavrou, pp. 154–78. Minneapolis: Univ. of Minnesota Press, 1969.

Wallace, Anthony F.C. "Revitalization movements," *American Anthropologist*, 58, No. 2(1956), pp. 264–81.

Weber, Max. "The Types of Authority." In *Theories of Society, Foundations of Modern Sociological Theory*, ed. Talcott Parsons *et al.*, trans. A.M. Henderson and Talcott Parsons, vol. 1, pp. 626–32. Glencoe, Ill., Free Press, 1961.

Weinstein, Fred, and Gerald Platt. *The Wish to Be Free*. Berkeley: Univ. of California Press, 1969.

Whitehead, Alfred North. *Science and the Modern World*. New York: New American Library, 1948.

Wildman, Allen. *The Making of a Workers' Revolution, Russian Social Democracy, 1891–1903*. Chicago: Univ. of Chicago Press, 1967.

Wilson, Bryan. *Religious Sects, a Sociological Study*. London: Weidenfeld and Nicolson, 1970.

Windelband, Wilhelm. "O printsipe morali." In *Preliudii, filosofskiia stat'i i rechi*. Trans. S. Frank from 2d German ed., pp. 252–77. St. Petersburg: Zhukovskii, 1904.

Wolf, Erik. *Das Problem der Naturrechtslehre: Versuch einer Orientierung*. Karlsruhe: C. F. Müller, 1955.

Zander, Lev A. *Bog i Mir, (Mirosozertsanie ottsa Sergiia Bulgakova)*. 2 vols. Paris: YMCA Press, 1948.

Zapiski Religiozno-filosofskikh Sobranii v S. Peterburge. Monthly supplements to *Novyi Put'*, Jan. 1903–Mar. 1904.

Zapiski S. Peterburgskago religiozno-filosofskago obshchestva. Nos. 1 and 2. St. Petersburg: "Herol'd," 1908.

Zenkovskii, Vasilii V. "Predchuvstviia marksizma," *Narod*, No. 1(1906), pp. 2–3.

———. "O Khristianskom obshchestve." *Zhivaia Zhizn'*, No. 2(1907), pp. 3–10.

———. *A History of Russian Philosophy*. 2 vols. Trans. George L. Kline. New York: Columbia Univ. Press, 1953.

———. *Russian Thinkers and Europe*. Trans. Galia S. Bodde. Ann Arbor: American Council of Learned Societies, 1953.

———, ed. *Sbornik pamiati Semena Liudvigovicha Franka*. Munich: 1954.

———. "Memoirs, 1900–1920," unpublished. Russian and East European Archive, Columbia Univ. Library, New York.

Zernov, Nicholas. *The Russian Religious Renaissance of the Twentieth Century*. London: Darton, Longman, and Todd, 1963.

Zhivaia Zhizn'. A Moscow periodical, 1907–1908.

Znamenskii, S. "Sovremennyi individualizm v eticheskom otnoshenii," *Bogoslovskii Vestnik*, 15, No. 12(1906), pp. 683–723.

INDEX

Aggeev, Constantine (b. 1868), theologian and church reformer, 79, 97

Anthony (archimandrite), (Granovsky), synodal censor, 63

Anthropological Principle in Philosophy, 29

Anthony (metropolitan), (Vadkovsky), (1846–1912), St. Petersburg churchman sympathetic to moderate church reform, 62, 78

Anselm, Saint (1033–1109), theologian, philosopher, and reformer, 39

Askol'dov (Alekseev, Serge A.), (1870–1945), philosopher and religious thinker, 63, 79, 81, 96–97

Asocial sociability, 127, 150

Asquith, Herbert H. (1852–1928), English liberal politician, 141

Augustine, Saint (354–430), father of the Christian church and theologian, 48, 172

Avenarius, Richard (1843–96), German originator of empiriomonism, 6

Bacon, Sir Francis (1561–1626), English statesman and writer on science, 17

Bakst, Leon N. (c. 1867–1924), painter and theatrical designer, 3, 61

Bakunin, Michael A. (1814–76), political writer and anarchist, 15

Baronov, G.A., 97

Basil, Saint (known as "Basil the Great"), (c. 330–79), one of the four great Greek Fathers of the Church, 11

Baudelaire, Charles P. (1821–67), French "art for art's sake" poet, 57

Bazarov (Rudnev, Vladimir A.), (1874–1939), Marxist empiriomonist philosopher and economist, 6, 61, 97–98, 156

Belinsky, Vissarion (1811–48), prototypical radical writer, 14–15

Belyi, Andrei (Bugaev, Boris N.), (1880–1934), Symbolist poet and literary theorist, 3, 55, 94

Benois, Alexander N. (1870–1960), theatrical designer and art historian, 61

Bentham, Jeremy (1748–1832), utilitarian philosopher and political reformer, 32, 124, 136–37, 175

Berdiaev, Nicholas (1874–1948), mystical philosopher, 8, 46, 61, 63, 71, 79, 81, 98, 154

Bernstein, Basil, sociologist of education, 18

Bernsteinism, gradualistic socialist doctrine of Eduard Bernstein (1850–1932), 108

Bishop Serge (Stragorodsky), (1867–1944), rector of St. Petersburg Theological Seminary and scholar, 62–63, 66, 87

Black Hundreds, 69

Blok, Alexander A. (1880–1921), leading symbolist poet, 3, 61, 94, 97–99

Bloody Sunday (Jan. 9, 1905), 58, 69, 73

Boehme, Jacob (1575–1624), German mystic, 95, 119, 172

Bogdanov (Malinovsky, Alexander A.),

(1873–1928), Marxist empiriomonist and economist, 6, 156

Bougle, Celestin C. (1870–1940), French social thinker, 141

Briusov, Valery (1873–1924), leading symbolist poet, 63, 94

Brotherhood of Christian Struggle: Christian socialism of, 74–78; political activities of, 59, 72–73; regarding the Russian peasant, 77–78

"Bruno", 49

Buchez, Philippe (1796–1865), French Christian socialist, 10

Büchner, Ludwig (1824–99), German popularizer of materialism, 107

Bukharev (archimandrite), (1822–71), monk and religious teacher, 11

Bulgakov, Serge N. (1871–1944): ambivalence toward radical intelligentsia of, 107–108; belief in socialism of, 108; on Bernsteinism, 108; on the Brotherhood of Christian Struggle, 95; on clericalism, 168; early life of, 44–46; and German idealism, 111; gnosticism of, 172–74; in the Kiev Religious-Philosophical Society, 53–54; liberal critique of, 169–72; criticizes literary intellectuals, 113; on love, 94, 116, 120–21; on Marxism, 45–48, 53, 110–11, 116–18; on the Merezhkovsky group, 53, 93–94; as organizer of the Moscow Religious-Philosophical Society, 70; as organizer of St. Petersburg Religious-Philosophical Society, 79; as personalist, 6, 102, 116–18, 153–56, 172–74; as philosophical idealist, 30; criticizes positivism, 30–33; at Prague University (1924), 176; as professor, 119; on progress, 48–51, 169; on radical individualistic moralism, 112; return to faith of, 95; on Russian idealism, 46–47; on Russian liberalism, 99–102; 105–106; on Russian Orthodox church, 108–10, 159, 170; on Russian Social Democracy, 106–108; on the Russian state, 164, 167; on Schelling's philosophy, 111, 115–16; on social science and the church, 110–11; Solovievian idealism of, 51–53; sophiology of, 52–53, 173–74; on subject-object unity, 115–16, 119–20; on theocracy, 168; on transformative ritual, 154–55, 162; originates the Union of

Christian politics, 95, 168; on the universities, 110

Camus, Albert (1913–60), French novelist and essayist, 49

Cantor, Georg (1845–1918), Russian-German mathematician, 49–50

Capitalism and Agriculture, 45

Capitalism and private property, 74–76, 111–12, 141–42

Carlyle, Thomas (1795–1881), English writer and historian, 57, 112, 139

Catherine II (1729–96), reforming empress of Russia, 12

Chernyshevsky, Nicholas G. (1828–89), radical social theorist, 15, 29

Chicherin, Boris N. (1830–1904), idealist philosopher and moderate liberal politician, 13, 29

Christian communitarianism, 73, 155, 159–64

Christian political economy, 110–14

Chrysostom, Saint John (c. 347–407), one of the four great Greek Fathers of the Church and an inspired preacher, 11

Chukovsky, Kornei (1882–1969), literary critic, 97

Chulkov, George I. (1879–1939), symbolist poet and literary critic, 61, 79, 94

Clericalism, 168

Comte, Auguste (1798–1857), French founder of modern positivism, 29, 47–48

Constant, Benjamin (1767–1830), French writer and liberal, 137

Dicey, Albert (1835–1922), British constitutional lawyer and political theorist, 141

Dionysius of Alexandria (the Aeropagite), (c. 190–c. 265), formulator of mystical theology influential in Eastern Church, 39

Dnieper River, 86

Don River, 86

Dostoevsky, Fedor M. (1821–81), novelist and philosopher, 11, 50, 68, 94, 147, 160

Douglas, Mary, anthropologist, 19

Dumas: First and Second, 59, 123–24, 133; Third and Fourth, 60, 167

Ecclesiastes, 176

Economic man, 137
Educational Statute of 1884, 162
Egorov (Levin, E.J.), Bolshevik thinker and politician, 98
Elchaninov, Alexander V. (1881–1944), Orthodox Christian writer, 58, 63, 70–72, 78–79, 84–85
Engels, Friedrich (1820–95), socialist theorist, associate of Karl Marx, 75
Epistemology: Kantian and Christian, 38–39, 43; positivist, 30–31; Schleiermacher's, 138; Solovievian, 51–52
Ern, Vladimir (1881–1915): belief in socialism of, 76–77; as contributor to *New Path*, 63; as creator of the Brotherhood of Christian Struggle, 72–73; against Merezhkovsky, 81–85; as organizer of Moscow Religious-Philosophical Society, 58, 70–72; Orthodox Christianity of, 7, 88–89; on Orthodoxy and the peasant, 89–91; peasant revivalism of, 77–78; as personalist, 154; on private property, 74–76
Ethics: Kantian and Christian, 39–40; Marxist, 117–18; relativistic, 33–34; utilitarian, 31–32
Evolutionism, 32–33
Ezersky, N.F., liberal politician, 103

Faguet, Emile (1847–1916), French liberal writer and historian, 141
Faust, 137, 144–45
Felicific Calculus, 32
Feuerbach, Ludwig (1804–72), German philosopher and critic of religion, 48
Fichte, Johann G. (1762–1814), German idealist philosopher, 9, 23, 150
Filosofiia Khoziaistva (*Philosophy of Economics*), 111, 173
Filosofov, Dmitry V. (1882–1948), religious and aesthetic writer, 61, 96–98
Florensky, Pavel A. (1882–*c*. 1952), religious philosopher, 49–50, 58, 63, 70–72, 84–87
Foucault, Michael, French historian of thought, 158
"Four Idols," 17
Fourier, Charles (1772–1837), French socialist thinker, 112, 131
Frank, Simon L. (1877–1950), religious philosopher, 8, 46, 60, 63, 79–80, 99, 103, 109, 171

"Free Theological University," 71
Freud, Sigmund (1856–1939), Austrian founder of psychoanalysis, 119
Friedrich, Paul, anthropologist, 19
Fuchs, Emil (1874–1971), German Christian socialist pastor, 10

Gellner, Ernest, English philosopher and anthropologist, 19
General will, 131, 133–34
Gere, Vladimir L. (1873–1919), professor of history at Moscow University, 35
Gnosticism, 172–73
"God-building," 99
Godlevsky, Sigismund F. (b. 1855), 98
Godseekers, 7, 57, 66–68; 91, 153–54
Goethe, Johann Wolfgang von (1749–1832), German poet, dramatist, novelist, and essayist, 40, 115, 137–38, 175
Goethean man, 137–38
Gogol, Nicholas V. (1809–52), writer and religious essayist, 160
Golubkina, Alexandre (1864–1927), sculptor, 72
Gorky, Maxim (Peshkov, A.M.), (1868–1936), radical writer, 61, 98
Gradovsky, Alexander D. (1841–89), professor and liberal theorist, 13
Granovsky, Timofei N. (1813–55), university teacher and liberal theorist, 12
Grot, Nicholas Ia. (1852–98), professor of philosophy, 29
Grotius, Hugo (1583–1645), Dutch natural law theorist, 135–36

Hauser, Arnold, philosopher and art historian, 154
Hegel, George William Frederick (1770–1831), German idealist philosopher, 9, 13, 28, 40–41, 111, 115–16, 129, 137
Heine, Heinrich (1797–1856), German lyrical poet, 19
Herder, Johann Gottfried (1774–1803), German clergyman and philosopher, 138–39
Herzen, Alexander (1812–70), Russian revolutionary thinker and prose stylist, 13, 19, 45, 74
Hesychasm, Eastern Orthodox mystical teaching, 119
Hippius, Zinaida N. (1867–1945), sym-

bolist poet and literary critic: as God-seeker, 7, 57; as organizer of St. Petersburg Religious-Philosophical Meetings, 61–62; revolutionism of, 96
Historical jurisprudence, 34, 130–31
Hobhouse, Leonard T. (1864–1929), English liberal philosopher and journalist, 141, 152
Holy Synod, 62
Human feeling, 138–39
Humboldt, William von (1767–1835), German liberal political philosopher, 124

Idealism: as "compensation," 19–20; and religion, 20–21; relation to "legal state" of, 147
Immortality, 50–51
In Defense of Materialism, 5–6
Individualism: academic, 163; conflict with majoritarianism of, 139–40; nonreligious nature of, 109; various types of, 22–23
Individualistic humanism, 99–101, 154–55, 163
Infinity, 49–50
Ivanov, Viacheslav I. (1866–1949), philosopher and symbolist poet, 4, 61, 63, 94, 97, 154
Izgoev (Lande, Alexander S.), (b. 1872), liberal journalist, 103

John of Kronstadt (1821–1908), revered preacher and writer, 66

Kablukov, S.P. (d. 1921), secretary of St. Petersburg Religious-Philosophical Society, 97
Kama River, 86
Kamensky, A.A., theosophist, 97
Kant, Immanuel (1724–1804); epistemology of, 31, 38–39; ethics of, 39–40; on natural law, 41–42, 135–36; on the person, 38, 137–38, 175; political thought of, 128–29; on subject and object, 149
Kapterev, Nicholas F. (1847–1914), professor of church history, 71
Karpovich, Michael (1888–1959), professor of Russian history and literature, 72
Kartashev, Anton V. (1875–1960), theologian and church reformer, 61–62, 66, 79–80

Kavelin, Constantin D. (1818–85), professor at St. Petersburg University, 13
Ketteler, Wilhelm, Bishop von (1811–77), German pastor and Christian socialist, 10
Khrustalev (Nosar, G.S.), (1879–1918), St. Petersburg lawyer and Menshevik, 98
Kierkegaard, Sören (1813–55), Danish theologian, 57, 161
Kiev Polytechnical Institute, 45, 53
Kiev religious-philosophical discussions, 53
Kiev Theological Seminary, 45
Kingsley, Charles (1819–75), English writer and Christian socialist, 10
Kistiakovsky, Bogdan (1868–1920), liberal social theorist, 8
Kizevetter, Alexander A. (1866–1933), liberal jurist, 13
Kliuchevsky, Vasily O. (1841–1911), historian, 35, 86
Kornilov, Alexander A. (1862–1926), historian, 35
Korolenko, Victor G. (1853–1921), socially minded writer, 97
Kotliarevsky, Serge A. (1873–1941), professor of law at Moscow University, 8
Kudriavtsev, Peter P., Orthodox Christian philosopher, 66
Kutter, Herman (1863–1931), German pastor and Christian socialist, 10

Laissez faire, 126
Lamennais, Félicité de (1782–1854), French priest and Christian socialist, 10
Larionov, Michael I. (1881–1964), painter and stage designer, 3
The legal state, 128–29, 134–35, 147
Lenin (Ulianov, Vladimir I.), (1870–1924), Bolshevik leader, 6, 14, 26, 99, 169
Leo XIII (pope), (1810–1903), socially concerned Roman Catholic leader, 153
Liberalism: criticism of, 99–102; as critique of Christian socialism, 169–72; as "new liberalism," 141–42; philosophers of, 43–44, 125; fear of religious politics, 102–106; in Russian history, 12–13; popular response to, 99–101, 166–67, 171–72, 176; Russian types of, 166; in

Western Europe, 9–10, 152. *See also* Russian liberalism

Literary intellectuals, 83–84, 113

Locke, John (1632–1704), philosopher and political theorist, 103

Lopatin, Leo M. (1855–1920), idealist philosopher, 29

Lossky, Nicholas O. (1870–1965), intuitionist philosopher, 63, 79, 97

Lotze, Herman (1817–81), German anti-positivist philosopher, 50–51

Love as a political force, 37, 40, 94, 116, 120–21

Lukać, George (1885–1971), philosopher and Marxist theorist, 154

Lunacharsky, Anatol V. (1875–1933), empiriomonist Bolshevik theorist, 6, 53, 55, 98, 153, 156

Lur'e, S., writer on politics and religion, 103

Luther, Martin (1483–1546), initiator of Protestant reformation, 174

Mach, Ernst (1838–1916), Austrian scientist and positivist philosopher, 6, 153

Malia, Martin, historian of Russian thought, 19

Mannheim, Karl (1893–1947), German sociologist of knowledge, 17–18

Marcuse, Herbert, social philosopher, 154

Martov (Tsederbaum, Iu.), (1873–1923), leading Menshevik, 99

Marxism: Christian revivalists' relation to, 74–76; on derivation of ideas, 17–18, 154; ethics of, 116–18; view of history in, 47–48; polemics of 1890s in, 45–46. *See also* Russian Marxism

Materializm i Empiriomonizm, 99

Mathiot, Madeleine, linguist, 19

Maurice, Frederick D. (1805–72), English Christian socialist, 10

Meier, Alexander A. (1875–1939), writer on religious-philosophical topics, 96–97

Merezhkovsky, Dmitry S. (1865–1941): creation of *New Path* by, 63; criticizes Russian Orthodox Church, 57, 64–69, 81; Ern's polemic with, 81–85; the "new religious consciousness" of, 7, 64–69, 81, 91, 153–54; opens pages of *New Path* to idealists, 93–94; as organizer of St. Petersburg Religious-Philosophical

Meetings of 1901–1903, 61–62; reports to St. Petersburg Religious-Philosophical Society of, 81, 98; responses of Churchmen to, 66–67; revolutionism of, 96

Michael (archimandrite), (Semenov, P.V.), (d. 1916), professor, priest-socialist, 63

Michel, Henri (1857–1904), French liberal political thinker and historian, 141

Middle class culture, 17–18

Miliukov, Paul N. (1857–1943), historian and liberal political leader, 27, 35, 148

Mill, John Stuart (1806–73), utilitarian philosopher and liberal theorist, 9, 32, 124–25, 136–37, 140

Millenarianism, 72–74

Minsky (Vilenkin, Nicholas M.), (1855–1937), poet, literary critic, and philosopher, 61–62, 66

Mir Iskusstva (*World of Art*), 61

Missionerskoe Obozrenie (*Missionary Review*), 62, 66

Modernization and the person, 21–23, 74–76, 154–58

Moleschott, Jacob (1822–93), German popularizer of materialism, 107

Morris, William (1834–96), English social theorist influenced by Christian socialism, 10, 153

Moscow Psychological Society, 29

Moscow Religious-Philosophical Society, 58–59, 69–72

Moscow University, 34–35, 45, 162

Moscow versus St. Petersburg, 84

Narod (*The People*), 95, 108

Natorp, Paul G. (1854–1924), German Neo-Kantian philosopher, 42, 131

Natural law: Kantian, 41–42; Neo-Kantian, 42–43, 135–36

Natural man: 48–49, 74–76, 102, 107–108

Naumann, Friedrich (1860–1919), German pastor and Christian socialist, 10

New liberalism, 141–42, 166–67

New religious consciousness, 7, 81–84, 91

Nietzsche, Friedrich W. (1844–1900), German philosopher, 33–34, 50, 57, 75, 139–40

Nikon, Patriarch (1605–81), vigorous church reformer, 88–89

Nineteenth-century Christian socialism, 10–12, 153
Nineteenth-century Russian liberalism, 12–13
Novalis (von Hardenberg, F.), (1772–1801), German romantic lyric poet, 137
Novgorodtsev, Paul N. (1866–1924), acceptance of German romanticism by, 137–39; ambivalence toward modernization of, 21–22, 37, 155–58; attitude toward masses of, 140, 143–44, 175–76; basic idealism of, 30; as Constitutional Democrat (Kadet) politician, 122–24, 133; contribution to *Problems of Idealism* of, 8, 27, 47; critique of religious politics by, 60, 99, 102–103, 168; critique of "scientism" by, 32–33; critique of utopianism by, 131–32, 144–46; distrust of love as political force by, 121; education, career, and personality of, 34–36, 46; epistemology and ethics of, 38–41; as idealistic liberal, 9, 149–51; individualism of, 22, 154–55; on Kant, Hegel, and the "legal state," 128–29; Kantianism and Russian Orthodoxy of, 37–40; on Marxism-Leninism and empiriomonism, 6; natural law doctrine of, 41–43, 135–36; Neo-Kantianism of, 41–43; "new liberalism" of, 141–42; personalism of, 9, 13, 38–39, 142–44, 156, 174–76; on radical moralism, 139; relation to Academy of, 159, 161–63; relation to class ideology of, 16–17, 154; relation to religious-philosophical societies of, 55–56; employs Simmel's thought, 139–41; religious attitudes of, 37–44, 146, 153, 175; on Rousseau and social harmony, 128–32; the Russian liberalism of, 124–28, 155, 165–67; on the Russian state, 164–65; on the *Vekhi* controversy, 148–49
Novgorodtseva, Lydia A., liberal political organizer, 35
Novikov, Nicholas I. (1744–1818), a leading liberal satirical journalist, 12
Novoe Vremya (New Times), 96
Novyi Put' (New Path), 55, 63, 93–94

Obolensky, Alexander D. (1855–1933), Over-procurator of the Holy Synod, 1905–1906, 79
October Manifesto (Oct. 17, 1905), 58, 69

On the Social Ideal, 5, 55, 145
Origin of the Family, Private Property and the State, 75
Orthodoxy, 85–89

Parodi, Dominique (1870–1955), Italian liberal philosopher, 141
Peasants: attitude of Brotherhood of Christian Struggle toward, 71, 73, 77; as integrated personalities, 142; impact of industrialization on, 89, 157; contempt for literary culture of, 91; impact of geography on, 86; lack of Christian revivalism among, 77–78; Orthodox Christianity of, 87–90, 104, 160; paganism of, 85–86, 90–91; probable actions of, 169; relation to delayed gratification of, 175–76; relation to individualistic humanism of, 166–67, 171–72; social democratic appeal to, 106–107; weakness of liberalism among, 99–101
Personalism: Christian and Kantian, 38–39; elite culture bearers of, 143–44; immortality in, 50–51; in modern societies, 74–76; inner controls in, 36–37; objective bases of, 156; philosophy of, 153–54; relation to individual in, 102; relation to peasant of, 172; relation to social ideal of, 145–46; against utopianism, 144–45; various manifestations of, 173–75
Pertsov, Peter P. (b. 1868), editor of *New Path*, 61
Pestel, Paul (1799–1826), leader in Decembrist revolt (1825), 15
Peter the Great (1672–1725), reforming Czar of Russia, 12, 89
Petrashevsky Circle, socialist discussion group (1845–48), 11
Petrov, Gregory (1868–1925), politically active priest, 62
Petrunkevich, Ivan I. (1844–1928), liberal politician, 13
Piaget, Jean, psychologist, student of mental development, 18
Pisarev, Dmitry (1840–68), radical writer, 15
Plato (d. c. 427–347 B.C.), originator of idealistic philosophy, 43, 131, 144, 150
Plekhanov, George (1857–1918), primary Russian Marxist theorist, 5–6, 61

Plotinus (c.205–207), principal Neoplatonic philosopher, 119
Pobedonostsev, Constantin P. (1827–1907), conservative statesman and writer, 57, 62, 78
Polanyi, Michael (1891–1975), Hungarian antipositivist scientist and philosopher, 36, 75
Poliarnaia Zvezda (Polar Star), 104
Popular sovereignty, 129–30, 132–33, 136, 142, 165–66
Positivism: critique of, 30–33; legal, 130; of Marxism, 5–6; political economy of, 110–11, 113–14; in universities, 28–30
Prague University, 176
Problemy Idealizma (Problems of Idealism), 8, 27, 47
Progress to perfection, 48–51, 111–14, 144–45, 158, 169
Prokopovich, Theofan (1681–1736), leader of religious reforms under Peter the Great, 12
Public opinion, 130

Radical intelligentsia, 14–16, 77, 107, 164
Radishchev, Alexander N. (1749–1802), liberal critic of serfdom and government, 12
Ragaz, Leonhard (1868–1946), Swiss Christian socialist, 10
Rasputin, Gregory (1871–1916), influential starets, 109
Rational-critical order, 157
Rationalization, 21, 140–41, 155–58
Rational man: embodies natural law, 135–36; Kantian, 38–43; in the legal state, 128–29; in Novgorodtsev's conception of man, 174–75
Religion and socialism, 73–77, 97–99, 105, 108–10, 112, 118–19, 159–61
Religion of humanity, 48, 101–102
Religious life and thought: as "compensation," 19; as ideology, 16–19; in conflict with idealism, 20–21; of Russian Orthodoxy, 85–91, 159–61; viewed by Brotherhood of Christian Struggle, 73–78
Renouvier, Charles (1815–1903), French idealistic liberal philosopher, 141, 152
Republic, 131, 144
Rerum Novarum (1891), 153
Revelation of John, 91, 169

Revivalism, 77–78, 95
The revolution of 1905–1907; activity of Brotherhood of Christian Struggle in, 72–73; danger for Orthodox church in, 89; development of, 26, 57–58; the first two dumas in, 59–60, 122–24, 133; impact on Bulgakov of, 93; Kadets in, 122–24; liberates universities, 162; peasant-worker class hatred in, 89; relation to religious-philosophical societies of, 69–70
Revolution of sensibility, 127, 174–75
Rickert, Heinrich (1863–1936), German Neo-Kantian philosopher, 110
Rising material expectations, 112, 174
Ritual, 89–90
Romanticism, 34, 137–39, 174–75
Rousseau, Jean-Jacques (1712–78), French writer and social thinker, 127–32, 146
Rozanov, Vasily V. (1856–1919), essayist, philosopher, and critic, 4, 7, 29, 54, 57, 61, 63, 79, 81, 96–97
Ruskin, John (1819–1900), English art critic influenced by Christian socialism, 10
Russell, George W.E. (1843–1919), English liberal writer and politician, 141
Russia: crisis of, 25–26; culture of, 3–4, 23; "exceptionalism" of, 76–77, 101, 107, 126, 142, 176; governing classes of, 165–67; as latecomer, 125–26; liberal forces in, 166; modernization of, 14–16, 157–58
Russian idealism, 8, 28–34, 46–47
Russian liberalism: academic setting of, 12–13, 163; against religion in politics, 60, 102–105, 170; characteristics of, 165–67; critique of, 99–102; in eighteenth and nineteenth centuries, 12–13; liberation movement in, 46, 59, 122; mood of Novgorodtsev's, 149–51; in 1905–1907, 122–24, 133; Octobrists in, 59–60; political development of, 59–60; relation of peasants to, 100–101, 170–72. See also liberalism
Russian Marxism: criticizes idealistic liberalism, 46–47; critique of, 106–108, 113–14, 116–18; empiriomonists in, 6, 53, 156; "God-building" in, 98–99; Lenin's, 6, 26, 99, 169; Mensheviks in, 113; Plekhanov's, 5–6; relation to Christian

revivalism of, 74–76; relation to Soloviev's philosophy of, 46–48; Social Democratic Party in, 15, 23, 26, 133. *See also* Marxism

Russian Orthodox church: competes with Academy, 159–64; concern for poor of, 11; condition of, 159–61; development of, 85–89; intellectual's discussion of, 70; peasants' relation to, 85–89, 169; polemic with Godseekers of, 62, 66–68; relation to Brotherhood of, 73, 87–89; relation to Christian socialism of, 109–10, 168, 170–71

Russian symbolist poets, 7, 93–94

Russian state, 163–72

Russian universities, 28–29, 110, 161–62

Russkaia Mysl' (*Russian Thought*), 103

Russo-Japanese War, 58, 69

St. Petersburg Religious-Philosophical Meetings, 7, 53, 57, 61–68

St. Petersburg Religious-Philosophical Society: differs from meetings of 1901–1903, 80; founding of, 78–79; Merezhkovsky-Ern polemics in, 81–85, 89–91; reports in, 1907–1908, 81; reports in, 1908–1909, 97–98; in Russian intellectual life, 60–61; turn to politics of, 96–97

St. Petersburg University, 29, 35, 162

Samuel, Herbert (1870–1963), English liberal politician and thinker, 141

Scheler, Max (1874–1928), German philosopher and sociologist, 18

Schelling, Friedrich W. (1775–1854), German idealist philosopher, 49, 95, 109, 111, 115–16, 119, 172

Schiller, Friedrich (1759–1805), German playwright and poet, 40, 175

Schlegel, August W. (1767–1845), romantic thinker and teacher, 137

Schlegel, Friedrich (1772–1829), romantic thinker and teacher, 137

Schleiermacher, Friedrich (1768–1834), German Protestant theologian, romantic, 40, 124, 137–39, 175

Science and "scientism," 32, 36–37, 110

Scriabin, Alexander N. (1872–1915), composer and mystic, 3

Serge, Archimandrite (Tikhomirov), rector of St. Petersburg Theological Academy, 63, 66

Sexual life, 63, 66–67, 75, 82–83, 94

Shchukin, S., Moscow priest and writer on religious topics, 160

Shestov, Leon I. (1866–1938), antirationalist philosopher, 3

Shipov, Dmitry N. (1851–1920), Slavophile liberal politician, 122, 166

Simmel Georg (1858–1918), German sociologist, 139–41

Sipiagin, Dmitry S. (1853–1902), minister of the interior, 62

Skvortsov, Vasily M. (1853–1932), director of Church missionary activity, 62–63

Slonimsky, Leonid Z. (1850–1918), liberal, Western-oriented journalist, 170

Smith, Adam (1723–90), first great spokesman for moderated laissez faire economics, 138

Social harmony, 128–33

Social ideal, 42, 145–46

Socialism as inevitable, 76, 105, 108

Social Revolutionary Party, 15, 26

Sociology of knowledge, 17–19

Socrates (d. 399 B.C.), Athenian philosopher, 150, 174

Solidarism, 141–42

Sollertinsky, S.A., theologian, 66

Soloviev, Serge (b. 1886), symbolist poet, 79

Soloviev, Vladimir S. (1853–1900): on beauty, 94; as philosopher of history, 47–48; philosophy of, 51–53, 71; on poverty, 126; on religion, science, and politics, 11–12; as religious mystic, 116, 119

Sophiology, 52–53, 173

Spencer, Herbert (1820–1903), English sociologist, 32, 47, 55, 134

Spirit of property, 74–76, 111–12

Stammler, Rudolf (1856–1938), Neo-Kantian German philosopher, 41–42, 131, 135

Stolpner, Boris G. (1871–1937), Social Democrat and philosopher, 98

Stolypin, Peter A. (1863–1911), minister of the interior, 23, 59

Strakhov, Nicholas N. (1829–96), publicist, thinker, and critic, 29

Stravinsky, Igor (1882–1971), innovative composer, 3

Struve, Peter B. (1870–1944): contributes to *Vekhi*, 148; as founder of St. Peters-

burg Religious-Philosophical Society, 79, 97; as idealist, 8; on religion and politics, 60, 102–105; on religion and socialism, 105, 119
Subjective religiosity, 104–105
Subject-object unity, 115–16, 119–20
Sventsitsky, Valentin, religious and political writer, 1905–14: attitude toward Godseekers of, 92; emotional state of, 72; on evils of property, 74–78; as founder of Brotherhood of Christian Struggle, 72–73; as founder of Moscow Religious-Philosophical Society, 58–59; in St. Petersburg, 1905, 78–79
Svet Nevechernyi (*Unfading Light*), 173

Tareev, Nicholas M. (1866–1934), professor at Moscow Theological Academy, 71
Tatishchev, Vasily N. (1686–1750), author of first modern history of Russia, 12
Ternavtsev, V.A., minor church official, 61, 63, 66, 79–80, 97
Theocracy, 168–69
Therapeutic society, 174–75
Thought and ideology, 16–20
Tocqueville, Alexis de (1805–59), French liberal political thinker, 124, 137
Tolstoi and Dostoevsky, 61
Tolstoi, Leo (1828–1910), novelist and moralist, 76, 112, 139–40
Total Unity, 51–53
Tragic sense of life, 43, 83, 110, 146–47, 175–76
Tretiakov Gallery, 72
Trubetskoi, Prince Eugene (1863–1920), idealist philosopher, 4, 103
Trubetskoi, Prince Serge (1862–1905), idealist philosopher, 4, 35, 161
Turgenev, Ivan S. (1818–83), leading novelist and poet, 142
Tyranny of the majority, 136, 139

Union of Christian Politics, 95, 103, 168
Union of Unions, 35, 122
Uspensky, Vasily V., Orthodox Christian teacher and writer, 61, 66, 79, 97

Utilitarianism, 31–33, 40, 125, 137
Utopia: critique of positivist, 49–51; critique of socialist, 107–108; "optical illusion" of, 169; repressive nature of, 144; uniformism of, 131–32

Valentinov (Vol'sky, Nicholas V.), (1879–1964), Marxist thinker of empiriomonist tendencies, 53
Vekhi (*Landmarks*), 61, 98, 148–49
Vernadsky, Vladimir I. (1863–1945), chemist and geologist, 35
Vestnik Evropy (*European Courier*), 170
Vladislavlev, Michael I. (1840–90), Neo-Kantian philosopher, 29
Voegelin, Eric (b. 1901), political philosopher and historian, 172
Vogt, Karl (1817–95), German popularizer of materialism, 107
Volga River, 86
Volzhsky (Glinka, Alexander S.), (b. 1878), literary critic and religious writer, 63
Voprosy filosofii i psikhologii (*Questions of Philosophy and Psychology*), 29, 46
Voprosy Zhizni (*Questions of Life*), 55, 78
Vvedensky, Alexander I. (1856–1925), Neo-Kantian philosopher, 29
Vyborg Manifesto, 124

Weber, Max (1864–1920), German sociologist and historian, 110
Western antinomies, 146–51
Wholes and Parts, 134, 143
Windelband, William (1848–1915), German Neo-Kantian philosopher, 42–43, 131

Yurkevich, P.D. (1827–74), idealist philosopher of the 1860s, 28–29

Zenkovsky, Vasily V. (1881–1962), religious philosopher and historian, 63
Zheliabov, Andrei I. (1850–81), revolutionary terrorist, 15

Russian Alternatives to Marxism was set into type on the Variable Input Phototypesetter in 10-point Times Roman with 2-point spacing between the lines. The book was designed by Bill Cason, composed by Moran Industries, Inc., Baton Rouge, Louisiana, printed by Thomson-Shore, Inc., Dexter, Michigan, and bound by John H. Dekker & Sons, Grand Rapids, Michigan. The paper on which the book is printed bears the watermark of the S.D. Warren Company and is designed for an effective life of at least three hundred years.

THE UNIVERSITY OF TENNESSEE PRESS : KNOXVILLE